I AM HAPPIER TO KNOW YOU

A Portrait of Egypt, Her People, Faith and Culture,
Viewed through the Heart of a Western Woman

I AM HAPPIER TO KNOW YOU

A Portrait of Egypt, Her People, Faith and Culture,
Viewed through the Heart of a Western Woman

Jeanne M. Eck

Angel Wings Publishing Partners
Wheeling , West Virgina

Published by Angel Wings Publishing Partners
Wheeling, West Virginia
Visit our website at: http://www.Angelwingspub.com

Publisher's Cataloging-In-Publication Data
(Prepared by The Donohue Group, Inc.)

Eck, Jeanne M.
   I am happier to know you : a portrait of Egypt, her people, faith and culture, viewed through the heart of a western woman /Jeanne M. Eck.

   340 p. ; cm.
   ISBN: 0-9753054-0-9

1. Eck, Jeanne M.—Biography. 2. Egypt—Description and travel—21st century. 3. Women travelers—United States—21st century. 4. Islamic countries—Description and travel—21st century. 5. Women—Egypt—Social conditions—21st century. 6. Egypt—Social life and customs—21st century.

DT107.828.E35 2005
962.05/5/092

Front cover photo of the author by Dr. Charles E. Shepherd
Back cover photo of the author by Joseph Sabry

Cover design by Peri Poloni, Knockout Design
Interior design by Dr. Suzanne Deakins, Spirit Press

Printed in the USA

Visit the author's website at: www.jeanneeck.com

Dedication

I Am Happier to Know You is dedicated to God. Without His presence in every exhalation of my life, I never would have left my native land and embarked on this precious journey.

△ △ △

My love always to my dreams come true:
Chuck, Bill and Dan.

Praise For
I Am Happier To Know You

"I Am Happier to Know You is an insightful portrait of the Middle East painted by an American woman living in Egypt. Jeanne writes with intellect, humor, compassion and love. Her life lessons are universal and resonate deeply."
Beth Rubin, author of "Split Ends," Maryland

"I Am Happier to Know You is a story of new life. Told with love, zest, grit, and extraordinary humor, it is the account of one courageous woman's engagement with a world totally new to her."
Linda P. Barnes, Washington, D.C.

"I Am Happier to Know You moved me deeply. It is insightful and compassionate and very much needed in today's world. It is a book with two sides—the learning and understanding of Middle Eastern customs observed through the nonjudgmental eyes of the author, and her personal struggle to find herself. Because it is written from the heart of her experiences, the author gives genuineness to the pictures she portrays."
Ruth Montllor, Virginia

"Through the open and accepting eye of the author, I Am Happier to Know You provides the reader with the opportunity to intimately explore the fascinating and rich culture of Egypt and her people. In this time of strife between the United States and other cultures, I think it is more important than ever for individuals to understand the lives and perspectives of people from the Middle East and around the world. With candor, love and humor, I Am Happier to Know You takes the reader a few more steps towards tolerance and understanding."
K.D., United States

"I Am Happier to Know You is universally appealing. Each chapter enlightens and enlivens, offering something for everyone. Some stories made me laugh; others brought tears to my eyes."
Ivy Hart, Maryland

"I Am Happier to Know You is not your casual read while sipping warm tea and munching crumpets. The author has taken the time to bring you to not only the beauty of the people, but the issues at hand in Egypt. Through her intimate portrayal of the details of life and circumstances there, you feel as though you are an Egyptian. This extremely visual, visceral account has an important place in our American libraries and universities."
Mary Lyn Matthews, Oklahoma

"Utilizing her honesty, wit and humor, Jeanne documents how she survived in a culture so unlike that of the United States. Hopefully, I Am Happier to Know You will bring our two cultures closer together."
Linda Soby, Virginia

"Written by an American woman living in Egypt, I Am Happier to Know You is a first-hand view with heartfelt understanding of the complex laws and lives of Egypt and her people. A frequent traveler myself, I Am Happier to Know You provided me with a rich perspective of the people and culture of the Middle East... I recommend it!"
Mary Lewis, Maryland

"As an American living in a Muslim country, Jeanne Eck provides political insights that helped me to understand the sociopolitical background to the conflict in Iraq and Afghanistan...so much more than the American press."
Susan Owens, M.D.Maryland

"I Am Happier to Know You proves that when traveling alone or moving someplace new without the benefit of family and friends, it's attitude and a good sense of humor that count most!"
M.B., Washington, D.C

Acknowledgments

Without the breathtaking willingness of a bountiful number of Egyptians who embraced, protected, and nurtured me, I Am Happier to Know You would never have been conceived. Their tender spirit enabled me to appreciate, understand, and value their culture; in the process, I learned to better appreciate, understand, and value myself.

My friends in the United States, in Egypt, and around the world sheltered me from the gales of life and embraced me with their wisdom and numerous acts of kindness. Because I changed many of their names throughout the book, to protect their privacy, I must refrain from listing them here. You have laughed with me in the brightest of times and sustained me in the most challenging. You know who you are and that I love you. *"Alf shoke"* (a thousand thanks)!

In Cairo, I am indebted to Audrey, Kim, Cheril, and Sharon who read the original manuscript and shared both their insights and enthusiasm. Sharon also performed the first edit before it was turned over to Kelly Zaug for fact checking and in-depth editing. Thank you!

In the United States, thank you to Fran and Paul Byers who have provided me with a home away from home and decades of unconditional friendship, love and support.

Introduction

I had only one close friend in Cairo. I call him Mo. We had met hours after I'd arrived in Egypt as a tourist. We felt instantly that the Universe had brought us together for a unique reason. Before I returned to Egypt to live, he had found me a flat, even stocked it with essentials. Without his help, I wouldn't have survived. For the first month, I was alone during the day. At night, Mo stopped by to "sit with me." I found myself thrown headfirst into a culture I didn't understand, a language I couldn't speak, and a country where I had only Mo to help me to adjust.

As a Western woman without the protection of a husband, family, or employer, I was at a distinct disadvantage. I was devoid of any understanding of the rules I would be expected to live by, or a comprehension of how our culture has been translated and typecast into misassumptions about a Western woman's values. Reality smacked me hard, then harder.

I had promised everyone I knew and loved in the West that I would stay in touch. I accomplished this via e-mail. I Am Happier to Know You evolved from my weekly (sometimes more frequent) communications titled "Notes from Egypt." Because those on my mailing list expected me to share Egypt with them, I was obliged to keep my eyes open and focused. This was an incredible gift to me; so was my aloneness.

Though I certainly didn't like it, I came to believe that God wanted me to go it alone, to face the realities and the illusions of my experiences solo. He wanted me to learn to hear, but to rely upon my budding inner wisdom. Being alone also forced me to overcome my introversion and to reach out to new people and experiences I wouldn't have had if I, like many expats, chose to limit my interaction with Egyptians. To my delight, my openness and journalistic hunger to learn everything I could about Egypt's people and culture opened doors to a world few foreigners access. Before long, "Notes from Egypt" took on a life of its own. I felt compelled to share my understanding of the culture so that others could more clearly see how the misinterpretation of our differences has widened the gaps in the road to peace. As you read I Am Happier to Know You, please remember that what I have written comes from my heart and my personal experiences. Any story that portrays a challenging experience does not define Egyptian people or culture, but of one or more individuals. Just as Timothy McVeigh is not a mirror image of the average American, these individuals are not a reflection of the average Egyptian.

At times, I felt that I would become brain dead from banging my head up against the backlash of rage I experienced when my Western cultural beliefs smacked up against those of Islam and the East. But, by far, the most difficult challenges came from within me. Egypt forced me to face the parts of myself still in need of healing, to see my country and culture through different eyes, and to understand that although our customs are different, we suffer the same fears and pray for the fulfillment of the same dreams. We are all one in our desire to fill our children's bellies with nourishing food and our hearts with love; we all seek to do the best that we can with this journey called life.

Throughout, you will be introduced to many Arabic words and their definitions. For your convenience, they're included in a glossary at the end of the book. If you're interested in making a printed copy of the glossary, visit my website:www.jeanneeck.com where you'll find photos and lots of other information.

The Arabic language overflows with mouth-watering nuances. A tire is not flat; it is asleep. The balcony of your top floor apartment isn't noisy because you're on a flight path; it's too close to the sky. I Am Happier to Know You is an English translation of the Arabic expression "Ana asaad" (pronounced ana ah-sod). It is used in two contexts. Upon hearing good news, Ana asaad is employed to say, "I am happier for you than you are for yourself." As in the West, when someone is introduced to you for the first time they will say, "I'm happy to meet you." An Egyptian will often graciously respond, *"Ana asaad"* (I Am Happier To Know You). I chose this title because it concisely expresses my gratitude for all that Egypt and her people have taught me. I am indeed happier and wiser for having known her.

It is with joy that I am able to share with you the stories of her magnificent people. The interpretation is mine alone. I have taken the liberty of changing names and places to protect the privacy of those who befriended me and that of those who bared their lives so you could better understand the Egyptian culture. Each moment of my journey has forever changed the woman I was yesterday and work to become tomorrow.

I ended each edition of *Notes from Egypt* by sending "Love and Blessings." I offer the same to you.

Jeanne

Cairo, Egypt

*May God make
it easy for you*

~ Islamic saying

Chapter 1

In October 2000, I traveled to Egypt as a tourist. Her sun-kissed, gritty breeze brushed back my hair exposing my upturned face to the scent of her essence. A sense of peace, one that had seemed to stop at the house next door instead of mine, cuddled me in gales of joy. It was as if I'd come face-to-face with the mother of my dreams, the one I had lost but silently yearned for. My soul recognized her immediately; my heart and eyes soon followed.

When I looked down, just above where the tips of my Travel Smith sandals were in the process of creating sensible ridges in the sand, a perfect imprint of a lotus flower appeared. A symbol of spiritual unfolding, it winked at me in the condensed morning sunlight. I stood frozen, my body swaying slowly in the shock of recognition. My eyes darted about, searching for others. "Surely it's a print made by a high-tech sneaker," I whispered. But it was the only one. Like the echo of laughter on a mountaintop, "Welcome home," bounced against the cells of my befuddled mind. The words traveled downward like a melody that spontaneously makes your toes wiggle and your feet perform a dance you never learned, but somehow have never forgotten.

Before my trip was completed, I knew I would relocate there. Within four months, Egypt became my home.

I followed an inner knowledge so deep and pure, even the terror of the drastic change I was about to make failed to deter me. I was fifty-four years old, spirited and single. My children were launched and my dog had moved on to celestial fire hydrants. If I lived frugally until my property in Washington D.C. sold, I had just enough money in the bank to cover my expenses. As a writer, I needed only my brain, a computer, a printer, and a phone line. I could work anywhere. I planned to stay for six months and then move on to Rhode Island. God and Egypt had other plans for me.

The reaction to my decision to relocate to a country over eight thousand miles away from my children and family caused telephones across the United States to overheat. Everyone worried about my safety, perhaps also my sanity. Some thought I was experiencing a crazed menopausal moment; others sighed and shook their heads, convinced that their mother, aunt, or sister was simply lapsing back into her role as the family's version of a New Age "Auntie Mame."

Most of my friends, the majority of whom share my dedication to spirituality, clapped their hands with elation while waving away the threads of trepidation that had them questioning whether or not they would have the same *courage* and faith to do what I was doing. Everyone, no matter how tepid or delighted, looked forward to living vicariously through me. I never felt courageous, only grateful to have the opportunity to track with my inner wisdom, secure in the knowledge that my journey would be an astonishing one.

After returning home from my trip, I packed up my life and placed it in storage. I deposited my four-unit building into the hands of a Realtor. I wrote a new will, arranged for on-line banking, lassoed my eldest son into managing my personal affairs, and began to say goodbye to everyone and everything I loved.

There was much I would miss: the sound, the touch, and the sight of my boys and the tender wisdom and blissful love of my family, friends, and teachers. I'd also miss my gentle tenants—men and women who supported my dream despite the tornado of havoc it inflicted upon their lives.

The week before the movers arrived in their unique version of a moving van, I walked through my apartment and inhaled the sight of the possessions I most cherished: my mother's pressed-glass cake stands, my father's pipes that still bear his scent and teeth marks, one grandmother's brass candlesticks and the other's delicately engraved silver sugar spoon. The Christmas ornaments that still dazzled me as they had when I was a child, the footrest in the shape of a cow I'd found at a craft fair, and the too large collection of paintings and prints I'd begun collecting before my children's first shoes had been bronzed, were packed with special care.

After my ex-husband moved out, taking with him the luxurious furnishings that defined his self-image, I created a space that reflected the newly cherished and emerging me.

I made carpets out of canvas. I searched for and found furniture designed to fit my curves, no one else's. I frequented the outdoor market a stone's throw from my apartment and wheeled home tired cabinets and cupboards rescued from historic homes undergoing the agony of restoration. Hours of dedicated stripping, sanding, and painting provided a background for the whimsy bubbling to be released.

Upon seeing the transformation of the home he had never lived in, only visited, my youngest son reflected, "Mom, this doesn't look like you!" A smile slid across my face like cake batter spilled onto a freshly waxed floor. "Ah, but it is me," I beamed.

Soon, my garden, the midlife child I had molded from raw earth, would begin to awaken from a fretful sleep anxious to tantalize me with its ever-changing horizon of hues and textures. But I would no longer be there to cheer it on, to feed it with my tender words and the compost nature prepared in massive batches for its nourishment.

The night before I was due to leave, I said goodbye to the small periwinkle room that served as my office, library, and infrequently used guestroom. I went through every room and thanked each for its warmth, comfort, security, and refuge. I put on a warm jacket and said goodbye to my small front garden, the boastful one that everyone who passed by declared the most beautiful in the neighborhood. Then I went to the big garden, Monet's palette hidden behind a private gateway. I sat in the frosty marble chips on a walkway I'd nearly dislocated my back creating, and wept.

My sense of loss caused my body to convulse with a rip-tide of fear that threatened to suck me down and toss me off course. I looked upward and focused upon the crisp spring sky and felt the current of my resistance retreat until I was delivered onto the shore of surrender. The tears of loss turned into a river of joy for what I was about to experience and gratitude for all that God had already given me. I thanked the garden, the sun that made it strong, and the rain that cleansed and nourished it. I even thanked the squirrels that had tormented me with their voracious appetite for yet another newly planted exotic bulb; then I walked away. Forever.

After protracted international flights and connection delays, accompanied by four suitcases overflowing with a few beloved books, staples, clothing, and my laptop, I arrived in Cairo. It was March 11, 2001—exactly six months before 9/11.

You are not a believer until you want for your neighbor what you want for yourself.

~Prophet Mohammed

4

Chapter 2

March/April 2001

With the exception of "the bird" and the peril that lurks in breaking cultural rules I don't even know exist, I'm settling into my new flat and embracing each interaction with the Egyptian people. It's easy to inhale their charm and Gaelic-like wit; the culture and Islam will take a bit longer

The "bird" is my doorbell. When activated, it sounds like the final bowel-loosening plea of a chicken whose neck is about to be wrung. If I were prone to brutality, within twenty-four hours of my arrival, I would have finished the job.

Auntie, my venerable landlady, is a reproduction of Winston Churchill minus the bowler and cigar. I don't know if nature gave them to her, or if the fistfuls of cash she regularly exhumes from between her breasts only makes them appear like double sand dunes. She heaves them shamelessly while rotating falcon eyes to explain away the deficiency of basic amenities in my flat. According to her, her last tenant, an Englishwoman, exercised "tote rights" when she left Egypt. If this is true, it's too bad the woman didn't steal the furniture. Two couches and eight overstuffed chairs dwarf my living room. They're as antiquated as the pyramids, but not as well maintained, and at their highest peak, less comfy to sit upon.

My two-bedroom/one bath furnished apartment has a cozy dining room. The kitchen and bathroom suffer from exhaustion. However, there is a washing machine and a new dishwasher. I don't use the dishwasher. If I fill it, I will have nothing left to cook in or eat from. My rent in U.S. dollars is less than four hundred per month plus utilities, trash, and *bawaab* (bow-ab) fee A bawaab is kind of like a guard, handyman, servant, and "virtue protector" who resides in front of the building. He escorts visitors to your door, handles problems in your apartment, carries packages, snoops for the landlord and the government, shares your business with the universe, and runs errands.

I have only one cooking pot, one frying pan, one wooden spoon, one sheet, two pillows distended with rocks, and a weary red chenille bedspread in need of Rogaine. As we've gotten to know each other, Auntie regularly appears at my door with little treasures: cooking pots, a sugar bowl, and a set of canisters. She speaks little English and I no Arabic, so we communicate through her children, Mo, or via pantomime.

Ah, Mo. His given name is Mohamed. Though linked in wisdom and spirit to the Prophet of his faith, his impish innocence beckoned that I dub him Mo; Peter Pan would suit him just as well. When I visited Egypt as a tourist, Mo was my first tour guide. A graduate of Cairo University, he's fluent in both English and French.

His hair is close-cropped, as coiled as a perm left in a tad too long. Though he's on the sweet side of forty, threads of platinum haphazardly imitate starlight on a moonless night. His nose, reflecting his Nubian heritage, is broad and almost as expansive as his smile. When stretched sideways in a grin, his cookie duster moustache lifts, exposing a child-like chasm between front teeth that are otherwise perfect. Eyes, as dark and rich as the soil of the Congo, are prone to overflowing like the Nile in springtime. They observe and nourish everything in their path. A former soccer star destined for greatness until his mother insisted he quit to focus upon his studies, he moves with the poise of a sinewy lion.

Mo works full time evaluating the risk of insuring maritime cargo, on weekends as a professional tour guide. Leisure is stolen from the hours he should be asleep; thankfully he needs little. He takes responsibility for everyone around him: his family, dear friends, acquaintances, friends of friends, orphans, those who live on the street, and for me. Mortal exhaustion cannot prevent him from serving as my father/brother/protector. Our friendship allows him to gnaw upon the life questions that trouble his heart and to quench his thirst for understanding a world beyond the horizon of his birth. I admire and ache for him.

Mo negotiated and leased my apartment. Auntie is the mother of an old classmate. He thought I would be safe here with "family" to look after me. Before I arrived, he had the apartment cleaned and stocked it with bread, coffee, sugar, and water. He told Auntie how kind I am. Apparently she believes him, but I'm not sure her youngest child, whom I've dubbed Moopiga, does. Although he's Mo's friend, I already recoil at the sight of him.

Moopiga is built like a Chrysler P.T. Cruiser; undersized arms and legs, squat in the torso, but plenty of room in the rear. He feigns disinterest in me as anything other than a source of income. Yet I can smell his envy and lust, which the language of his deportment translates into disdain whenever I am in his anointed presence. He's a kilo short of ugly, as covetous as a burglar peering through the window of a mansion, and as perverse as a pimp who traffics in children. I guess you could infer that I don't like him.

He's married to gentle Fatma, the mother of his young son and daughter. Sometimes I hear her crying in their bedroom, other times I marvel at the force and brevity of their lovemaking as it pummels down upon me from two floors above. Both make me sigh in sadness, but only for her.

The whole family lives in the building. Those I haven't met are inquisitive about me, so they come with Auntie when she is visiting, or ring my doorbell in an attempt to ascertain whether or not their grandmother, mother, or brother has pegged me correctly. They say nothing, only stare and then pantomime that they rang the bird by accident. Fat chance. They have a need to examine a Western woman who is unmarried, but quite marriageable, who lives alone, but may be a stereotypical Western version of a *sharmoota* (loose woman). Even on the street, I feel like a pigeon that everyone but Mo is trying to thrust into a triangular hole.

$$\triangle \, \triangle \, \triangle$$

Repairs need to be made. The traffic in and out of my apartment is like Wal-Mart on a Saturday afternoon.

Workmen are not allowed to enter unless my bawaab is present to hover like a fly the size of a Buick no repellent could deter. A woman is never to be alone with a man who is not her husband, brother, uncle, son, or father. Because they have known Mo since he was a college student—and therefore he is considered to be morally beyond reproach— it appears that even bawaab Mohamed and Auntie have exceptions to society's rules; the exception is the rule. I just don't know what they are yet.

Mohamed has a pleasing weathered face, the hue of a chestnut pulled from the fire a century ago. A flowing native robe (a *galabaya*) covers his lanky frame. Long underwear is revealed when he sits or hikes up his robe to squat. I do not know if he has any hair. His skull is never without a turban created from old, but clean cloths; some are white, others are agreeable prints. I like the print ones best. They seem to bring out the depth of his smile and the twinkling behind his cataract-glazed ripe olive eyes. Although it's a bit chilly, he wears only sandals. One of his big toes is twisted, a swollen, leathery appendage.

So they won't track more sand onto the faux oriental carpets and freshly planted white ceramic tile floors, before they enter, my bawaab and workmen leave their shoes outside. Unfortunately, dirt from their feet is the least mess they are likely to leave behind. The concept of cleaning up after one's self is nonexistent. It's left for me to do. In the social pecking order, cleaning people are considered lower than laborers or repairmen. It would shame their status to take on this task. This had me a tad confused. I am considered "superior." So, if they think it's beneath them to do so, how come it's not beneath me? I guess they think I have a maid who will materialize and do what a superior woman in their culture would never tackle. It would twist their knickers to know that I'm a rather accomplished charwoman.

I turned the dining room into an office/den and created two seating areas and a dining niche in the living room. Like containers of Dijon mustard lined up on a grocery shelf, Egyptian furniture is displayed in identical groupings and colors. Apparently, putting chairs or couches anywhere but against a wall is unheard of, as is the use of complimentary fabrics and patterns. Mushroom, in every hue, my least favorite color, surrounds me.

Last night, Auntie wanted to know how I had moved the furniture, then questioned why I hadn't requested that Mohamed do it for me. At the time, it seemed easier to do it myself.

Auntie and her family guffawed appropriately as I demonstrated how pushing with my bottom can move mountains; Moopiga almost smiled. They found it amusing when I added, "I was afraid Mohamed would hurt himself." He's prone to carrying everything on his back, including rolling suitcases. How would he have moved the china closet? Besides, even though I'm to pay him a monthly "fee" of 20 LE (Egyptian pounds), I'm required to tip him for extras. I've been cautioned to be fair, but not too generous. If I give too little I'll insult him; if I give too much, I upset the delicate economic balance and encourage him to take advantage of me. Yikes!

There are so many rules. Thank God dear Mo is available to unravel them for me. My questions make his eyes crinkle in amusement until he looks like a smile on legs. He takes pleasure in answering my questions. It gives him the opportunity to observe his culture through an unfiltered lens.

△ △ △

El Maadi (which means riverboat crossing in Arabic), the section of Cairo where I live, is a charming merger of old Egypt and a poignant interpretation of suburban U.S.A. The semi-paved road in front of my building is nestled between Road 9—a main shopping lane—and an open, nearly green spot. The foundations of historic villas retain their secrets amongst wild vines and donkey carts of trash circuitously dumped to save affluent landlords from paying a monthly rubbish removal fee. McDonald's is just down the street.

My flat reminds me of an oceanless version of Key West. Every room has wooden windows that open in or slide sideways. Since I live on the ground floor, the doors to the outside have miniature grated inserts that can be unfastened to allow for ventilation or to see who's ringing the bird without opening the whole door. Some work, others were painted shut a generation ago. Wooden shutters, invented and manufactured by Auntie's husband, connect to pulleys concealed in the cinderblock walls skimmed with plaster. They rarely reach the windowsill without bouncing up, so when lowered, they don't provide complete privacy, but do allow for airflow.

There are bars on all the windows and a separate entrance to my personal garden. With Mohamed on guard twenty-four hours a day, who could possibly get by? He sleeps just outside the entrance to the building on a hand-hewn bench he makes up each morning. He naps a lot during the day, perhaps because at night he dozes like an owl. Other bawaabs and their families live in one-room huts on top of elegant buildings or in dirt-floored areas carved from a crater resembling a basement.

I've already started a compost pile to nourish some of the tropical vegetation we use as houseplants in the West, and to feed the plants I've begun to move to augment the skimpy flowerbeds.

There are different, merrily dressed birds that croon while I work. Some are permanent residents; others are tourists on a stopover from South Africa and the Middle East. During the day, with the exception of a wind chime tuned to the pitch of cascading shards of glass, it's very quiet.

Mo takes very good care of me. He has propelled me around El Maadi to purchase food, adaptors, supplies, and a fistfull of phone cards. I will need a different card to call cell phones (mobiles), the United States, and to access the Internet. I can only use my home telephone to call residences within Cairo. The only really reliable phone service is a mobile. I'm thinking about having Auntie's eldest granddaughter arrange for me to purchase one, but Mo thinks I should wait. They're expensive and I don't know how long I'll stay.

Tonight another one of Mo's friends will come to help me install my Internet connection. This morning, my lovely, fresh-faced young American acquaintance, Kim, is taking me on a taxi tour of El Maadi and the expat community center, the Community Services Association (CSA) where I may sign up for some classes. Her Adonis husband, Raed, who speaks English with less of an accent than many Americans, was in charge of coordinating my trip when I was here as a tourist.

It turns out that Betty Atherton created CSA when her husband was the U.S. Ambassador to Egypt. She saw that a lot of the wives had too much time on their hands and founded the center as a haven where they could gather, make friends, work out, and learn something new. I met Betty in Washington when we took a healing certification course together. Even here, the circle of the world is infinitesimal. Through CSA, Betty's wisdom and energy continue to make life easier for every expatriate who moves to Cairo.

△△△

The days require a light jacket. The sun is too far away to generate more than a whisper of spring. The nights are colder. I'm so grateful to Auntie for surprising me with a thick blanket. I'd been sleeping in several layers of clothing beneath a sheet borrowed from a guestroom bed and the balding spread. I've been told to expect excessive heat in the summer. Apparently global warming has created humidity even in the desert. This is a reminder of home I can do without.

Now that my computer has been transformed into one that works on this voltage, I'm able to listen to my CDs while I work. Mo continues to be protective of me; he's also obsessive about obtaining the lowest price for anything I need. It's not unusual for him to firmly stride away from a merchant while spitting in disgust, "This is too expensive. We can do better." Unfortunately, since the price is fixed, he can't negotiate the cost of phone cards.

To go online, I use a card good for ten hours. it took a century to send my first letter so I doubt it will last very long. My connection kept burping. Egyptians are used to sporadic phone service. I'm not. While Americans are obsessed with the capacity to do things quickly, the average Egyptian is grateful if something works at all. With the exception of traffic, a buffet, or a sale, they're an incredibly patient people and hardworking.

Since most working-class Egyptians hold two or more jobs, they sleep little and are usually only available to fix things long after my bedtime has passed. The flow of nocturnal workmen has not abated.

I'm adapting to many new ways of doing things. I've learned creative ways to make coffee (with a strainer lined with a paper towel) and to mash beans with my lone wooden spoon rather than in a food processor. I don't miss my clothes dryer; I rather enjoy hanging things out in the fresh air. At the market I can usually figure out the contents of a product even when the label contains only squiggles of Arabic. I'm making do with less.

I've settled into a schedule. In the morning I walk to the local markets to buy food for dinner then do my chores: laundry, watering the garden and removing the skinny layer of sand that continuously covers the floors and furniture. In the afternoon I write. In the evening I have dinner with Mo, eat at my desk, or read.

This morning I ventured out to run errands. The first obligatory stop was at a money machine located in the vestibule of a neighborhood bank. Although I carefully enter each debit in my checkbook, since the exchange rate varies almost daily and access fees differ, it is already hopelessly off. I'm also learning to get over my IRS-inspired mania for receipts. I haven't quite figured out how to keep records. One is expected to pay repair people and the landlord in cash without the benefit of a receipt. To avoid Egyptian taxes, my lease says I pay 850 LE per month in rent. I'm really paying 1,500 LE. Obtaining proof of payment from Auntie has as much potential of success as a horse cantering on two legs.

I've also learned that it really is slightly less treacherous to walk in the street rather than on the sidewalk. Most are quite narrow. Haphazardly deposited trees obstruct the path; splintered cement has created treacherous fissures and ankle-twisting craters. The traffic is much lighter in El Maadi than in downtown Cairo, so much so that I've even crossed some main streets. This might not sound like a coup, but it is. There are approximately 1.5 million cars on the streets of Cairo—usually at the same time—and few traffic lights or stop signs. Many tourists take a taxi to the other side of the street rather than trying to cross by themselves. Crossing guards? Get real!

On my way to the market, I pass young police officers ensconced in groups on nearly every street corner. Since summer has yet to arrive, they're still dressed in midnight blue uniforms consisting of long-sleeved shirts, black belts, berets, and ankle-high boots that must be terribly uncomfortable because they're seldom fully zipped. In the summer they'll wear white cotton pants and shirts. Other than their capacity to mask the presence of street corners and to collectively leer at female pedestrians, I'm not sure they have a function. Based upon how disrespectfully they hold their weapons, I hope they're not loaded. I think they're pretending to be soldiers rather than young men from the farmlands and ghettos of Egypt consigned into mandatory service.

While out, I found a neighborhood office supply store to buy paper for my printer. The size is quite peculiar. It's far longer than eleven inches. I fear the editors I work with in my freelance work will fail to appreciate its flight of imagination.

Further along the street I stopped at a dry goods market. I was seeking my favorite cleaning product, ammonia. To my surprise, I learned that it is sold only in concentrated form in pharmacies. In desperation, I spent the equivalent of $6.50 for a bottle of Mr. Clean.

At the produce stand, I bought vegetables to create some of the Egyptian dishes I have come to enjoy. In particular, I like the salads fashioned from eggplant, cabbage, beets, tomatoes, cucumbers, or carrots.

After lugging my purchases home, I went outside to hang a load of laundry. It is fortunate that my clothesline is protected from the apartments above by a slight overhang. One of my neighbors, obviously suffering from a chest cold, hung over his balcony and used my garden as a spittoon.

There is so much I want to see and do. I'm still searching for the right Arabic immersion course. I've learned how to say thank you—*shokran*, no thank you—*la-a shokran*, and the names of a few native dishes.

If her schedule permits, one Saturday morning Kim and I hope to go horseback riding at the base of the pyramids. I was able to do this when I was here as a tourist. It's nearly impossible to describe the exhilaration of gently cantering over sand dunes in the shadow of sites so lush in history and spiritual significance you virtually inhale their energy.

Though they took up valuable space, I'm so glad I thought to pack my boots and breeches. I hope they'll be used often. I brought my shiny purple helmet, too. I attached it and my down pillow to a handle on my wheeling backpack. As I pulled it behind me, I must have looked like Snoopy's version of a middle-aged Hell's Angel.

Last week I stopped by the local antique store to meet the owner, Mo's friend, Amin. Part philosopher, student of human behavior, and a devotee of deflowering as many heterosexual men as he can in one lifetime, his eyes wear a perpetual mask of amusement. He insisted that I sit and have coffee while he smoked tobacco through a native water pipe called a *sheisha*. Expats from around the world wandered in and out to bask in the rarefied atmosphere of his court. I met a European decorator and a professor from the American University in Cairo.

Because he knows how dear it is to me, Mo took me back to my beloved Sakkara, the home of King Zoser's Step Pyramid. While we were there, a guard whispered that terrorists had shot and killed several tourists and a police officer on the pyramid grounds in Giza. Needless to say, this was very unnerving. We left immediately, but not before another officer yelled in Arabic that he wouldn't be upset if I, and the other Westerners who milled about the sacred site, suffered the same fate. I haven't learned how to swear in Arabic yet; Mo's retort was clearly a vibrant one.

There is no "instant" news analysis so we didn't learn the real story for several days. A Japanese resident of El Maadi clashed with a hawker. This is really an oxymoron. One cannot interact with a hawker without, at a minimum, a verbal battle. "No" in any language bounces off them as if their brains had been left on the last car of a train leaving the station. In this case, the hawker attacked the woman with a knife. He was shot in the leg by a guard. I guess she tried to say "no" in too many languages. He'll probably spend the rest of his life in prison. Physical violence against anyone, but particularly a tourist or expat, is a major crime. The Egyptian government does a reliable job of protecting foreigners. They don't take kindly to terrorists or thieves. The incident at the Pyramids was quite unusual. Central Park it isn't—thankfully.

> *Each day that goes by*
> *and I'm okay is a feast.*
>
> ~ Egyptian Proverb

If you stay with people for forty days, you'll become part of them or they'll become part of you.

~ Egyptian Proverb

Chapter 3

April 2001

A gangly poinsettia dangles over the wall into my garden like an adolescent whose torso hasn't caught up with its arms and legs. Each day a breeze leaves gifts of clothing and children's toys that plunge or glide from the balconies and clotheslines above. I've been neatly stacking everything on the staircase leading to the units above me, but I keep the clothespins as my recovery fee. I didn't know it, but I'm supposed to give everything to my bawaab to redistribute, even the panties.

There are stray cats everywhere. A pumpkin-colored tabby guards my door. If the mating reverberations I hear each night are any indication of their fertility, before summer starts, the feline population will double.

There are two Western-run animal rights organizations. One of their primary purposes is to capture, spay and neuter strays. It's a problem with no beginning or end. They also attempt to place homeless and abandoned cats, dogs, kittens and puppies with loving owners.

Some are adopted by expats. However, when summer comes and they leave on holiday or for good, it's not unusual for them to dump their pet at the shelter or leave them on the street. Of course many take them with them, but countries with stern quarantine laws make it difficult for a pet to move with its family.

Few Egyptians have pets; those who do are wealthier and usually opt to purchase or adopt animals with pedigrees. In general, wild cats and dogs survive by scouring through garbage; locals feed some.

As is true in other underprivileged countries, cats and

dogs are seen as a menace. There's the fear of rabies—which is rampant here—but also a discomfort with the whole Western adulation of animals. After all, if one does not have enough money to feed their family, why would they worry about a hungry stray animal?

Unfortunately, when the novelty wears off, pets are often abused and local children have been caught and stopped by expats as they take their aggression out on puppies and kittens. Thankfully, most of the animals are too smart to get caught. Stories of the children's creative methods of torture are rampant. In this culture, unlike ours, abuse of animals is not seen as the precursor to the creation of legendary serial killers.

This weekend, when I went to the country, I noticed that *gamoosa* (water buffalo) are used as often as horses to pull ploughs. They're also bred for their meat. Gamoosa is quite tender, virtually fatless, hormone-less, and not as rich tasting as American beef.

Trunks of trees flanking country roads are clad in white paint. Since drivers rarely use headlights—they keep them off so as not to bother other drivers, or because they think using headlights will drain their car battery—the paint, in theory, is supposed to assist cars from straying off the road and hitting them. The custom of not using headlights is not quite as hair-raising in the city. With so many cars on the road, brake lights and street lamps offer some illumination, but in the country only the moon and stars are available to light the way.

Even at home, the Egyptian concept of adequate lighting for different tasks seems odd to the Westerner. Most Egyptians don't own lamps. They use multiple overhead fixtures or chandeliers. They're usually hung lopsided on a hook, leaving a crater in the ceiling exposed.

△ △ △

I stopped up the sink again, a near daily occurrence. My bawaab shuffled in carrying the most wretched plunger I've ever seen. Heaven only knows where it has been and what it has seen. I wish I had my tools. I could take the trap apart and fix it properly. The last ten plumbers sure didn't.

I'd also like to wash the cover to the overhead fixture in my office, but that will necessitate Mohamed getting on a ladder—if Auntie even owns one. I can't just ask for a ladder without his thinking that I think he doesn't know how to do his job; this would be a major insult. The vestige of flies and mosquitoes is solid, barely allowing the wattage of a taper.

One thing more about ladders, because workmen don't arrive with one, it's an item every expat should own. They're expensive and many workmen come by taxi or metro; even if they owned one they couldn't carry it with them.

If no ladder is available, repairmen often use the furniture or jump up and down a lot. Some buildings have makeshift ladders similar to the ones used to storm castle walls. They're created out of two poles with planks of wood attached to form steps. They are single, not stationary stepladders. Thus, unless held upward by two or more men, they don't work for reaching anything in the center of the room. When used in the perimeter, they wreck the walls.

Auntie told Mo that she's installing a mirror in my dining area. I told him I'd much rather have a food processor, a blender or a hand mixer. Do you have any idea how long it takes to mash a pot of garbanzo beans with a fork or spoon? I can only imagine the muscles I'll build up when I whip cream; egg whites I think are out of the question.

Last week I attended my first meeting of the Women's League hosted by the local community church. I grasped it as an opportunity to meet other women and to learn about volunteer activities.

The guest speaker was a missionary who works at a private, Christian-run orphanage in Upper Egypt, the south of the country. The Nile flows upward from Central Africa so it hits southern Egypt first. I became quite uncomfortable when he made what I considered to be some rather condescending comments about Egyptians and Islam. It hurt to hear him speak so unkindly of the people who, without any benefit to themselves, have taken me into their hearts.

As well as meetings and shopping events, the Women's League sponsors volunteer opportunities. I had the chance to participate in a visit to a cancer hospital they support. The building was exhausted. It looked as if it was built in the 1950s. We passed out toys, juice, cookies, and baseball hats to the children lying in rows of beds in the overflowing, children's ward. The children come from all over Egypt. From the moment they're admitted, their mothers and other family members never leave their side. There is not enough trained staff to care for the children or to do what the nurses can't or won't. Their families bathe them, monitor them, clean up their vomit and diarrhea, cuddle them, and cook their meals. The family also provides supplies for their child's care: soap, rubber gloves, needles, blood, bandages, disinfectant, and medicine.

If I hadn't had extensive hospice experience, it would have been impossible not to crumple in grief. Thankfully, I was able to look beyond their naked heads, withered bodies, intravenous drips, and the used syringes scattered haphazardly on and beneath their beds. We shared the universal sign of love, a smile which most of the children eagerly returned despite their pain or nausea. They ranged in age from infants to teenagers. There was so much sweetness and wincing horror.

I told Raed about my experience. I said, that I'd like to do more than passing out juice, baseball hats, and small toys. The language barrier makes it difficult. "Remember Jeanne," he reflected in the dear Egyptian way of cutting through the gauze that hides us from communing with others, "They'll feel your love. There will be no barriers."

△ △ △

As my journey begins to gel into a veneer approximating normalcy, my aloneness and desire for the friendship and companionship of other women has begun to bounce off the walls. While I relish my alone time and Mo is there for me as often as he can be, I want to meet other expats. I think it would be enlightening to see if their experiences jibe with mine. I'm sure they could also provide me with information to help me adjust. Most of all, I miss having a variety of friends around with whom I can share adventures and stimulating conversation that doesn't center around toilet training, the horrors of teenagers, gossip, or shopping. I've begun to make friends with a few Egyptian men, but as in the West, their focus upon the vitality of my mind all too quickly shifts to attempts to discover not what is in my heart, but beneath my jeans.

My situation is limiting. I don't work in an office; therefore I don't have the opportunity to make friends with colleagues. Since I'm not part of a duo, married women may feel uncomfortable including me in couple events.

The mask of self-assurance that covered my fear of not belonging, has, out of necessity, been mothballed. If I don't risk letting others know that I'd really like to meet new people and make new friends, they may assume that I don't need any. So, I've gone out of my way to ask everyone I meet how I can find women who are interested in the same things I am. As I've learned to do, I've also asked God for his help.

As a result of my prayers and openness, Clara, one of the women on the hospital trip, kindly offered to take me along to a birthday luncheon on the Nile. Unfortunately, most of the women I met have small children. Their husband's companies and children's schools are the apex of their social life. We have little in common. Still, it was a beautiful fall-like day and a joy to be out on the water in a native sailboat, a *felucca*.

Many of the women lease horses and ride three times a week. This is too much expense and time for me, but they said they'd "ring me up" soon to go with them. We'll see. I think they were doing the "Y'all come" routine, European style.

Anyway, in between the hospital and the luncheon, I went to the Community Center with another woman I met last week at the church program. Her name is Molly. I think she's the answer to my prayers. She has four children, three in college in the U.S. and one in her senior year of high school here. Molly is from Maine, rounder than she'd like to be, and authentically kind. She's about my age, tall, with short sandalwood hair that frames a fair, heart-shaped face and mirthful blue eyes.

Expat women lead interesting lives. Since most have young children, they do volunteer work, ride, go out to lunch, shop, and take golf lessons while their children are in school. Apparently, at night families stay in.

Tonight I went to my first yoga class. It was boring. Rather than doing many different postures, the instructor has choreographed an inflexible workout that is unlikely to vary.

During the day, I walk everywhere possible. Each time I find my way, I rejoice as if I've just competed and won an Olympic event. As long as I stay away from the diagonal streets and the circles that torment El Maadi as they do D.C., I don't become lost. At night, I take a cab. I must learn how to give my address in Arabic. My poor driver was apoplectic when he tried to bring me home tonight. Until I learn more basic Arabic, I will utilize a map and my daylight wanderings to direct drivers where I want to go.

I find the days confusing. Due to the Islamic Sabbath, Friday is the first day of our weekend and everyone else is involved with their families so there are no events for me to attend until Sunday, the first day of the week, rolls around.

Each morning I awaken to the reverberation of Muslims calling fellow worshipers to the first prayer of the day (there are five) about an hour *before* sunrise. The melodic summoning begins, with *Allah*, the first of ninety-nine names of God. It resounds like an immense sigh from a loudspeaker atop a neighboring mosque crowned by a minaret that looks like an intricately carved candlestick. Sometimes it rudely awakens me. If I'm nestled beneath Auntie's velour blanket that looks more Native American than Egyptian, it sounds like a sweet lullaby encouraging me to nuzzle deeper into my dreams and to forget how great the gap is between our cultures.

I've been having a very difficult time with my Internet connection, or lack thereof. If I'm able to get online, I'm immediately cut off. Apparently I need to install Netscape. It works better here than Microsoft. If I can stay online long enough, I'll download it. At the moment, I'm sitting in a cyber café. Actually, unless I'm interested in sipping on a hard drive or munching on a keyboard, café is a misnomer. There are three computers in a small room you can only reach by walking through what could loosely be defined as a real estate office. The guy who works here is actively typing away. Although he appears very busy, whenever I rise to ask him a question, he immediately changes his screen. He obviously has no problem accessing whatever rings his bell.

Each small challenge met becomes a major victory. Events from home are distracting me from adjusting here. The last few days should have earned me first prize in the frustration triathlon.

As soon as my plane left Washington, a purchaser, who had lost out on the bidding on my building, approached my tenants directly. Under D.C. law, tenants have about thirty days to match the terms of a ratified contract or to assign or sell their rights to a third party. They chose the last option. By using D.C. tenant laws to his advantage, the new purchaser, who wanted my tenants to leave for reasons he never shared, paid them to do so. While I have no problem with my tenants making money off the sale of the building, if he defaults on the contract after they move out, I'll be without the income to pay over $4,000.00 per month in expenses. Ever since I was notified of the situation, my stomach and heart have been on a marathon roller coaster ride. I hate roller coasters. If I were going to die or end up losing my building through bankruptcy, I'd rather start the process standing on the ground.

This turning worm necessitated my locating FedEx and fax facilities to finalize a deal with a person I had no desire to do business with. Upholding my end of the law was more difficult from here than walking across the Nile without contracting a deadly disease. At least I have a general idea where the Nile is.

It took two days of monumental frustration to accomplish what would have taken minutes in the U.S. The Yellow Pages is available, but not commonly distributed. I couldn't find a cabbie that understood what I needed. Without the intervention of Molly's husband's secretary, I would still be walking the streets, begging everyone I met for help in locating an international delivery service. She was able to provide a telephone number for FedEx. Trying to take a taxi to their office wasn't an option because I couldn't find it on my map, so I inquired about pickup and shipping charges and how long it would take them to come to my flat with an envelope for me to place the papers in. They don't take checks or credit cards. I didn't have enough cash.

The first problem I encountered was that the banks were already closed. The money machines I frequent were empty. I walked to the other end of Road 9 to locate another machine. Success! I went home, called FedEx and was told they would come within three hours. This was in what I have begun to understand is Egyptian time. Three hours turned out to be about six.

After the papers were launched I needed to find a place where I could send an international fax. The new purchaser insisted that I immediately send a copy of his signed contract with my original signature. He couldn't wait for it to arrive with the other papers. I'm always amazed by how a cunning individual expects everyone else to act like them.

I went back up Road 9. After numerous attempts to get help, I found an expat who assisted me. He steered me to a shop on Road 9 that has a fax machine. Of course, because the employee didn't know how to dial the international access code for the U.S. before the fax phone number, it took many attempts, hand wringing and my tears to convince him to please try "one more time." It should be an interesting three months until settlement.

On the stable side of the coaster, I can now return home without a hassle. Mo taught me how to say "*Shara tessa gamb McDonald's*" (Road 9 next to McDonald's). From there I tell the cabbie, "*Ala tuul*" (straight ahead/away) until we get to my street. Then I say "*Yemeen*" (right) and when we get to my building, "*Hena kwayyis*" (here's good). Whew!

It's going anywhere else that's still a challenge.

I've learned the necessity of keeping at least 100 LE around (currently about $38.00). I was a bit shocked the first time the gasman came to the door with a bill. They don't mail bills. Like FedEx, you can't pay by check. This is basically a cash-and-carry society. They come to your door, hand you a bill and you pay it *now*.

Since I'm still not good at reading numbers in Arabic, I had the money collector go to Auntie to pay the bill. Then I reimbursed her. As it turns out, this was wise. He told me I owed 75 LE, then 25 LE. My street-smart experience in D.C. has come in handy. Although my bawaab escorted him, he wasn't, in this case, much help. Who knows, if the guy gets more than he's supposed to, perhaps Mohamed receives a cut.

△ △ △

As a condition of their husband's employment, the Egyptian government does not allow most expat wives to work in Egypt. Their husbands often work longer hours than they would at home. Therefore, women my age face long days and are forced to learn to live the life of the suddenly idle rich. Western men joke that in their next life they "want to come back as an expat wife." Their husbands' companies are usually, but not always, very helpful in assisting them in settling in. Most families are paired with another family who serves as personal mentors. If I had a husband, I could have just sent the real estate papers with him to the office where they would have been shipped and faxed.

Some women have their own car and driver. Everyone seems to have a maid at least three times per week. Others have a nanny and/or a cook. If they live in a villa rather than an apartment, they may have a gardener and their own security guards or bawaab. Depending upon how large their flat or villa is, a housekeeper is as much a necessity as it is a luxury. Dust constantly covers and permeates everything. It's nearly impossible to stay on top of the cleaning.

Expats, no matter what their social or economic status

at home, are considered by most Egyptians to be rich. Of course, based upon what they earn working two or more jobs, by comparison, we are rich. Sadly, this society also appears to embrace the mentality that any product or person from outside Egypt is superior to anything or anyone locally produced.

I hear that many expats quickly begin to suffer from memory loss and mental *littleness*. They come here as middle-class men and women, but because of tax incentives, company paid housing, higher salaries, and bonus incentives that lure them into accepting positions overseas in a second or third world country, they're living far better than they would at home and sometimes forget who they are.

With the exception of Western products and housing, everything is cheaper than it is in the West. If they're not into saving, expats have a lot of money to spend on stuff they'd never be able to afford at home. What's interesting is that while many make it their goal to buy as much gold, precious gems and silver as they can carry and store, they think nothing of haggling with a souvenir merchant, for what seems like hours, to negotiate a price that's fifty cents lower than what they'd already agreed upon. They're masters of the art of barter. Sometimes it's embarrassing to watch the tap dance that begins with: "I'm really a poor" Brit, American, Korean, German, French, Scandinavian, or Japanese. When it comes to paying fair salaries to the local people they employ and tipping for the services of a taxi driver or waiter, many are preposterously tight and often out-and-out rude.

Because inexpensive help is available, as soon as they arrive, some young couples begin to produce children at an amazing rate. If they're able to stay here until their last baby is in school, some mothers totally avoid the grunt work of childcare. I'm envious.

In addition to cooks, nannies, and personal drivers, people actually have gardeners who come and water the plants on their balcony. Manicurists who, in addition to taking care of all their nails, will exfoliate and cream their arms and legs and a masseuse who will knead their overfed bodies.

Women who utilize all these services find themselves with a lot of extra time. Some take classes or volunteer in the community. Others learn how to ride, play darts, or golf. Some women begin to drink too much. AA meetings would swell out onto the street if everyone who has a problem recognized it. Others have so much time to shop, rather than saving, they return home bankrupt. A few have affairs with their own or their husband's driver, or a cornucopia of afternoon liaisons with repairmen, delivery boys, and merchants whom they dub "toy boys." I wonder what the toy boys call them.

Some quickly begin to believe they really are wealthy and upper class. Heaven only knows what happens when they go back home. It must be rather horrible. Thankfully, since I'm paying my own way, I've yet to be bitten by this illusion bug.

△ △ △

Auntie supervised as her worker installed "the mirror." Now, for entertainment, I can stand in front of it and watch myself mash beans. Since my ability to cook is quite limited, I've decided to just chill. I don't eat that much so it's easier to feast on fruit, salad, mashed beans, cheese, yogurt, and carryout (or carry home, as they say here).

I've discovered a divine German bakery where everything is covered. This is important. One quickly learns to not trust the "purity" of the bread sold in open-air bakeries. If it's not baked there, young men on bicycles deliver it. The bread is often carried on enormous uncovered metal disks balanced on their heads. When they stop suddenly, or swerve, some of the bread falls off. Passersby are quite helpful. They pick up whatever has fallen onto the road and put it back on the tray. Before the guy who sells the bread gives it to you in a bag (sometimes there are none unless you bring your own) he knocks it together to get rid of the dust. There are also bread men on bicycles outfitted with huge iron trays. They drive through neighborhoods so everyone can buy their bread at their front door. Thankfully, I am seeing more and more plastic being used to cover things.

The German bakery sells a beautiful leek quiche for 10 LE that lasts for a few meals. I've found a butcher who sells gamoosa, a bonus since everyone is a bit afraid of mad cow disease.

There seems to be no overt racial discrimination here amongst Egyptians (though light skin is appreciated more by some than dark). Egypt has been occupied by half the world, so her people range in hue from the African heritage of the Nubians, to the pastiness of Europeans. One of the children in the cancer ward had the most beautiful sapphire blue eyes, yet his skin was the color of burnt brown sugar. Perhaps it's economic, but there seems to be animosity towards the growing population of Ethiopian and Sudanese refugees.

I have a temporary housemate. She's about a week old. I think she was deserted by her mother because she's so cranky, or was. She had fleas and passed them on to me. She's a tabby kitten with gray-and-black markings. Amin (from the antique store) sent her home with me on Friday after her mother left her in his shop and enjoyed the peace and quiet so much she didn't return. Since most cats and dogs run wild here, he assured me I could let her loose once she is weaned . . . we'll see. I've named her Sphinx. Amin asked if I like dogs. Oh dear, I wonder what he has in store for me this week.

△ △ △

I had a lovely visit with the sister of a colleague of my brother John who works at the U.N. International School. Last Friday night, Lydia and her husband invited me to visit their home. They're Coptic Christians so I was able to learn a bit about the role they play in a society in which they are the minority.

They live on the other side of Cairo in a beautiful apartment that's been passed down from one generation to the next (this is normal, people often live in the same place from birth to death). She teaches high school chemistry and owns a daycare center. He is a builder/developer who tells me that the recession is so severe there is no money to lend. Obviously this makes it a challenge to sell what he has built.

They have two children, a teenage son whose Apollonian face and physique will break many hearts, and a young daughter who speaks English as well as I do.

I thought I'd been invited for lunch (our dinner). It was strange. Everything was brought to the living room in stages. Only I was fed. First I was served juice, then fruit cup, then a strange ice cream made out of gum and pistachios and fruit, then cookies and tea. "Where's the beef?" Not! I learned later that Copts fast a lot. Since Easter is coming, they're fasting now. As their guest, it was required that I be treated like royalty. Fasting rules vary throughout the year. Sometimes Copts can drink only liquids during the day. Other times, for weeks on end, they are not allowed to eat any animal product.

They were so kind and generous. I felt blessed. To top it off, their dog obviously adored me. He kept humping my leg. It's so wonderful to be wanted by a much younger man, even if he has four legs. Speaking of which, it's great having to keep my legs covered. I'm afraid that I'll never be able to wear shorts again. I've discovered that my thighs keep moving after the rest of my body stops. In addition to yoga, some extreme measures need to be taken.

Like various parts of my aging body, each day offers a new challenge. I have come to clearly see that the biggest obstacles I face are internal rather than external and will follow me no matter where I live. Everything is a mirror and an opportunity to grow and to create additional space within myself to fill with peace and joy.

△ △ △

I had lunch with Mary. We met through another contact. Mary is from Annapolis; she's been here two years and expects to stay one more. She has a *quiet* healing practice in El Maadi. I say quiet because the Egyptian government frowns upon such practices—okay, its illegal. To protect herself from being arrested or deported, Mary only takes on new clients via referrals.

Depending upon the interests of the individual, I'm finding that the expat community is a circle that constantly curves back to its beginning. One receives names of other people who then give you the name of someone else until you begin to duplicate contacts. Since we're all in the same pod, no one hesitates to initiate a call. The expat spiritual community is a flourishing one. You just need to know how to find it.

Mary and I bonded instantly over the phone and knew our lunch together would be a long one. It was. We have much in common and enjoyed sharing our thoughts and perspectives. Unfortunately, because she works long hours, it will be difficult for us to see each other often.

I participated in a different volunteer activity, the Baby Wash Program. Women bring their newborns for weekly checkups to a clinic in the poor village of Giza located at the base of the Pyramids. The babies are weighed and observed to see if they're thriving or are having any physical problems. The volunteers then bathe the babies and dress them. Although most of these women don't have running water, I certainly can't believe they don't know how to bathe their babies. Perhaps the title of the program is a misnomer and would be more appropriately titled the "Baby Check" program.

As an additional incentive to participate in the program, the mothers receive a free outfit for their child and a cloth diaper that's quite different from the ones we have at home. It has a narrow hourglass shape. Instead of diaper pins, there's a cord you wrap around the baby's waist and then tie in a bow.

After the volunteer is done, the mother takes the baby back to the waiting room, undresses it and trades outfits with another mother. The mothers seem to prefer the colors of the desert, ones we would find a bit dull to dress a child in.

△ △ △

For the first time since arriving, I returned to my beloved Pyramids. It was an adventure, but probably not for the reasons you would imagine.

Although I told the cab driver "Pyramids" in Arabic (Al Ahram), he ended up taking the wrong exit off the Corniche, a main boulevard that runs parallel to the Nile.

We must have crossed and recrossed the Nile five times before a haze of steam began to rise from beneath the collar of my blouse. I didn't need Arabic to convey my fury. Smiles and rage don't need translation.

He stopped quickly and asked another cabbie to speak to me. Thankfully cabbies are really helpful to each other. I pushed down my window (most window cranks are missing) and explained my destination. "Ah ha!" off we went.

As we approached the entrance, a young boy asked, in Arabic, for a lift. My poor driver was in such a state over my obvious displeasure with his performance that he allowed the child to join us.

The boy spoke passable English. He turned around and addressed me as if he were a tour guide, but the tour he wanted me to take was one I had zero interest in participating in.

He immediately began to try to sell me postcards, a camel, and/or a horseback ride, rare antiquities, etc. Ah ha! A Bedouin child from the village literally nestled adjacent to the foundation of the Pyramids. He was the son of hawkers. Hawkers are just trying to earn a living, but they don't hear *no* in Arabic or English unless an Egyptian guard comes up behind them and boxes their ears. Politeness doesn't work.

When the child told the cabbie to turn left onto the rutted dirt road leading to the top of the village instead of straight ahead to the entrance to the Pyramids, he was scorched by the tongue-lashing of an apoplectic woman who knew exactly what he was up to.

"La-a! La-a!" I screamed in indignation. The cabbie hit the brakes and backed up. He was shaking in terror. When I shamed the child by screaming, "You are a bad boy. Allah will be angry with you!" he flew out of the cab and down the path he had tried to take us on. Putting the fear of God into him took on new meaning!

After reading numerous books, including works about Edgar Cayce, *Initiation* by Elisabeth Haich, *Initiation in the Great Pyramid* by Earlyne Chaney, and volumes one and two of *The Ancient Secret of the Flower of Life* by Drunvalo Melchizedek, that discuss the spiritual significance of different areas in the pyramid complex, I went specifically to

31

visit the King's Chamber in the Great Pyramid. It's only open at certain times. Twice a day, one hundred tickets are sold. I needed to be there at 12:30 p.m. to get in line before the tour operators bought them all. My assertiveness training continued when tour guides cut in line and I had to point out that there were others ahead of them.

A Japanese man stood in line in front of me. He was trying to pick me up so I used his interest to my advantage and gave him money to buy my ticket. He asked if I was married. When I didn't respond, he handed me my ticket and went on his way, alone.

As you enter the Great Pyramid, the granite walls first leading downward and then up into the Queen's and King's Chambers virtually pulsate with energy. They are as cool and smooth as the finest silk; in the diffused light, their patina glows from deep within.

The climb upward is quite rigorous, over a hundred steps at a 90-degree angle. One has to bend in half to enter the King's Chamber, which is located directly above that of the Queen.

As you enter through a U-shaped stone doorway, on the right, at the end of the room is the sarcophagus where Initiates of the Sacred Mystery Schools experienced their final initiation. (Those who see the Pyramids as spiritually significant believe, unlike archaeologists, that the pyramids at Giza were never used for burial, but for teaching and initiation ceremonies.) I believe that the smaller ones were used as classrooms, the Great Pyramid for initiations. It is also said in spiritual literature that carved into the wall above the sarcophagus is a history of the world's religions; it shows when we will share only one. I read somewhere that the Egyptian government moved the sarcophagus after visitors who climbed into it had mystical experiences. Of course, prohibiting visitors from climbing in and out also serves to preserve a priceless antiquity. According to some sources, the sarcophagus was located directly beneath the apex of the Great Pyramid where a capstone, fueled by an Ark of the Covenant, pulsated energy directly into it.

Under the Sphinx lies a great hall archaeologists are attempting to uncover. There are also smaller rooms that were used for meetings and events. Some spiritualists believe that the Sphinx was the "office building" for the complex.

After being prepared through many years of training and a week or more of fasting and meditation, for their final initiation, Initiates were placed in the sarcophagus for as long as two or three days. While there, they had to face the parts of themselves still attached to their ego. Many died because their bodies were unable to absorb the incredible energy that pulsated into the sarcophagus when the capstone was energized.

When I placed my hand inside the granite-and-crystal sarcophagus, I could actually feel a heartbeat! Energy thumped from my hand, into my body, and then exited through the bottoms of my feet. As I stood there with my hand caressing its interior, people began to gather around me watching in curiosity. I ended up teaching a mini lesson about the Mystery Schools. When I felt energy pouring into my heart, I knew I had experienced an initiation, but without the neurological burnout.

When I was finished, a young British woman asked if she could join me in meditation. For about an hour we sat next to each other; our backs rested against the sarcophagus.

Because many tourists have no concept of the chamber's spiritual significance, the strong energy can make people uncomfortable; they react by talking loudly or laughing. When they see a weird woman doing strange things such as chanting (me) and meditating, their voices raise another decibel level in discomfort.

There are just as many tourists who come for the same reason that I do. When I opened my eyes and looked around, I was touched to see the perimeter of the chamber filled with silent visitors deep in meditation. As I stretched, an American woman approached me. "Thank you for being here," she said. "Because of your example, I was able to do what I came here to do." I nodded in astonishment, unable to verbally respond when she inquired, "Do you speak English?" The young Englishwoman also prepared to leave. We hugged and she too was gone.

For a few precious minutes I was able to visit the Queen's Chamber. It was a wonderful experience. Spiritual theories are mixed about its use. I *felt* intuitively that it was used for the sixth out of seven initiations, but other literature says that after initiation in the King's Chamber, Initiates were brought to the Queen's Chamber to recuperate.

Classes of school children visit the Pyramids each day. My friends who are tour guides tell me that teachers from nearby schools bring the children primarily for the opportunity to practice their English on tourists. They stop tourists and request that they have their picture taken with them. They ask a lot of questions: "Where are you from? What is your job? Do you like Egypt? How old are you?" No matter what the response, they giggle. Since age is so important here, they don't understand that to Westerners certain questions, especially age-related ones, are considered rude. They're just being friendly.

Thanks to *Dynasty*, *Falcon Crest*, *Baywatch*, and the flotilla of Western smut available on the Internet, some Egyptian men think Western women are, shall we say, actively available for their pleasure. In my personal experience, this is true across every level of society. In addition to misperceptions perpetuated by the Western media, some European women here on holiday let it be known that they are available for "a bit of the nasty." Mo told me that a number of European women have been referred by their friends to certain tour guides who, for an additional fee, will provide indoor recreation.

I bought a bottle of water from a hawker. Because I knew the price was inflated three times beyond his profit margin, I negotiated the price down from 3 LE to 2 LE. I don't mind paying more than an Egyptian, but I won't pay as much as a tourist.

A group of young men casually sitting upon a 10,000-year-old block of stone, observed the exchange. They thought it was great that a foreigner was able to do what they would do. One of the boys inquired about my marital status. His friends doubled over in waves of hysteria when I responded firmly, "Why do you want to know? I have children who are two times your age!" Their culture requires that they learn of a woman's marital status. It's a big deal. That a woman is unmarried and happy is a foreign concept.

How could I be happy without a husband, a protector?

When dealing with verbally aggressive male strangers, it's best to reply that you're married to an Egyptian named Mohammed. Eighty percent of Muslim men seem to have that name. Incidentally, *Mohammed* is spelled several different ways. Since they usually won't mess with a woman with an Egyptian husband, they immediately leave you alone. They also will leave you alone when you say in Arabic, *"Ana men hena"* (I'm from here). This lets them know instantly that you know the ropes and won't be tricked into taking "free" gifts or an overpriced camel ride. In closing, I'll share a story that may help to explain why I find Egypt so delightful and scrumptiously capricious.

My friend Mary was watching a man ironing clothes in an "outdoor" laundry. An outdoor laundry is kind of like a storage unit that is too small to work in so the ironing guy sets up his board on a flat tiled area between his shop and the sidewalk. The irons they use are the kind heated with coals or very old, professional electric ones.

When he needed to dampen a part of the garment, instead of using steam or a spray bottle, he filled his mouth with water and spat upon it!

Wear your size, mingle with your equal, and know the one who knows your father and grandfather.

~ Egyptian Proverb

Chapter 4

April 2001

Wizened women reside downstairs. The majority suffer from the perversity of Alzheimer's that steals the mind and leaves behind a healthy body; the rest are crumbling from the brutality of old age.

Upstairs, discarded angel-cheeked infants and toddlers skirt around precious babies who, due to their profound disabilities, wait lethargically for their fresh lives to end as hastily as they began. Two disabled teenagers lie twisted by their deformities on mats. They are amused by, yet vulnerable to the mayhem surrounding them. All but one are girls.

We arrived at nine in the morning and left at noon. Maria, a German volunteer, picked me up and dropped me off in front of my building. Since it's so difficult for a newcomer to get around, this small kindness was a thoughtful gift. Two budding Dutch occupational therapists and several Western nurses accompanied us. They go there often.

We traveled on major roads, past posh villas and half-finished human chicken coops waiting patiently for the appearance of a *faloose* (money) wand to transform them into habitable abodes.

As we approached an area of cliff-like hills overlooking the serendipity of Cairo, we began to ascend like a message caught by the wind that knows exactly where it's going. The condition of each road exposes jagged veins of crocodile skin bordered by mean villages; but our destination was the cruelest of all: the Muqattam Hills.

Maria willfully maneuvered her heaving van through

rivers of mud that just as suddenly slipped into rolling ravines of spent earth. The ancient streets narrowed. If we had been so inclined, we could have reached out and retrieved handfuls of decaying mud bricks from the sagging hovels residents call home.

My eyes widened with both interest and dismay. My journalistic curiosity found our surroundings fascinating; my heart was not as detached. I felt as if I had stepped back in time, perhaps one or two centuries. This was a side of Cairo I had never before seen. I waited for it all to become real, to touch it, to smell it.

Nonstop convoys of trucks unload waste onto a site located on the other side of the village. The garbage dump is the "office complex" the women and children of the village "commute" to each day. Their job description requires that they sort through slimy hills of trash in search of the gold of recyclables they can then swap for *piastres* (small change). Medical waste is commingled; hands, arms, and legs speared by contaminated needles, twisted metal, and shards of glass are standard occupational hazards.

The empty trucks sail through the village, leaving behind wallpaper remnants of debris caught up in their draft. Plastic and paper merge with mud until they clot into surreal renditions of papier-mâché sculptures.

Flies dive-bombed us. The stench was medieval. It was impossible to simultaneously hold one's nose, swat flies, and walk without slipping into a sea of mud. We blundered from an alleyway barely wide enough to house the van while still allowing a small donkey cart room to pass, turned left and struggled forward toward an anonymously gated compound.

It's not anonymous to the residents of the village. Women dressed in a soiled rainbow of galabayas waited impatiently to be admitted. Some were seeking medical attention; most were hoping for a sinewy chicken or milk for their children.

As we approached, the compound's bawaab pushed the first woman. Like dominos they were thrust backward, but only far enough for us to slip single file, between impenetrable wooden doors.

We entered a sunlit compound run by Mother Teresa's

sisters. Straight ahead a whitewashed villa twinkled in welcome. It reminded me of an Egyptian artist's rendition of a hacienda. Somewhere on the first floor there is a medical clinic where local women and their children come for treatment. The nuns are sadly lacking in medicine, particularly bandages and ointments to treat burns. Burns are rampant in poor communities where butane/kerosene cooking burners and heaters explode or are overturned.

Nuns, summoned from around the world to serve the people of Muqattam's garbage-collecting community, scurried about. I surmised that most are nurses. They were dressed in white saris trimmed in Virgin Mary-blue that are covered by darker blue-and-white-striped cotton aprons. Their headscarves billowed in the breeze or sat nonchalantly on strong, determined shoulders. Maria told me that their Mother Superior, who was just thirty-nine, died suddenly of a cerebral hemorrhage. Sister Anna has taken over. It is difficult for her to live in the shadow of her predecessor's exalted memory.

The orphanage is clean, and so are the children. The nuns are competent, sweet, and dedicated to service, but there aren't enough of them to go around so they hire women from the village to help. Still, without the Egyptian and foreign volunteers who come each day to do whatever is asked of them, the staff couldn't manage.

We ducked our heads beneath a hand-hewn doorway to meet the elderly women who live downstairs. We entered a small, dark room with an oppressively low ceiling. Having lost my father to the indignity of Alzheimer's, my pain was still too raw to visit with them. I stayed only long enough to appear polite.

I was led up a stairway attached to the outside of the villa. We climbed to the second floor and entered a small space, more the essence of a room than a real one. Just beyond it, a mesh baby gate blocked the neck of a doorway. One of the volunteers opened it. We entered a playroom overflowing with the most beautiful collection of little human beings I have ever seen under one roof. A few toddlers lifted their arms in expectation. Several watched shyly through butterfly lashes. Others scooted away on their bellies like Marines who have just landed on an enemy beach. Like miniature kamikaze pilots on tiptoe, the rest propelled themselves forward in wheeled baby walkers. Occasionally one would run over one of the little Marines or pin a delicate butterfly child against the wall. There were many stuffed animals no one played with or cuddled and few toys. Many of the babies sat quietly in lethargic contemplation while others oozed with joy.

We each chose a baby or toddler to cuddle and feed. The children were fed from the same cereal bowls, from the same spoons, and from the same bottles. Runny noses were shared as well.

The employees were efficient, yet the behavior of one was identical to that of a matron in a prison for women. When an infant or small child would not stop crying, she would reach for an arm or leg and meanly pinch it. I noticed that several of the children recoiled when she approached. I wondered if the appendages of the child that filled her pregnant womb would suffer the same terror.

Other employees picked children up by one arm and half carried, then tossed them like rag dolls across the room. Before we left, I told the volunteer leader what I had observed. "This is why it is good that we come," she replied sadly. "I will tell Sister Anna."

When we had finished feeding one baby, we reached for another, then another. There was a lone infant boy. I retrieved him from his slatted cell unobtrusively placed just inside the doorway of the playroom. He is blind, probably deaf. He cannot suckle. I held him anyway. He didn't meld into my arms in the instinctive desire for the embrace of a mother's warmth. I held him tighter. He didn't respond.

At lunchtime, toddlers were placed in mini molded lawn chairs arranged around a diminutive conference table. As little chins bowed and tiny fingers interlocked in subjugation, one of the Egyptian employees led them in a Christian prayer that went on for so long an adult would have become impatient. When they were finally allowed to eat, plump fingers or demitasse-type spoons smeared a rice dish toward and into their mouths. It had tomatoes in it. Their hands and faces turned diverse hues of tangerine.

Immediately after lunch, those ranging in age from about twelve months to three years were stripped from the waist down and placed on portable potty chairs glued in line in a hallway off the bathing-diapering room. They sat like obedient puppies placed on newspaper. As one potty was vacated, another child filled it. Our task was to clean and re-diaper those who were finished. Two large sinks are used to wash bibs and babies. One washcloth was used to wipe each mouth.

Children who had been made ready for their afternoon nap, accompanied by a bottle of juice donated by one of the volunteers, were placed into their own cribs in another room adjacent to the play and cleanup areas. Until they move on to another facility, their crib seems to be their only possession.

The sleeping room is arranged with cribs in two sizes. The smaller ones are for the infants, the larger for the toddlers. They're lined up back-to-back and side-by-side in mirrored rows. Each child has a "sibling" to gaze at or to defend against as they drift off to sleep.

For many reasons, my experience was disheartening. Through my work with the dying, I have come to see death as a natural part of life. We are born. We live. We die. Sometimes I saw terrible, hard deaths. Other times, the process was so tender that death brought an overwhelmingly gentle sweetness to the closing of a life.

The sweetness in the orphanage is saccharin-based. It's unnatural for children to be warehoused without the benefit of a parent or family of the heart to love and nurture them.

If adoption, as we know it in the West, were allowed, at birth, these gorgeous children would be snapped up and placed in homes around the world. But even Egyptians can't adopt them. Islamic law forbids it. An Islamic child cannot lose its father's name or its religion. An Egyptian family can take an orphan into their home and assume responsibility for them, but they cannot legally change the child's name. Mo told me this has to do with the fear that a child who is adopted could end up marrying a sibling; therefore, even Coptic children remain homeless.

Some of their mothers died in childbirth. Their fathers work. If he has a small child, it is difficult to find another wife. If there are no relatives or siblings to care for it, the infant is taken to an orphanage. Sometimes a new wife will agree to mother the child and it is brought back home. But in Egypt, as in most societies, stepmothers are assumed to be of the ugly variety. And, as in so many other cultures, girl babies are less desirable than boys, even more so if the child has special needs.

Because the people in this area are poor, most cannot take in another child, even one who is related to them. Yet without a family, these children are ostracized by society for the rest of their lives.

Before couples marry, both families want to know the history of their child's intended. Coming from a "bad" family can destroy a person's marriage prospects; coming from no family is even worse. The discrimination doesn't end there. Orphans find it difficult to get a job. Families hire family members first no matter how extended their relationship.

One incident at the orphanage was amusing. One of the small children spat up sun-laced rays of lunch all over my white shirt. I decided to treat the stain immediately. To do this I had to remove my blouse, put soap on it, rinse it and then put it back on while it was still wet. This was very shocking to the female employees who walked into the potty/diaper area and found me standing in front of the sink dressed only in my bra and jeans. In another chapter I'll explain why this seemed so strange to me, though it may have had more to do with my being a Western woman than anything else and the surprise factor of my spontaneous strip tease.

While modesty among women doesn't exist in the same way it does with Western women of my generation, between men it's a big deal. Mo told me that when he was a member of the National Egyptian soccer team, they all showered and dressed as privately as possible. Unlike in the West, there's little occasion for comparative analysis.

Chapter 5

May 2001

In this culture, Samson is alive and well.

Although interpretations of the Koran are mixed about how female modesty should be manifested, to show a woman's purity, devotion to Islam, and to avoid tempting a man who is not her husband, the majority of Egyptian Muslim women keep their heads covered when they are not at home or visiting family. To a Westerner, surprisingly, if not pressured by her family to do so, it is often the woman who decides whether or not she wishes to cover her head. Some even opt to cover their heads over the objections of their husbands.

Head and body coverings vary. Some women don a cape-like garment, usually made from polyester, that covers them from head to waist, others, with the exception of their eyes, are covered from head to foot. But most wear a large scarf fastened around the neck, at the chin or chest. Cleverly, they create folds at the crown of the head they then secure with straight pins so the scarf fits quite snugly. The scarf covering, called a *hijab*, may also cover a portion of the forehead so one cannot even see a hairline. For practical reasons, some women consider a hijab to be a good thing; they never have a public 'bad hair day.'

I was rather taken aback to learn how Egyptians handle body hair. Egyptian women remove *all* the hair from their bodies! This is a cultural, *not* a religious practice. They use a mixture of sugar and lemon juice that's cooked until it is very thick then cooled and stretched like taffy or they buy a mix that does the same thing. There are women who will actually come to your home to perform this ritual for you!

The lemon-sugar mixture is then placed on the skin and pulled in the direction in which the hair grows. In the larger cities, they use chemicals such as Nair, but one would hope not on their pubic area. I'm dying to ask my gynecologist about the health implications of such a practice. Men remove only their pubic hair.

Women without pubic hair are considered clean and pure like a child. I learned recently that by removing her pubic hair, a woman loses the sexual sensation harbored in the roots, which is probably the reason we grow it in the first place. Of course hair removal isn't that unusual. Looking back in history, head and body hair seem to have played a major cultural role in societies around the world.

Another cultural twist I find unsettling is the national identification system. Everyone must register when they turn sixteen. A friend showed me his card. It lists his name, his religion, and that of his wife and the names of his children. This certainly makes it difficult to check into a hotel with someone who's not your spouse. Egyptians can't stay at a hotel without showing this identification. Passports also include the bearer's religion. My friend was surprised that this is not done in the U.S. and by my explanation that in the United States, one's religious choice is a privacy we take for granted.

This issue was highlighted again when I went to the government center to extend my visa. I was able to get it for one year with multiple reentries. The layout for the process looked a lot like the D.C. Department of Motor Vehicles, but more efficient. Because the woman couldn't understand that my passport had been amended—I'm registered under my former married and maiden names versus just Eck—I started to explain, but Mo (who was kind enough to take me to get this done) kicked me really hard and gave me a look that could wilt concrete.

I was shocked that they asked for my religion on the application. "What do I put down?" I asked Mo in indignation. He suggested that "Christian" would be sufficient. He didn't think it was funny when I began to make up a name for a religion based on the best of all religions: *Budjewcathmushindhunachr* . . .

Egyptians have a subtle, marvelous sense of humor. My friend Mo regales me with stories about the tour groups he leads. Because he works another full-time job determining the risk of insuring maritime cargo, he isn't available to lead a lot of tours during the regular workweek. As a result, he doesn't get the pick of the litter when it comes to choosing with whom he will work. Therefore, he often finds himself leading tourist groups from countries where frugality is a virtue.

Mo was my private tour guide to Sakkara and Memphis. The tour company charged me $125.00 for entrance fees, lunch, a driver, and guide. I was shocked to learn that he received less than 75 LE for escorting me (currently about $19.00). Since the pay is so awful, tour guides rely upon tips to survive. Sometimes they stay with a group for as long as fourteen days. They should be tipped a minimum of $10.00 per person per day, but frugal tourists tip $1.00 per day and think they're J. Paul Getty.

The frugal love to shop, but rarely buy anything. It's a bit embarrassing when their guide has to take them to a market where every vendor virtually spits at him when they learn he's escorting certain nationalities. When I was at the Pyramids, and said "No thank you" to a hawker selling postcards, I heard him murmur the name of a frugal nationality in disgust. This was not a compliment.

Mo works with a particular bus driver on a regular basis. One day the driver asked, "Is there a bank called the 'Thank You Bank'?" Mo looked at him in confusion. The driver sighed before continuing, "Well, every time one of your frugal groups get off the bus they all say thank you, thank you, thank you, but give me no money, so I wondered if there is a Thank You Bank where I can go to collect my tips?" In defense of the penny-pinching, they may be under the illusion that everyone is well paid and the cost of their tour is all-inclusive.

While tourists are being served gorgeous meals in lovely hotels or sampling inexpensive Egyptian foods in restaurants that cater to herds of tourists, I usually dine at home. This of course means shopping and cooking.

I bought my first raw chicken today. They're so small a whole one fits nicely in the palm of my hand. One needs a magnifying glass to find the breast. However, they are also quite tasty and the lack of hormones makes up for the size. Like chickens, many of the local melons are much smaller than what I'm used to, but delectably sweet.

When I returned home from marketing, I discovered that the wind left a rather large pair of women's black lace panties in my garden. Frederick's of Hollywood-style underwear and negligees are available everywhere. They're even sold from carts where garbed women, without any pretext of embarrassment, hold them against themselves in public to check for size. My puritanical upbringing makes me still feel uncomfortable about giving the lacy droppings to Mohamed to return. Therefore, I tried to throw them up to the balcony above me, but they kept coming down and landing on my head.

Apparently, the weeds from my D.C. garden hid in my suitcase and transplanted themselves into my new garden. Watering is quite an adventure. While in Aswan last year, I had the opportunity to learn how to do it properly in this climate. Since this is the desert and the soil is quite parched, one fills each area as if it were a basin. I wish I'd brought the garden clogs my son and daughter-in-law, Bill and Adrienne, gave me as a gift last Christmas, for as soon as the pool fills, it turns to mud. It's not a good idea to walk around barefoot given the pesky little things looking for a home that can enter through the bottoms of your feet and become a non-deductible dependent in your intestinal tract!

Speaking of D.C., I observed that the poor condition of the roads here are quite similar. An Egyptian friend who has been to D.C. paused, then responded dryly, "Actually, they're better here."

It may be that the roads are no worse than those in D.C., but when you find yourself lulled into thinking that what you want is available, that business practices are the same as in the West and cultural practices aren't that different, you're quickly brought back to reality.

My tomato seedlings have begun to sprout. I asked the local florist where I could buy seeds. He politely informed me that one could acquire them from fresh vegetables. Duh! I dried some on a paper towel and planted the towel.

I probably could have just opened a tomato and planted the whole thing. I still don't have a shovel or spade. I've been using a soup spoon.

Banking is also a challenge. I lost my debit card. I went to the money machine in the vestibule of the bank around the corner from my flat. Since one can only take 500 LE at a time (this enables the bank to charge duplicate fees because you have to use your card again to get more), I foolishly left the card in the machine between transactions. Slurp! It was gone. The bank was closed, but the guard told me I could return to retrieve it when the machine was opened the next morning. I did. "Ah," I was told. "It is really a weekend so the machine cannot be opened until tonight. Kindly return tomorrow." I did.

I explained the situation to the lovely young woman sitting behind a desk in the lobby. She returned with my card, but cautiously asked to see my passport before giving it to me. "Is this really your signature?" she inquired in disbelief. I had to prove to her that it was. What's interesting is that bank officials really expect your signature to match another document, exactly. Mine doesn't match within a document. Sister Victoreen would feel vindicated. She found it impossible to believe any child could have such illegible handwriting. I truly believe she went to her grave convinced I was just being willful.

Family gatherings are different here, too. The family is truly the backbone of the culture. Each Friday afternoon, most get together for a Sabbath feast. It's not unusual for grown children and their families, even if they live in the same neighborhood, to move in with their parents for a week so they can "visit." Visiting is interesting. It does not require conversation. Family members will sleep, watch television, or just stare at each other.

In many Egyptian homes, the mother is the matriarch. No matter how wide or narrow her perspective, her word is often law. Since a marriage is considered to be a reflection upon the whole family, if a couple is having problems, it isn't unusual for everyone to get together to solve it—right down to the most intimate details. Everyone knows everything! Divorce is allowed, but some families believe it brings shame on the whole family and the marriage prospects of the couple's children, so they will sit with the pair and tell them of the sacrifices they made to convince them to stay together.

Coptic couples *cannot* divorce except under the most extreme circumstances. Muslim women can obtain a divorce for several reasons, one of which is if their husbands are unable to, um, "perform." But if she initiates the divorce, she may leave empty-handed. Muslim men can get a divorce if their wife agrees. If she doesn't, he can get one anyway by saying three times, "I divorce you." This apparently doesn't happen very often. If it does and they get back together at a later date, they cannot remarry unless she married someone else in the meantime and then divorces her second husband or is widowed.

As strong as the family is, I've been told that the majority of the marriages are not particularly happy ones. Men complain among themselves that their wives don't take care of themselves, aren't interested in sex and lose interest in pleasing or taking care of them after their first child is born (sound familiar?). Once a woman is past childbearing age, many feel they no longer need to participate in "horizontal recreation."

The average married woman has the same spreading-hip problem common in the U.S. But unlike the West, obesity doesn't make women less attractive to men. Many like having a lot to touch and hold onto. While the women spread at an early age, the majority of men don't seem to get beer bellies. Perhaps, since it is forbidden by Islam to drink alcohol, they don't need a portable shelf to hold a beer can.

To compound marriage problems, when men aren't working, many don't hurry home but hang out with their friends until the wee hours of the morning. Men can have up to four wives, but they're supposed to treat each one equally. Good luck. Why anyone would want more than one spouse is a complete mystery to me.

Many women work outside the home. They come home, cook lunch (which is served around 5:00 p.m.), help the children with homework then prepare dinner (which is served around 10:00 p.m.). If their husband works another "day" job, they wait up to serve him dinner. They're exhausted.

Egyptians also deal with death quite differently than we do in the West. When someone dies in a hospital, depending upon their financial situation, the family may place the body upright in a car and bring it home. They wash it, wrap it in a simple white cloth, pray over it and immediately bury it in the grave they have dug themselves or paid someone else to prepare. Burying a body in the ground is actually illegal, but if a family is poor they have no other option other than to ask that their loved one be buried above ground with someone else. If they're rich, the body is placed in the family's mausoleum. The next day, the family rents a colorful, narrow rectangular tent erected near or adjacent to a mosque, or next to their home where male friends come to pay their respects and to pray. Women callers visit the home.

Since families are so close, everyone goes into mourning for the requisite forty days, even for "extende" family such as cousins, uncles, in-laws, and so on. If a couple wants to marry, they're supposed to wait a year from the time of death of a close relative, but a widow/widower may remarry after forty days.

△ △ △

Making an international call was by and far my biggest challenge this week. One of my credit card bills was sent to D.C. (even though I had asked that it be sent to my son, Bill, who gallantly has been helping to keep my online banking straight). He called on my behalf to ask that they send it to him, but for "security" reasons they said I had to call again. "She can call collect," they offered. You can't do that from here and I can't make international calls from my home phone without a card. I had only a card for international calls that can be used from a phone kiosk on the street, not from my apartment. So, at 11:00 p.m., with mini flashlight in hand, I found myself standing at a phone kiosk in El Maadi. When I finally reached the credit card representative, I was every service person's nightmare.

The next day I was able to purchase a ten-minute international card to use from home to call my son Dan to wish him a happy birthday. So far, the biggest denomination I've been able to find is for twenty minutes. They do make a sixty-minute card, but no one seems to sell it.

I've had a new gizmo installed on my computer that's supposed to allow me to make international calls for a small fee. Thus far it's only succeeded in screwing up all my other programs.

When you know the language of another people, you're safe from their evil.

~ Egyptian Proverb

Chapter 6

May 2001

This week I started Arabic class. Camilla is our teacher. She's half Austrian, half Egyptian, Catholic and married to a Copt of identical cultural background. She has three grown children. Molly introduced us. We're thrilled. Camilla is a few years older than me. She's a full-size, motherly woman with a vast smile, Oreo eyes, and an easy, raucous laugh. She's giving us the lessons for free because, although she's taught French in the past, her self-confidence is pretty low. We see this as a wonderful opportunity to get to know each other, to learn Arabic, and to help her see why we already adore her.

I've gotten Arabic numbers down. I practice by reading license plates. Now when I shop I don't always have to ask, "*Bikam*?" (How much) unless the price tags are smeared and difficult to decipher. I've learned to say good morning —"*Sabbah el kheir*," and good evening — "*Massa el kheir.*"

I still haven't learned how to use the Metro. That's next on my to-do list. I'm told I don't want to go during rush hour for it's like a sausage factory (sorry, bad analogy since pork is a no-no). The first car is for women only, the rest are unisex. Great, I can either choose to be stared at as if I had a braid hanging from my nose or get groped.

Before leaving the U.S., my brother John cautioned that as much as I love Egypt, when I am no longer a tourist, I will begin to see the parts of her that are not kind and gentle. Over time I will integrate this knowledge and become more balanced in how I see things. I'm in the "Isn't there anything kind and gentle in this *@&%* country?" stage. Hey, it only took six weeks!

Sometimes the only thing that keeps me sane is my sense of humor and the knowledge that I don't have to stay here. I have come to see that there are many things that are in total opposition to my belief system. But just as quickly, I remind myself that it is not my country, it is not my culture, and I must be respectful even when the differences make me want to lose my lunch or break out in hives.

I become most annoyed when I feel that the system is trying to shove a gag down my throat. This is guaranteed to get my nose out of joint to the point where I respond by becoming "warrior woman."

I think it's probably a bit easier for Western men than it is for Western women to live here. I constantly get myself in trouble by being, what I consider, merely kind, polite, and moderately friendly.

I have not yet been able to control my penchant for smiling. I always dress appropriately, never in shorts or revealing outfits, but I'm told that by being polite and smiling I may be giving the local men the impression that I'm available.

For example, you're not supposed to smile at a merchant, waiter, or repairperson even if you know them. Rather, you're supposed to treat them like dirt or nod toward them sort of solemnly. To me, the challenge is to not appear as if I'm flirting, or arrogant, and to remain true to the part of me that seeks to be loving and kind to everyone I interact with.

Walking to the market this morning, I was amazed when some preadolescent boys sitting on the curb stared up at me in an openly sexual way. At first it's flattering to be perceived as attractive by so many men, but it gets old quickly when you realize that they'd find the comedienne Roseanne hot. Gradually you begin to feel dirty, as if all you have to offer is the fact that you have a uterus, or as in my case had one, but we won't go there.

Yesterday, I was talking to some expat women about this. One in particular has had some nasty experiences, which is one of the reasons she had her breasts downsized via liposuction.

It's an interesting dichotomy. Egyptians are really uptight about sexual conduct. They're not allowed to show physical affection to the opposite sex in public, even with their wives. The tourist police watch hotels to make sure unmarried couples aren't sneaking into each other's room to play doctor. Islam seems to have a finger in every part of daily life from how the government is run (although it's not an Islamic government) to personal hygiene.

The upside to this is my renewed appreciation for the freedom we take for granted in the U.S. and the incredible wisdom of our forefathers when they separated our government from religion. Yet the difference is that Islam is practiced as a way of life, not as a private choice where one picks and chooses the ways in which they worship God. The majority of the population is Islamic so everyone else is expected to adhere to many of the same rules a Muslim is required to live by.

To help me understand, I've begun to read an English translation of the Koran. I've been told over and over again by Egyptians that its beauty cannot be translated adequately from Arabic so one can get the "real" flavor; others say a foreigner can't get the real flavor because a lot of the aggressive stuff is left out of the translation.

Seeing how people live under the laws of one religion makes me also appreciate and better understand the Middle East conflict. Islam is an outgrowth of Christianity, therefore a stepchild of Judaism. They practice many of the same beliefs as Orthodox Jews, but they believe that Jews and Christians have turned their backs on God. And just as Catholics and some Christian sects believe their religion is the only true religion, so do they. Yet the first chapters of the Koran appear to come directly from the Bible and subsequent chapters quote heavily from it. Many forget that the Prophet Mohammed said that any good person should be treated the same as a good Muslim.

How difficult it must be for the Palestinians to live in the shadow of a religious state that is not theirs and how difficult for the Jews to be surrounded by those who consider them to have turned their backs on God. Of course, conflict over religion has reared its ugly head around the world. How did we get away from the love that is the foundation of all religions and become so afraid of our differences that we no longer find it within our hearts to remember how to show our love for God by loving one another?

The conflict between Israel and Palestine is often used in the West as a means to label all followers of the Islamic faith as terrorists. Nothing could be further from the truth. The assumption is also made that expatriates, Americans in particular, are in constant danger while living in an Arab country. Just as those in the West who live in a major city rather than a small town are more vulnerable to random crime, because expats are easily identifiable, we're more susceptible to retaliation by terrorists. And, like Western cities that have larger police forces to protect their citizens, the Egyptian government has increased its armed forces to protect expats and foreign businesses as well as to insure that those who seek to replace the existing government with a fundamentalist one, won't have the opportunity to do so.

Police officers are stationed on every street corner in El Maadi and throughout Egypt, particularly at the historic sites.

The last thing Egypt or her people want is to become involved in a war. In addition to the physical/ecological devastation of nuclear/germ warfare, a war will destroy an already fragile Middle Eastern economy, Egypt's in particular.

Egypt depends upon the Suez Canal and tourism to survive. The majority of the Egyptian people are trying to live on less than we spend on cleaning products or gasoline each month. I think this is a major reason why there is so much hanky-panky in business dealings.

The average street cleaner makes 100 LE per month (about $26.00) and pays 2 LE a day to get to work; the average guard at the Pyramids makes about 75 LE. This gives you a small indication of how vulnerable everyone is economically.

There are few government programs to feed or clothe the poor. The poor depend upon good Muslims to share a small percentage of their salaries each month to help them survive. (Giving a percentage of what you earn to the poor is called *Zakat*, one of the Five Pillars of Islam).

Unfortunately, the Egyptian government can't protect us from nature. The weather at this time of year is a sandy version of Camelot. With the spring winds, *khamasiin*, the phrase "eat dirt," takes on new meaning. It's sunny every day, clear and warm (probably high 70s–mid 80s), but the dust storms covers both animate and inanimate objects. Since my computer is my lifeline to the outside world as well as a valuable aide in my work, I keep it covered to protect it from being destroyed by dust.

△ △ △

Molly sent me an e-mail titled, "You know you're in Egypt when . . ." It reminded me that I haven't mentioned the other side of public displays of affection. While it's inappropriate between men and women, it's acceptable between men.

Male friends are often seen walking down the street holding hands, with their arms around each other, kissing hello on the cheek or affectionately addressing each other as *habibi* (my sweetheart).

Because it's against Islam, the general population takes it for granted that there is no homosexuality, therefore no one thinks twice about showing their male friends how much they care for them. Of course, yours truly has many gay friends in the U.S. and has already met several gay Egyptians, but she can't tell anyone that they exist! Based upon how and with whom my gay friends express their sexuality, bisexuality also exists. A gay man willing to drop 20 LE can find straight partners if he chooses to.

I'm so busy trying to understand the nuances of the culture and the Arabic language that my head is spinning. Unfortunately, as soon as I leave Arabic class, what I've learned stays behind. Molly is more advanced than I (she lived here before). I really want to be able to communicate on a basic level. I don't care about how you address a male versus a female. That will come later. I'm like Joe Friday, "Just give me the facts." The other problem is that because Molly, Camilla, and I have fun together, we aren't working as hard as we should be.

If my Arabic were better, getting around outside the areas of El Maadi I'm now familiar with wouldn't be such a hassle. I went to the American Embassy. I had to have papers notarized for the sale of my building. I interviewed four cab drivers before I found one I *thought* understood me. When he headed in the direction of Molly's apartment instead of downtown Cairo, I knew I was in trouble. We were able to stop a pedestrian who spoke English so I got there just fine . . . eventually.

The American Citizen's Center at the embassy was very efficient, however, I found it rather offensive that it costs $55.00 per seal in U.S. dollars or the equivalent in LE! Using a check or credit card was not an option. Based upon the number of people who came for the same service, I'd say that the expat community is supporting the embassy without the contribution of any taxpayers other than us.

When I returned home, I discovered that the mess deposited by a sudden khamasiin storm added more frustration to my day. I'd left clothes on the line. This was not smart. They're now tie-dyed various shades of beige. My floors are covered in white ceramic tile. When the dust gets in, the floors become decorated with shoe tracks. I think I'll keep switching *gazmas* (shoes) to vary the pattern. The big joke is that cleaning during khamasiin will cause the winds to come right to your door, re-covering anything that isn't moving.

Since I only have a broom and a mop, I borrowed Auntie's vacuum cleaner. Actually, it looked more like something displayed at the Smithsonian to serve as an example of an earlier version, pre-Civil War. The hose was sort of connected to the machine with lime green tape. I say "sort of" because in order to get any suction I had to hold my hand over the gap between the tape and the hose, and hold the canister upright so it wouldn't twist and increase the fissure. This left me without a free hand with which to hold the wand.

In frustration, I searched my apartment for materials I could use to "fix it." I wrapped the gap with bubble wrap and a piece of ribbon. It worked like a charm. The cord retractor wouldn't retract, so when I was finished, I put it in an empty toilet paper tube. I've learned to never, ever throw anything out that could possibly be useful! In any case, when I called Mohamed to ask him to return it to Auntie, he looked at my handiwork with interest. I think he's concerned that Auntie will fire him as the handyman and take me on as his replacement.

I also asked to borrow an iron, but Auntie doesn't own one. She suggested that I take my clothes around the corner to be pressed. I think I'll go wrinkled. I really can't stand the thought of wearing someone's dried spit. Anyway, based upon the condition of the vacuum cleaner, if she had an iron, it probably would require me to fill it with heated coals.

To clean floors, Egyptians hose everything down (or throw on buckets of water) and then use a huge squeegee on a stick to dry the floor. I haven't been able to master the technique without leaving dirt lines.

Most public areas are made of native marble or granite. Mohamed was cleaning the staircase and hallways with a flood of water last week and wasn't concerned when it began to seep under my doorway. He's very good with the squeegee.

Although Auntie is a dear, her son Moopiga continues his Machiavellian intrusions. He believes their tenants should pay for any repair. Last week, I gave up on the kitchen sink and asked that they summon a plumber. While he was here, I had him fix the toilet whose guts turned out to be comprised of a combination of plastic bags and ribbon. I made a big mistake by not asking that all this be done correctly before I signed the lease. Now I have to pay for it. Auntie was right. I'm kind—stupid, too!

△ △ △

I'm always happy to see Moopiga's wife, Fatma. She brought me a piece of cake and a flower to celebrate Egyptian Mother's Day. In return, I purchased a small box of chocolates for her children to accompany the empty plate when I returned it. I hadn't seen her so, while Auntie was here supervising the plumber, I gave her the dish and the chocolates to give to Fatma. Auntie promptly sat down, opened the chocolates and began to eat them. Mo told me that she knew they were for her grandchildren, but she loves chocolate so she played dumb.

In addition to my rent, I learned that I'm to give Mohamed 20 LE each month for guarding me and another 4 LE for trash. Of course, if he does anything extra he expects *baksheesh* (a tip). The country relies on it.

Yesterday I tipped him when the lock to my front door stripped and I couldn't get into my apartment, and more when he handed me the air envelope from UPS he had hidden under his bed outside the building. Mail is never put in the mailbox. I don't even have a key. Mohamed can't read English so he brings all the unidentified mail to me to decipher. Perhaps I should charge him for this service.

Apparently flat roofs cause the bouts of heavy winter rain to flow down the inside of the walls. In every room of my apartment, the new paint and plaster has begun to crumble just above the floor molding. I pointed this out to Auntie. She says this is normal. It's called "wall cancer." That's fine. I just don't want to be hit with surgical reconstruction costs for that, too.

My hair requires surgery as well. I need to get a haircut. I've been checking out the "dos" of expats I meet, but their cuts don't come close to what I'm used to. Most go to a European hairdresser who's apparently a bit flamboyant. From what I can gather, her prices are too. I've been told that they're based upon one's nationality. It's extra if she washes your hair, but she will wet it for free before she begins to cut. Egypt, like Puerto Rico, seems to have cornered the market on henna. There are some very unusual shades of red decorating a variety of heads. They range in hue from clown orange to fire engine, and at the most extreme, eggplant.

Chapter 7

May 2001

The electricity keeps going out. I don't think it's uncommon, I just don't know why. Perhaps Mohamed is fixing something. My computer has a battery backup so I wasn't turned off. It's kind of cozy writing in the dark.

I keep forgetting to tell you about the streetlights. Mo told me that there actually is someone whose job it is to manually switch them on at night and off in the morning. The problem is he sometimes misses a few. If his mind is on his personal problems, he misses most of them.

Molly and I enjoyed a full day together. She taught me how to use the subway. It's very clean. With the exception of having to get into line to buy a ticket to your destination and a lack of air-conditioning, it's just like the D.C. Metro. I learned how to get to the railway station when I want to take a train out of Cairo. We spent the day in Heliopolis (sort of like going from downtown D.C. to Silver Spring) and attended an exhibition at an Arabian stud farm.

On my way home, I bumped into my friend Amin in front of his antique store. When I told him about my day he had some rather pithy comments. As much as I'm itching to, I'm not going to go there except to say that the horses were magnificent and quite spirited when trotted out to demonstrate why it costs millions to purchase their bodily fluids.

On the way back we took a detour and went downtown by bus. Camilla just called to ask how our day was. She spent hers fielding a family crisis in Montreal where she and Yosef own a home. "You took a bus?" she exclaimed.

"Oh my God! I've never done that!" "Stick with us, Camilla," I laughed. "We'll expand your horizons!" With the exception of an ice cream cone, we didn't buy anything.

Since we were near the Egyptian Museum in downtown Cairo, we were stopped often and asked if we needed help finding our way. This kindness was immediately followed with, "Please come upstairs to my shop." One native who observed the exchange wryly commented, "Isn't it wonderful how helpful Egyptians are?"

△ △ △

I haven't told you about Egyptian toilet paper. I quickly ran out of the few U.S. rolls I was able to squish into my suitcase. They come in packages of three. It's not too bad, double thickness, and sort of soft. The problem is the tube is about twice the size of an American-made brand and the amount of paper on the roll is about ten times smaller.

I had dinner with a fellow member of Hexagon (a D.C. theatre group I was involved with) who's working here in Cairo for a firm that's revamping the Egyptian tax code from one based upon the Russian system. I'm not sure this is progress.

Stan has been overseas for a while so we'd never met. My friend Rick, who taught me how to use a follow spot during my short career as a techie (he's living in Alexandria and working on a different USAID contract), gave him my number. Since I don't have an answering machine it took him two months to reach me. It was fun to spend the evening with someone from D.C. who knows a lot of the same people. Unfortunately, he says he hates Egypt as well as Egyptians. He also believes that Palestinians force their children to serve as human shields when Israeli tanks invade their land. According to him, this is because they don't love them. Obviously we have a totally different perspective on Egypt and the Middle East.

While it's often maddening trying to play by new rules, if one isn't open to understanding and laughing at our differences, a Westerner can't be happy here.

In addition to basking in the glow of a people who are funny, kind, and gentle, I've learned that there isn't very much I can't live without. I don't feel deprived sometimes frustrated, sometimes sad, sometimes furious, but always grateful. Even in my meager surroundings I have so much more than 80 percent of the population. Egyptians have taught me to remember my sense of humor and to slow down.

I keep a suitcase in my dining room. I've put a few things in it that I don't readily need like books I've read and U.S. voltage cords I can't use. It serves another purpose. It's a reminder that I can leave whenever I choose to, something my Egyptian friends cannot do. I can go home and buy a house and fill it with my wonderful books, artwork, small appliances, beautiful clothes, family heirlooms, and the furniture I've refinished and painted. I can create another garden. Those from home who love me will be just a phone call away or a few hours from the nearest airport. It's also a reminder that to flourish all I really need is the ability to maintain a sense of humor, human contact, love, and laughter (a jar of Hellmann's mayonnaise would be nice, too).

I've worked very hard to make friends here, to fill my life with opportunities I may never have the chance to experience again. In the scheme of things, it really doesn't matter how the toilet in my apartment is held together; at least I have one. So what if I have to sweep out sand, it's only sand.

I've come to see the parts within me in need of healing on a deeper level that may never have been unveiled at home. I've also come to identify, embrace and cherish my strengths, to hug myself for a job well done. I've come to appreciate the smallest experience as a gift, an opportunity to learn and to grow.

While looking for a travel company recommended by my new British friend Jennifer, I saw the most incredible bird, a hoopoe. Its feathers were laden with black-and-white polka dots. As it flew away, it slowly unfolded a magnificent headdress topped by a flaming plume. I was in awe.

It's these little moments I've come to treasure. This incident may seem insignificant, but isn't that what living is about, taking time to slow down and to appreciate and savor the beauty and flavor of the tiny but unexpected experiences that make up a day rather than rushing past life as if wearing a blindfold? I think if I learn nothing else here, my time will have been well spent.

I asked,
"Why are you so polite?"
He replied,
"It is the art of God."

~ Egyptian Proverb

Chapter 8

May 2001

Stan isn't the only one who makes unkind judgments and assumptions. It's a universal weakness we all fall prey to at one time or another. Recently, I've been verbally harassed on the street. I've come to understand that simply because I'm a Western woman, some individuals will take it upon themselves to suggest that I'm a practitioner of the world's oldest profession—not a lawyer or a mother.

Given my age, this leaves me in a bit of a quandary. Do I say, "*Shokran,*" "*Inshallah*" (God willing), "*Ya Kelb*" (you dog), "*Om Mack*" (your mother), laugh, or send them love? So far I've been too taken aback to say anything when someone passing me on the street calls me a *sharmoota* (loose woman).

I'm dying to use the line made famous by an Englishwoman, Om Sety, who called some of the sacred sites in Upper Egypt home. As she passed by, a native woman hissed the equivalent of, "Go home, foreign whore." Purportedly she responded, "What! And leave all the business to you?"

It's sad that some young boys have been raised to be disrespectful. Camilla has promised to teach me to say, with a sympathetic, motherly smile, "Don't worry, it really will get bigger!" to the *waldeen* (boys) who think it's funny to juggle a part of their underdeveloped anatomy for my benefit and Molly thinks we could make a fortune off adult males by smuggling in suitcases filled with jock itch cream. Because men are required to wash their genitals as well as their anus, face, hands, and feet before praying five times per day, some apparently become chafed. One can't help but notice how much scratching and rearranging goes on in public.

On different levels, I'm doing some rearranging in my home as well as in my attitude and assumptions. I seek to approach every new experience with wonder and a sense of humor. I need the humor in particular.

I now have an iron, an answering machine, a battery-operated radio, and a toaster oven! I'm in heaven. The iron and the oven are not so gently previously owned. I had to have the plug on the iron replaced. The man at the electrical shop encouraged me to replace the cord, but it looked fine to me, so for 5 LE it's good as new. The couch in my office covered with a towel makes a dandy ironing board. The toaster oven goes from dead to incinerator in seconds so I'll have to play with it, but it has to beat trying to toast a piece of bread over the burner on my stove using a metal fork.

The summer should be interesting. Most expats will be gone for all or part of it: Molly for a month, Camilla for three, Mary nearly a month, but thankfully, my British metaphysical friend Jennifer whom I've enjoyed visiting with on many evenings, will stay.

The winds really picked up again one afternoon this week. There's something lacy stuck in the tree outside my guest room window. A Batman mask hangs from a limb. I'll use the broom to get the lace down. At first it was a bit startling to look up and see Batman staring down at me, but I kind of like having him there. He'll stay until the wind decides to move him.

We had a thunderstorm! I was so excited about the prospect of seeing my first rain I rushed outside to watch, but it merely spat and died. Still, the local mini grocery store just a few blocks away was flooded. When I went by, they were drying everything salvageable on the sidewalk. Since the lot will go right back on the shelf, I took a quick inventory of what not to buy in the foreseeable future.

I went to the bank to get Auntie's rent money. There was a four-day holiday coming up so the lines were worse than they would be in front of a port-a-potty at a beer drinkers' contest. At 2:30 p.m. the guard locked the doors, but he let in those who strongly objected to being kept out. Yelling really works here.

The lights went out three times. Employees quietly stood up from behind the counter and disappeared until the electricity came back on. Even so, with the interruptions, it took less time to complete my transaction than at Riggs Bank on payday.

Employees hired specifically for the purpose of serving office workers coffee, tea or lemon juice (the Egyptian version of very sweet, warm lemonade) bring trays of drinks to staff throughout the day. They're called "tea boys." I gather that some businesses contract the service out for it's not unusual to see a tea guy walking down the street with a full tray. There are also guys who saunter around with huge metal containers filled with hot tea strapped to their backs. They carry small glasses in the harnesses that cover their chests. You buy a glass of tea and immediately gulp it down so the guy doesn't have to come back for his glass. Egyptians don't sip things. They drink and eat quickly. Since the glasses are probably not washed between customers I haven't indulged.

△ △ △

When she receives the Ben Gay my dear friend Mary Lewis is sending me as a surprise for Auntie and Moopiga, Auntie will probably offer me to her husband as a second wife.

Mo negotiated with her to extend my lease without any rent increase. Moopiga probably went nuts when he found out. I offered to do an energy healing on her lower back, but she backed out of the apartment, past my crystals and other good stuff before I could explain. For some reason she prays a lot when she's with me . . . wonder what that's all about? Seriously, Moopiga is trying to protect his parents, and Auntie is a kind woman. We've become great friends, as close as one can be when you communicate via pantomime or an interpreter, and money is involved.

I'm blessed to have her and all of you in my life. I received two pieces of mail from my son Bill. Mohamed handed them to me when I arrived home from various destinations. I was distressed to discover that customs officers or one of the security guards for the assistant chief of police who lives in my building had opened them. I assume they were checking for money or illegal substances. Since children rarely send their parents money or illegal substances, if they'd known whom the letters were from, they probably wouldn't have bothered.

On Thursday, Molly and I took a quick overnight trip to Alexandria by express train. It's a beautiful city nestled along the Mediterranean coast, similar to Athens, but cleaner and less congested when the weather is cool. I spent a perfect day with my friend Rick talking and exploring the area around my hotel adjacent to the Egyptian president's summer palace that was once occupied by King Farouk. It looks like a huge pink-and-cream gingerbread castle decorated with turrets and charming covered balconies in many shapes and sizes, each topped by a lofty needle (probably antenna). My room had a balcony overlooking the Mediterranean.

The next day Molly and I had a 2:00 p.m. train back to Cairo so I was up at the crack of dawn to take advantage of every moment. By 8:00 a.m. I was on the tiny hotel beach enjoying the early sunshine and a delightful swim. I'm a bit sunburned.

Today I'll take the subway to meet Stan in Zamalek where he lives. It's an island on the Nile in Cairo and part of the high-rent district. We're going to take a walking tour. I'll come back to El Maadi early in the evening for a party at the home of Maria, who drove me to the orphanage. I haven't been back because she's had an eye infection and can't be around the children.

While I was disappointed to learn that Amin wasn't able to pull off the party he had promised to host at his country house this weekend, I was equally thrilled by Maria's invitation and delighted that I'll have the opportunity to expand my circle of friends.

It's almost time to harvest my first batch of compost. I've transplanted my tomato seedlings, and Molly gave me her basil plant since she has a balcony rather than a garden to plant it in. The basil here has tiny leaves, but it's fragrant and flavorful. My tenant, Marika, wrote to tell me that our garden back home is particularly beautiful this spring.

The eye is looking but the hand is short and cannot reach it.

~ Egyptian Proverb

When God divided minds
everyone was satisfied with
his own, but no one
liked his share in life.

~Egyptian Proverb

Chapter 9

May 2001

"You know you're in Egypt when your ideal holiday is anywhere you can go to eat pig." The party was delightful, truly an international night of great German food that included roast pork! Maria's husband is the headmaster and a teacher for the elementary section of the German school. I met several French couples, as well as others of German, Swiss, and mixed nationalities. Maria failed to mention that the party was in honor of her fifty-first birthday. Apparently it is a common practice in France and Germany to host a lovely party for friends to help you celebrate.

It was very hot, probably close to 110°F. I was out all day; not on the promised walking tour of the gardens or interesting sites of Zamalek, but on an expedition in search of restaurants Stan wants to visit. I'm still feeling the consequences of a touch of heat stroke.

Although I could have walked to the party and been there in about fifteen minutes, since it was still hot, I decided to cab it. This has been a week of lost taxi drivers. A five-minute trip took thirty minutes. He really didn't know where he was going and made so many wrong turns I too got turned around. When we finally arrived, I handed him 3 LE (which is on the high side of the going rate within El Maadi). He tried to tell me I should pay more, but I assured him sternly, *"Kefya faloose!"* (enough money). I wasn't about to pay him extra for his foolishness. He sulked away.

This is a major problem. Taxi drivers often have no idea

where you want to go or pretend to get lost to make a few extra pounds. There's the shame thing about not knowing what they think they're supposed to know, the hope they'll make "sympathy money" by getting you lost, the "I'll pretend to get lost to get more money," or just a need for business no matter how long it takes. My Egyptian friends tell me this happens to them, too.

How do you know what the rate is from one place to another? You never ask the taxi driver. Before you go somewhere new, you call an Egyptian friend or another expat and ask what it should cost, and then you carry the exact change you'll need including tip since the driver "may" not have any change. If you ask the average driver, he'll double or triple the fare! So, you get in the cab and tell him where you want to go. When you arrive, you get out of the taxi, hand him his fare (on the high side of what the fare should be), and walk away. Usually, the driver is very happy, but when they get lost (on purpose or not), they expect you to pick up the difference. I don't think so!

One of the most difficult realities that constantly rears its head is to see firsthand how Egyptians are treated by expats (in particular Americans, British, and Koreans). The things they say among themselves about Egyptians are shocking. At a dinner party I attended with Stan and his American, Canadian, and British colleagues, a guest commented that all Egyptians are stupid. I was horrified and asked if perhaps he wasn't being a bit condescending. Neither he nor the other guests thought so.

Mind you, it must be difficult to work here and try to upgrade systems to Western standards. Westerners have to deal with hidden agendas, for everyone has one, primarily to see how they can make extra money by doing things a certain way. As I've mentioned before, the pay scale is so low, making money in other ways is a matter of survival, so trying to figure it out and to work around agendas is a real challenge.

Of course, Egyptians aren't the only ones with hidden agendas. Although the American people as a whole are extremely generous, I suspect that our government's generosity has more to do with oil, for whoever controls politics and the oil in the Middle East, controls the world.

The attitude of the wives of these men can be even worse. Last week I heard about an incident involving the wife of a U.S. executive. She attacked her husband's Egyptian driver with an umbrella! An expat women's organization refuses to allow the Egyptian craftspeople displaying their products at their events to eat from their buffet table. They want a separate table for Egyptians! An Egyptian woman was filling a plate with food when a member of the organization sponsoring the event angrily approached her and told her that the food was not for her. The woman had to put the plate down and walk away in humiliation. As a friend commented, "Perhaps you should put plates of food on the ground like you do for your dogs?"

Saddest of all is that the woman who told her she couldn't eat at their table, showed in the most glaring way the lack of desire on the part of some Westerners to understand the culture she lives in. Her insult, while uncalled for, was also one of the greatest *faux pas* she could have committed.

In Egypt, if someone is a guest in your home, no matter how little you have, the best is served to the guest. If there is only one piece of meat, it is not only offered to the guest, an Egyptian would be insulted if they didn't take it. They are a hospitable, generous people.

Some expat women treat Western women married to Egyptians just as poorly. No matter how lovely they are, they're not always welcome by members of some expat women's organizations. It's not unusual for another woman to hiss within her hearing, as if she had a social disease, "Don't say anything in front of her, she's married to an Egyptian!" On the other hand, it isn't unusual for an expat married to an Egyptian to be a bit oversensitive to any criticism of the culture even when it is reality-based or just a funny example of our differences. Balance goes both ways.

I'm very fortunate. I can choose with whom I wish to associate. If I were married to an expat executive, club politics could make it difficult to speak my truth without hurting his career. Because of my status, or lack thereof, I've been able to make friends with truly magnificent people from every culture and social level without giving a flying farthing what someone else thinks. This has enabled me to see the culture from many perspectives, not merely from my narrow vantage point. I'm getting an incredible education and loving it! And yes, for the most part, if I'm at an event and someone does or says something I consider inappropriate, I can excuse myself. I'm not going to change anyone's mind, but I don't have to participate.

As I've begun to become a tad more comfortable with the Arabic language, I've come to appreciate how magnificent it is. Egyptians have a way of saying things in one word what we can't express in a paragraph. For example, rather than having a single word for romantic love, Arabic has many, each carrying different levels of meaning depending upon the circumstances. This makes it nearly impossible to do justice to the translation of an Egyptian love song.

Hib means love. *Ishq* is love that entwines two people together. *Shaghaf* means that love nests in the chamber of the heart. *Hayman* is love that wanders the earth. *Tech* means losing yourself in love. *Walah* is love that carries sorrow with it. *Sababah* means that love exudes from your pores. *Hawa* shares love with air and falling, and *gharam* is love you're willing to pay the price for.

Kim called the other day to say that she and Raed are expecting their first baby. It will be a beautiful one! She's suffering from constant nausea and sleeps all the time. She's approaching the three-month mark so hopefully she'll be feeling much better soon. I guess we won't be doing much horseback riding.

Chapter 10

May 2001

Egyptian men are under considerable pressure to marry and have a family. From several perspectives, this is a real problem. First, they must have an apartment of their own and enough money to pay her a dowry. Even with a university education, salaries are so low it can take many years to be able to afford the rent for a place of their own.

Second, sex outside of marriage is against Islam, which is why there are so many young, horny men walking the streets. Of course, premarital sex is no stranger to many of them.

Third, many young men don't want to rush into marriage, but their mothers put so much pressure on them to do so, some give up and marry the young woman down the street "who's very kind" to get Mom off their back, or even today, their cousin.

Birth control is widely practiced, especially in the cities where young couples choose to have smaller families.

Ah. The children here, especially the toddlers, are delicious! From birth, to about the age of two, they're attached to their mothers by an umbilical cord of devotion. If their mothers could breathe for them they would. The needs of their child comes before all others, which means that many wives ignore their husbands after their first child is born. Historically, to some, a child is the payback for "enduring" intercourse.

A small child is seldom put down or allowed to cry. If their mother is busy and can't hold them, they're passed to their father, another relative, or a sibling. Many sleep in their parents' bed. Older siblings often take marvelous care of their brothers and sisters. It's not unusual to see them hugging and kissing them or holding their hand protectively, particularly if the younger sibling is a boy.

Twenty years ago, it was considered shameful for a father to be seen carrying his child. This is no longer the case. The young father of today can be seen walking the streets with his child in his arms, or with one balanced on a bicycle fender or handlebars. Children are not put on schedules or told "no." As a result they develop the security of knowing that they are lovable and acceptable just the way they are to everyone around them. They also feel protected and come to the conclusion at an early age that the universe revolves around them.

Education is highly prized. Egyptians know, despite low wages even on the professional level, it is the key to their children's future. Because the public schools, like in our inner cities, are sorely lacking the ability to provide a good education, families make great sacrifices to send their children to private school, many that are bilingual: English, French, or German in addition to Arabic. Once children have mastered a second language, many are then sent to another immersion school to learn a third.

A recent series of tongue-in-cheek cartoons in a local newspaper depicted what happened to a wealthy family when their children began school. Tuition payments caused them to sell their luxurious villa and to move to smaller quarters with chickens and goats as neighbors. As the years passed, their home became a park bench.

How one dresses is very important, so it puts an additional financial burden on families here as it does in the West. Parents want their children to fit in with those who come from families a bit better off. Anything from the West, in particular jeans and sneakers, is highly prized over Egyptian-made products. Thankfully, more and more schools are switching to uniforms.

The whole family participates in the child's school day. Parents spend hours each night helping their children with their homework and drilling them on what they have learned.

Even the extended family waits in anxious anticipation

when grades are due. To facilitate "full marks," they hire the children's teachers as private tutors. Many complain that this is a racket perpetuated by the teachers to earn extra income, but they also see the additional expense as a necessity. When a child is ready for college, their grades will determine what career they can choose.

There are no public parks, few green spaces, but many high-rise buildings and busy streets. Most children do not play by themselves outside unless it's right below their apartment window. This enables their mothers to keep an "ear" on them. If they have a dispute with another child, she will swoop down like an avenging angel to protect them, often causing strained relations and/or a rumble with the mother of the offending child. The other child is always the offender. A mother does not think it possible that her child could be at fault, at least not publicly.

Children stay at home under the watchful eye of their mother, aunt, or grandmother. If they're in school, they're involved in a variety of after-school activities: religious lessons, football (soccer, the national passion), horseback riding lessons, art classes, swimming lessons, birthday parties, and tutoring if they're not getting full marks in a subject.

A child's day is very long with no specific bedtime. They're often allowed to sleep over at their grandmother's or another favorite relative where they're loved, spoiled, and cherished. Outings consist of visits to see relatives. The children sit around and listen to adults gossip. Life is an open book whose lessons are learned early.

Toys are not big here (though scooters, Barbie, and Pokemon have become status symbols) but television and computer games are. As in the U.S., television is often used as a babysitter. With the advent of the Internet, older children spend more time online. This exposes them to "things" and to the moral values of the West. This will probably eventually cause more problems, especially the expression of their sexuality as they grow up.

Like Western parents, many parents here believe that denying their children anything is harmful. This of course does not help children to understand financial reality or the stress their fathers are under, working two or more jobs to keep a roof over their heads. It also makes them a bit spoiled and unrealistic in their expectations.

Boys are usually not taught how to cook or clean; girls often don't learn until they are ready to marry. Until then, their mother or a cook and maid do it all.

For their whole lives, women take care of men. It's very unusual for a man to ever live alone. A young, unmarried woman never lives alone. She must be under the protection of a man.

There's a little boy who lives in the flat above me. He's probably five or six. He has an old man's gravelly voice punctuated with a zest for life that must leave his mother exhausted. He has a little sister who's much more demure than he. She takes him in her stride, except when he hits her, which happens often. This is allowed. He's a boy. She's a girl. He's superior.

He's a cyclone, each movement an exclamation point. I hear him when he comes home from school, as he directs life from the balcony above, when he cries in frustration or anger. I collect the bits and pieces of his creativity and junk food wrappers that glide downward into my garden. He plays in the hallway. The echo of his exuberance floats into my flat. His words make me laugh aloud, though I don't understand anything he's saying.

Each time I hear his voice I want to create a pretext for bumping into him, to see if the picture I've shaped in my heart matches the one I'd see with my eyes, but I don't. I prefer to imagine how he puffs up and transform himself into Batman or one of a million other characters he creates each day. I never want to see him as just another child.

When we do meet, for surely we will, I'd like to be able to tell his mother how grateful I am to have him in my life, how much I appreciate his passion for living. With the exception of his penchant for beating up on his sister, I want to ask her to always protect his essence, for the world would suffer a terrible loss if it were harnessed. He's like a little alarm clock that buzzes with the reminder that we can choose to live life with joy and excitement or through the cellophane of fear.

I want to tell her of my own boys who filled my heart and life with joy and the same exclamation points of wonder and chaos. I want to tell her to enjoy these moments because before she knows it, he will become a man and the sounds she hears today will be but a memory that whispers past her home like a freshly fallen leaf caught by the wind.

Lastly, I'd like to tell her that if she's as lucky as I, he'll grow up to be kind, gentle, healthy, and strong. I hope that when he has to bend at the waist to kiss her hello, she'll stop with wonder and say to herself with awe, "Wow. I had a part in creating this magnificent man. He's become everything I've ever wanted, and more." I hope she's as blessed as I have been.

*Build your son
without building for him.*

~ Egyptian Proverb

Walk straight and make no mistakes to confuse your enemy.

~ Egyptian Proverb

Chapter 11

May 2001

Whoops! I think I committed a major blunder! When Molly and I got on the train to return from Alexandria, the bellman broke my carry-on. I can't pull the handle out. It's no longer a suitcase I can pull. It's been sitting in my living room. Last week I saw Osama, the guy who fixed the lock on my front door. Knowing that he's pretty handy, I asked him to stop by to look at it. Rather than fixing it himself, he took it to a repair shop. Now I realize I should have given the luggage to Mohamed, my bawaab, and asked him to take care of it for me. Live and learn. I'll ask Mo to please apologize to him for me. I insulted Mohamed by not asking him to take care of it.

I've gotten very good at ordering things over the phone. You can have anything delivered, even a Big Mac. There's a bit of a challenge when ordering groceries.

Today I called the local market and asked them to deliver a few things (including six eggs and one container of milk). Instead of the eggs, I received six small containers of yogurt. Rather than one container of milk, he brought a case! No problem. The young delivery boy went back to the store and returned promptly with the correct amounts. It's also important to tell the person taking your order that you want the least expensive version of a product or you'll end up with the most expensive brand, by "accident."

Speaking of eggs, I've been a little apprehensive about buying them after observing how they sit out in the sun all day in front of stores. Even inside the store, they're never refrigerated. They come in packages of ten rather than a dozen, or you can buy them loose in any quantity. I had my heart set on making rice pudding. I pray the heat from the oven will kill anything that could cause my digestive system to rebel.

Today I signed up for horseback riding classes in Giza. I took a test drive on a petite, gorgeous chestnut gelding named Ramses. He's gentle with an incredibly smooth, slow canter that he can go into on autopilot if he so chooses. It's nice not to have to kick the hell out of him to get him moving, most of the time. My instructor will be Hussein. He's about my height, on the slight side with ebony hair and really great bridgework. He's probably in his forties, but it's hard to tell. Egyptians often look far older than they are. Of course it could be me. I tend to forget how old I am and think everyone else shares the same birth decade. I don't know why, but I continue to be surprised when they don't.

He had me cantering in the jump position over sand dunes a breath below the Pyramids. I found it much more comfortable than staying seated. I seem to have left my Velcro rear end in D.C.

Hussein is trying to talk me into leasing Ramses. He told me that the woman who used to lease him left Egypt and he wants someone who will be gentle with him. Remember the expat circle? I believe that the woman who leased him was the one whose birthday was being celebrated on the felucca! She hasn't left Egypt. Anyway, we'll see. It's a long metro or cab ride to Giza from El Maadi and I'd need to ride 3–5 times per week to make it worth my while. In addition to the expense, it would take a great deal of time, but if I go in the early evening while it's still daylight that might be an option.

I went back to the King's Chamber in the Great Pyramid on Monday with Mary, the healer from Annapolis. The tourists were far and few between so we took turns lying in the sarcophagus. Wow! Eventually we were caught on the security camera and had to bribe the guard. He let us continue to do it if we promised to jump out as soon as we heard someone coming. No problem! However, there is a problem.

In the past, you could stay in the King's Chamber as

long as it's open, but things are changing. They only want you to go in for a few minutes and then leave immediately. They say it's because human carbon dioxide is threatening the Great Pyramid. While that may be true, if it was their major concern they would put a time limit on the tickets they sell to gain entrance. My guide friends tell me that they are never asked to limit their time when they escort guests. I suspect that another reason is that spirituality is seen as threat to Islam. Of course, Islam aside, it may also have to do with a scam the guards have created to snooker spiritual tourists into giving them extra money.

I've been really busy doing other things as well. Last weekend Molly and her husband Tim invited me to go swimming at a local private club where they're members. It was wonderful until a major dust storm hit. There was a tent set up in the garden. We watched from the clubhouse bar as it moved about like a giant daddy longlegs desperately trying to escape from quicksand.

On another night, Tim and Molly took me to the Ace Club (a private British club/bar in El Maadi) for trivia night. We lost, but it was a lot of fun matching wits with expats, the British in particular.

Wednesday, Camilla took Molly and me to get our haircut. Molly had hers colored. She now looks like a short-haired version of the woman from *The Munsters*. I look, shall we say, almost bald. Camilla looks better than we do and she didn't get felt up by the shampoo boy the way Molly and I did. She was happy he left her alone, but she told the owner and none of us left baksheesh.

The hairdresser grabbed a bunch of hair and with a sharp screeching sound, lopped it off with a razor. When he was finished with his dull tool, he finally used scissors. By then I was minus a lot more of the hair I'd arrived with than I'd counted on. Thankfully, it will grow, in what pattern I don't know, but it will grow. Hey, what do you want for 40 LE (less than $10.00)?

Later in the week I attended a dinner dance at the American Embassy residence. It was a lovely garden party with food catered by the Four Seasons. The food looked a lot better than it tasted. It was fun to get dressed up and to show my legs on the street for the first time since arriving here. I was very fortunate in another respect. Apparently, while I was at the buffet table, our round table collapsed. The catering manager made up for it by giving us more wine. I told him we'd totally forget the incident if he brought us chocolate! He didn't.

It's funny how when you begin to think in LE you forget what it's worth in U.S. dollars. When a merchant wants 5 or 10 more LE than the going rate, you become outraged until you realize it's only a few dollars more. Everything is relative.

Although I have several Egyptian male friends, I'd really like to become friends with an Egyptian woman to get her perspective. The last time I rode the metro, I sat in the women's car. In addition to many Egyptians not being concerned with the issue of personal space and the use of deodorant, they love to stare at Western women. If you meet their gaze, they don't drop their eyes the way we do in the West. They keep on staring. If you're light haired, they like to touch you to see if you feel the same way they do.

Mary said that one day a little boy began to stroke her arm. Later she realized he was petting her like a puppy to feel the hair on her arms. As I've mentioned before, the women here remove all their body hair so kids don't get to experience this with the women in their family. Of course, the universal admiration of a child in its mother's arms breaks the ice, but I find the women reserved around me and I really don't like being dissected by their eyes.

The young woman who works at the bakery now greets me with a smile. One day I was trying to explain to her that I wanted a small loaf of bread. "I'm alone. Most of a large loaf will go to waste," I said. She looked at me in shock and replied, "Oh. I'm so sorry!" To her, my aloneness is sad because I don't have a protector, someone to look after me, or anyone to help run my life. Go figure!

Chapter 12

June 2001

I no longer believe that the Suez Canal, tourism, and foreign aid are Egypt's greatest sources of revenue. After my recent experience with Egyptian customs, I know it's the fees they charge for the privilege of receiving a gift from home that keeps the country running. The "free" stuff cus-toms agents help themselves to from the packages they inspect are their undeclared bonus.

Just like at home, there are days when the stupidity of regulations makes you feel as if you should check yourself into a hotel room with padded walls you can bang your head against.

Before I left D.C., I visited the city's version of a torture chamber: the Department of Motor Vehicles. Since my dri-ver's license would expire within three months, I needed to obtain a new one while I was still in the country. However, D.C. doesn't allow you to forfeit remaining months. Why? According to the bored clerk who waited on me, it's because I had paid for them. Hello! I explained that I would bear the loss. Nope. Still couldn't do it.

Eventually I located a supervisor who understood my dilemma and allowed me to obtain a new one. Egyptian customs policies remind me of D.C. They're no better, no worse; dealing with either of them is fraught with frustra-tion.

The Egyptian government, like D.C., expends so much energy controlling the minutest details of the lives of its cit-izens and anyone else they can pull into their net, one has to begin to wonder if that's the reason they've made little progress on the important issues like exporting more than they import. Case in point, receiving a package from overseas. Mind you, my dear friend Mary, who is even more anal retentive than I, spoke with FedEx before putting the package together to make sure she didn't inadvertently send something on the no-no list.

I don't know if it's the variety of the contents of the package she sent, its weight or size, but the last few days have been challenging for me and for the Egyptian representative of FedEx who's been trying to get it cleared through customs and delivered to me.

On *Saturday*, the rep called to say they needed to pick up my passport to take to customs at Cairo airport. Mind you, not a copy of my passport, *my passport*. I was also instructed to write a letter stating that everything in the package was for my personal use, not for resale.

Sunday morning, the rep called to say that I needed a doctor's prescription to receive the tubes of Ben Gay and Icy Hot and the bottle of Tylenol enclosed in the package. I asked Mary to send these to me as gifts for Auntie, her son Moopiga, and for a friend of Mo's. I had given Auntie and Moopiga the small samples of Ben Gay I brought with me and they found it helped their arthritic symptoms. The Tylenol was for Mo and me. You can't get it here.

Before I arrived in Egypt, Mo had asked me to bring several tubes for his friend, a young man who suffers from crippling arthritis. It worked so well the first time he used it, he decided that more would work even better. Apparently, although Mo told him per my instructions to use *very little*, he lathered it on like shaving crème. The poor man was screaming in agony and spent several hours in the shower trying to wash it off. This probably made it even worse! Anyway, rather than going into outraged American Rambo mode, as gently as possible I explained to the agent that these are *not* prescription drugs but creams sold over the counter, like shampoo, to anyone. He said he "understood, but didn't know if customs would." I didn't add that you could go to any local pharmacy here and buy any prescription drug without a prescription! A few minutes later, the young man who picked up my passport on Saturday arrived at my door with a form I had to sign stating that I was releasing the package to FedEx.

Monday morning the same FedEx employee returned my passport. A while later, Camilla and I went to the doctor with Molly before heading off to the American University in Cairo bookstore. The doctor, a beautiful Egyptian woman with a mane of free flowing ebony hair, pink nail polish and matching lipstick, saw us at the appointed time. She speaks English and French fluently. She was kind enough to throw in a prescription for the nonprescription products along with Molly's diagnosis. By the way, her medical group also has a holistic/homeopathic component to their practice.

When I returned home Monday afternoon, there was a form in my door from the Egyptian Post Office stating that I had another package, this one from my friend Beth Rubin. (She just published her first novel, *Split Ends*. It's a hilarious and poignant story about divorce from the perspective of a mid-life woman.) Of course I didn't know what the note said until it was translated by Osama the repair guy/carpenter.

Tuesday morning Molly came by with some fresh bread and change so I could pay Mohamed to go to the post office for me to retrieve my second package. As it turns out, I had to go with him. Therefore, with riding helmet in hand (since I was on my way to Giza) Mohamed and I jumped into a cab and went to the post office. A tired, squat building, it looks as if it had once been used as a railway station. I followed his flowing galabaya through a mass of people to a woman sitting behind a cage. She was busy, meticulously entering figures by hand in a ledger book. Eventually she looked up. Mohamed ceremoniously handed her the card. She filled out another form and handed it to me to sign. Thankfully, I carry my passport with me. I had to put the number on the form. I should have it memorized by now. She retrieved the package then asked me for 11 LE. "Why?" I asked. "It's for customs," she replied with a disinterested shrug.

Tuesday afternoon the bird screamed. There stood the FedEx guy holding the package that had been held up in customs! I was thrilled. As he handed it to me, he casually mentioned that I needed to pay 260 LE for the privilege of receiving it! Later, when I did some calculating, I realized that the customs charge in LE was the equivalent of the packages' declared worth in dollars. Thank God Mary and Beth fudged the numbers!

Now I understand why those visiting the U.S. return with overflowing suitcases, cartons, and refrigerators strapped to their backs! They're trying to avoid the hassle and expense of receiving gifts from abroad. This is also why whenever an expat leaves the country, despite the additional shopping, they kindly take lists of items their friends need.

Still, it is very difficult and expensive to bring electronic equipment back with you. You can bring a personal computer and video camera, but their serial numbers are entered on your passport. Color ink jet printers are generally not allowed. The Egyptian government is afraid they'll be used to make counterfeit money.

The aggravation cannot take away from the love and kindness of Mary and Beth who went to so much effort and expense to send me things I really need. I now have stocked medicine and spice cabinets, real toilet paper, and I can actually dig in my garden without catching anything, I can fix anything Egyptian style with glue and duct tape.

Sometimes I'm very lonely. I'm never homesick for "home," for Egypt is now my home for as long as it is supposed to be. The dark times have taught me to appreciate what really matters. I truly love Egypt. I love her people. I love her culture. I love the opportunity I have every day to see life from a broader, richer perspective. As we all know, real growth is not without challenge and pain. I have much to be grateful for.

Yesterday, my riding instructor had me cantering over sand dunes without a saddle. My feet were bare! It was one more challenge that rebalanced me and gave me confidence in my ability to hold on to life with joy and wonder while spitting out flies. I pretended that they were customs officials.

Chapter 13

June 2001

Going to and from Giza is an adventure by itself. I've been blessed with a regular taxi driver, Said. He's Palestinian, married to an Egyptian, and the father of five. He's on time, kind, reliable, a safe driver, age hard to guess. For 40 LE he picks me up, takes me to Giza, waits while I ride, brings me home, and teaches me new Arabic words.

Today, he saw that I was tired from my ride. He brought the cab to a screeching halt, opened the passenger door and gently placed my arm on a handmade armrest.

Each time we go to or from Giza, I see things that make me laugh aloud.

Earlier in the week, as we began to cross the Nile, on our right we saw a man on a bicycle. This was not unusual. What struck me as delightful was that although he wasn't pedaling, he was sailing along as fast as we were. His sandaled feet were firmly on the pedals, his galabaya ballooned around him like an inflated version of the Michelin man. His left hand was clasped around a strut on the side of a truck's bed. His right hand steered his cycle. It took a lot of strength and balance to keep his wheels from twisting which would have sent him either under the truck or propelled him over the decorative fencing on the edge of the bridge and into the Nile. Since few bicycles have brakes, I shuddered at the thought of what would happen if he had to stop.

Today, on the way to Giza, we saw men carrying old-fashioned crates of live ducks on their heads. The crates are also used to hold vegetables, rabbits, and pigeons. They

look Asian in design with a lid that fastens with a toggle.
They're rectangular with bamboo-type slats made from the
spine of branches from date palm trees.

On the way home today, as we approached the exit to El
Maadi, in front of us was an open pickup truck filled with
camels! I did a double take. How they got that many into
such a small bed I can't imagine. Although the camels were
reclining, knowing how large they are when you're up close
and personal, they had to have literally been on top of each
other. Their bobbing heads hung over the truck bed's
perimeter like a basket overflowing with puppies. They
seemed unconcerned about the conditions of their transport. If they had known their destination, they may not
have been as docile. Said said they were on their way to the
camel market where they would be sold for meat or as
beasts of burden. I don't think I've eaten camel meat yet,
but I'm not sure.

Police checkpoints are set up regularly along the highway. I don't know if this is for security, but I do know that
if a taxi driver or his front seat passenger don't have their
seatbelts on, the driver will receive a 50 LE fine, an outra-
geous loss for someone who drives a taxi for a living. Of
course, there are no seatbelts for backseat passengers and
because most front seat belts on taxis don't work anyway,
the driver pretends to have his fastened.

Taxi drivers take great pride in personalizing their vehicles. Some have festive seat covers created from rag rugs.
Dashboards are often covered in faux fur, others with an
array of small animal toys whose heads bob unceasingly.
Most drivers carry a box of tissues in a holder on the ceiling of the cab or in the center of the dashboard. The majority of rearview mirrors hold an assortment of prayer beads.

To and from Giza we travel along the Corniche (there's
one in Alexandria, too). It runs parallel to the Nile. It's a
pretty drive with many restaurants on the shore and feluc-
cas and fishing boats dotting the water. There's no area
where people can walk along the shore. It reminds me of so
many places in the U.S. where regular folk are barred from
access to the ocean.

I rode a different horse today. She was a bit strong headed. We have a few similarities. For the second time in my

life, I galloped. I might mention that both times were not voluntary on my part, but I was able to slow her down to a lovely canter before terror overcame me.

I met a delightful English woman at the stable. Her name is Lynne. She's lived in Egypt for twelve years and is a psychologist who works with children, in particular those with learning disabilities. She's been riding since childhood and also teaches children how to ride. It's her therapy.

She was helpful in another way. Hussein, my instructor, has been getting a tad too friendly. After my last class, he "casually" put his hand on my thigh. This may not seem like a big deal, but remember that most Egyptian men would never do that to an Egyptian woman. Today, on the way back to the stable he invited me to dinner at his house. He suggested I do this when I come to ride one evening (which I'll begin to do now because it's too hot during the day, like D.C. in July). Since he's told me he's single, this is not an invitation to meet the family, but probably to have me as the main course. To agree to go with him to his home would be asking for trouble. Although one can assume he doesn't live alone, it doesn't mean that he can't arrange to have everyone gone. I told him that sounded nice, then added, "But I think my Egyptian friend should come, too. You'll really like him." He shut up.

I asked Lynne's advice about the touching and dinner invitation. She thought I handled the dinner invitation well, but was outraged about the knee grope. She marched over to his brother (family-run business) and told him what was going on. She did this, she said, because if I don't nip Hussein in the bud, no one there will respect me. I had spoken to Mo about the problem. "You will have to be *very* tough" with him, he advised. I knew Mo was really angry. He usually says, "I think you need to be a *little* bit tough."

Hussein's hawk-like eyes observed the drama from a distance. He was suspicious, and afraid. As a diversion, he offered to take me into the stable to meet a pregnant mare about to deliver. Cagily he asked what Lynne had been discussing with his brother. I almost laughed aloud when I realized that his greatest fear was losing the income I provide. He thought I was about to fire him and hire Lynne.

I told him that he had overstepped my boundaries. From

now on he was to treat me as he would a Muslim woman. The touching was to stop. His denials slid down the stable walls like a man who has landed against it after meeting the hooves of one of the residents of the stable. I knew he was furious, but also that he will now behave himself . . . for a while.

When I arrived home, I found a message from Molly. I was invited to join her, her mother-in-law (who had arrived for a visit from Maine), and her husband Tim for an afternoon at the symphony. I grabbed a bite to eat and hit the shower.

The Cairo Opera House is new and magnificent. The works of Debussy, performed by the Cairo Opera Orchestra, surrounded us in total rhapsody. The Opera House has an active program of plays, operas, ballets, concerts, and vocalists. They even offer programs outdoors where patrons can sit on pillows under the stars. Unfortunately, those programs, due to the heat, don't begin until 10:00 p.m.

Dear Camilla left yesterday for three months to visit family and reopen their home in Canada. I will miss her so much. She's brought gales of laughter and joy into my life. Molly, who's become my social secretary as well as a dear friend, leaves in a few weeks. I've been asking God for replacements to tide me over while they're gone. They're coming right and left.

Thursday the Three Musketeers (Molly, Camilla, and I) went to the member appreciation luncheon of the Cairo Petroleum Wives Association (CPW). We had a grand time feasting on authentic Egyptian dishes, visiting with each other and partaking of the services of fortunetellers who use pebbles or coffee grounds to forecast the future. Each was surprisingly accurate. One even told me I would marry soon. My groom will be an American who will love me even more than I love him. Hum.

Chapter 14

June 2001

I had a glorious experience. It will stay with me for the rest of my life.

Said was late picking me up from my riding class. I think he didn't understand when I said, "one hour." In any case, as so often happens, when there's a delay or change of plans, it's an opportunity for a miracle to come into your life.

On the way home from the stable, he pulled the car to the side of the road and pointed to the Pyramids in the distance. As I watched in awe, the sun, nearly the size of the smallest pyramid, hung suspended like an enormous swirled lollypop of mango, firecrackers, and gold bullion. Like a shade on a window being leisurely lowered, it slid behind the Pyramids and vanished into the horizon. The incident lasted about two minutes, 120 precious seconds I'll never forget.

As we headed home, I examined the zillion apartment buildings line either side of the Ring Road leads to and from the pyramids. Many, though occupied, remain roofless. This has a lot to do with the fact that unfinished buildings are not taxed. Since it only rains occasionally in the winter, the liability for damage is limited. No problem (*Mafish mashkilla*)!

Although women here are controlled in ways we might find disquieting, based upon the domestic disagreements I hear being played out through the hallways, walls, ceilings, and open windows of my building, they're not shrinking violets when it comes to expressing their displeasure to their husband or anyone who gets in their way. They scream, cry, and yell at a decibel level that shakes my doorbell into tweeting. Sometimes they make it difficult to sleep. Even the jet engine that masquerades as an air conditioning unit in my bedroom fails to muffle the drama as it takes off or lands every five minutes.

Thanks to Camilla, at night I'm no longer being dive-bombed by mosquitoes. At her suggestion, I purchased little electronic devices. You put a pellet in it and as the device heats up, it slowly melts the coating on the pellet that emits a subtle fragrance of eucalyptus and keeps them away. I wish I could carry them with me when I'm riding because the flies make the hawkers seem like sleeping kittens. I was speaking literally when I said I spit them out. I cover myself with insect repellent but they seem to particularly like ears, noses, and mouths. Egyptians don't appear to be bothered by them. There must be something in their diets, perhaps all the B vitamins they ingest in bread and rice.

Speaking of electrical things, after using an appliance, particularly a large one such as an air conditioning unit, the dishwasher or washing machine, you must turn it off via a cutoff switch on the wall before touching it. Grounding can rarely be counted upon.

The repairmen came and took all my AC units outside and cleaned them. They cool fine, but they didn't level them correctly so now the runway in my bedroom has been extended to the rest of my apartment.

I would estimate that for a few days this week it's been close to 110F. The British psychologist (Lynne) told me that she buys rehydration packets at the pharmacy, sort of the local version of Gatorade. What's interesting is Hussein gives me a banana to eat when we return from a ride. The potassium seems to help me quickly revive from the heat.

The Sahara Desert surrounding Giza is very beautiful. The wind creates immobile waves of sand that contrast with a palate of every shade of fawn imaginable. At their zenith, they're the size of small mountains that tower above flat plateaus and ancient tributaries where the Nile once flowed.

There's a lot of excavation going on or near the Pyramid

complex. Currently, Egyptologists are uncovering an area half the size of a city block. I just finished a book about the visions of Edgar Cayce. It describes the Temple Beautiful and the Temple of Sacrifice. I think this site is the Temple Beautiful where, around 10,000 B.C., aging and genetic mistakes were corrected to create a new level of mankind to serve God in perfection. This is kind of an oxymoron. If God creates all people, aren't they already perfect in his eyes?

I had a rather busy week, thanks in great part to Molly. Tuesday night we went back to the Ace Club, the British dive that hosts trivia night each week. Our score moved up. This was largely due to Tim's knowledge of geography and esoteric science. I'm helpful on metaphysics, some literature, and the human body. Molly's a whiz at movies, music, and literature.

Thursday we savored a home-cooked Korean luncheon. Molly's friend, Dorathea cooked. She was kind to include me. The food was plentiful, exotic, and delicious. I ate everything placed before me. It didn't have to travel very far to my mouth. We sat on the floor beneath what we would consider to be a coffee table.

Wednesday night I attended a high school graduation party. Thursday night I gave a presentation to a group of spiritual women about the Sacred Mystery Schools.

I was up at five-thirty this morning to go with Molly and Tim to their daughter Jan's high school graduation. The ceremony was held right in front of the Sphinx!

I always hoped that one day my own boys would look back in awe on their years on Capitol Hill and think about the significance of the sites that surrounded them as they played touch football on the grass at the Library of Congress and skate boarded or went sleigh riding on the Capitol grounds. What memories Jan will have as she heads off to college this fall.

There's a new addition to the stable. I got to see him five hours after he was born! He's chestnut with a white blaze on his forehead. He was a little unsteady and his mother very protective. What a thrill! Hussein said that once his mother sees that no one will take him from her, she'll relax. Right now, it's not a good idea to get too close to her stall.

Who can blame her for being a bit cranky so soon after delivery? It's hard enough delivering a two-legged child!

Obstetrics aside, diseases of the liver are rampant here, perhaps due in large part to the pollution of the spirit. I've been reading everything I can find about Egypt's recent history and the stories of her people. According to one book, *Whatever Happened to the Egyptians*, by Galal Amin, Nasser, Egypt's first Egyptian president, became an Arab Socialist who sought the fair distribution of wealth, opportunity for all Egyptians, and to increase Egypt's GNP. Sadat was a capitalist impressed by everything Western. Based upon the environment and the imbalance of trade today, what neither focused upon are the long-term consequences of pollution and the ramifications an imbalance of trade would have on the economy. Today, Cairo is covered, like the dome of a stadium, in noxious clouds second only to Mexico City. Rather than providing enough for their people, rice and flour are imported to augment what is produced here.

Many Egyptians left their families behind and moved to neighboring Arab countries where well-paying jobs were more plentiful. When they returned, they brought with them a more fundamentalist practice of Islam. Amin makes the case that they had to have been receptive to fundamentalism to embrace it.

Today's leadership is neither socialist nor democratic. Although Islam does not run the country, it is still reflected in the Egyptian constitution and many of the hard-core fundamentalist beliefs that the government practices. Personally, I see fundamentalism as a falling away from the love upon which Islam, as well as all great religions, was founded.

Rather than taking care of their people, politicians and their bank accounts become overfed. The joke among Egyptians is that it would be best for everyone to keep the current administration in office. So much has already been taken by government officials, it would be cheaper not to replace them with those who would start from scratch.

Today, most women are still controlled by men: how they dress, where they can go, whom they talk to. Amin quoted his father who, upon returning from Europe, shared his conclusions about why European nations are more advanced than those that are Muslim and Arab. He cited two factors: "The higher position of women, and the abundance of rainfall."

From a spiritual perspective, if women are not allowed to share their nurturing energy, their creativity, intuition, and yearning for peace, the whole society loses its ability to nurture, create, and flourish.

Then there are the men. While they're very emotional and cry easily, the societal/religious belief that they're superior to women lulls them into thinking that they're powerful, at least outside their workplace.

Their wages are obscenely low. Under Islam if a wife works, she gets to keep all her wages. It is the man's responsibility to support his family. Because men have to work day and night, many are too tired to think outside the narrow scope of their existence, to question, or even to believe that their lives could be better.

It's illegal to protest, to speak your mind, but most men are so tired they wouldn't have the desire if they were allowed to.

Male energy dominates the culture as well as the region. It's out of balance. The people do not demand change or monitor their government. In effect, neither men nor women are benefiting from the God-given right of free choice.

I go nuts occasionally. It happens when I feel that my rights are being trampled upon. This is the biggest obstacle a Western woman faces here.

It happened when I went to get my visa extended. My passport is in my married name, but in the back, it's been amended to my maiden name. The woman processing my extension couldn't understand this and asked why I had changed my name. I had to tell her! Of course, divorce is not uncommon here, but I felt violated when I couldn't tell her it was none of her business.

Along with any electronic equipment or a video camera you bring into the country, the purchase of liquor at the duty-free shop is also entered in your passport. One has to wonder if there isn't a file on everyone.

Apparently, there is no "town" in the world smaller than

Egypt. Egyptians love to gossip, and no tidbit is too trivial to share. Even license plates reveal secrets.

An Egyptian, who happens to be a physician, came to see me for a consultation. Lynne, the woman I met at the Pyramids, referred him. Within minutes of his arrival, Mo received not one, but three calls on his mobile saying that there was something wrong with me. Why? Because a doctor was with me. Moopiga and his mother told him that he needed to come immediately to check on me, which he couldn't do since he was working. He hadn't gotten a new phone card so he couldn't call me either. Auntie, her son Moopiga, and my bawaab Mohamed were genuinely concerned about me, but also titillated and upset because an Egyptian man was alone with me even if he is a doctor.

How did they know my guest is a physician? Since he drove to my apartment, they saw it on his license plate. To further complicate matters, the Cairo Assistant Chief of Police lives in my building (he's Auntie's son-in-law) and his security men check out everyone who comes inside, no matter whom they're visiting. They even follow guests.

While I was touched by their concern over my health, I was also spitting mad. I felt violated. Here it's assumed that you're doing something wrong until proven otherwise! On top of that, phone cards haven't been available for nearly a month. Mo's mobile calling card had no minutes left on it. Neither did mine. While he could receive calls, he couldn't make any. He was leading a tour and had no way of reaching me. Being an Egyptian man, he was close to hysteria.

When I went to the American Embassy black-tie event, Mo got a full report on what I was wearing, who picked me up, and the time I arrived home.

My bathroom backs up to the room my bawaab uses to shower and prepare food. He's probably more familiar with my elimination schedule than I am.

My friend Rick says that his landlady stops by his apartment often to hang out alone or with friends while he's at work. A woman I know hired a private driver because taxi drivers began to know where all her friends live. Of course, now her driver can tell everyone where she goes and what she does! Molly had this happen with the guy who parks his taxi down the street. Anyway, it's all part of the experience, the really irritating part that includes the malfunction of just about anything powered by electricity.

Apartment building elevators, like wounded animals, need to be approached with compassion and prudence. Most are quite small, a tad larger than a phone booth. A maximum of four slender people without packages can squeeze inside.

There are two sets of doors on *most* elevators, I say *most* because if they're not there, they should be. The outside door is metal. When you enter the elevator, you need to wait until it slams shut by itself. Sometimes this happens. Next, you have to close each of the two inside doors until they're secure. They're very narrow. If you're carrying anything, you have to put it down before getting the elevator to work. Trying to get into one with a package larger than a can of tuna fish is a challenge. If you've gotten on the correct elevator, after you've closed all the doors, you get to press the button to the floor you want to go to. Some buildings have two elevators. One goes to even floors, the other to odd. If you get on the wrong elevator, you walk up or down a flight.

Since the floors aren't numbered on the inside of the elevator or on the doors you pass, you're really never sure if you've arrived at the correct floor. If the light is out inside the elevator, you have to guess which button to push. When you stop at what is hopefully the right floor, you must wait until you hear the metal door click. If you don't wait, you're locked in. The elevator stays put until you push the button to go up or down. You take another ride until you can return to the floor you want. My impatience has caused me to ride to far more floors than I ever intended.

Those who live beyond the sixth floor of a building have learned although their view is magnificent when the sky in Cairo is clear (about 10 percent of the time), when the elevator isn't working, they get far more exercise than they planned on. This is a rather frequent occurrence.

Apartment buildings that I have been in have no freight

elevators. When one moves in, everything that can't fit in the elevator must be carried up narrow winding staircases by the resident bawaab or movers. Although it's good for the environment and easier on the landlords' budget, most stairways have lights that turn off after fifteen seconds. It must be a real thrill to feel a dresser sliding down your back when the lights go out.

There's another problem with elevators. Sometimes the light will tell you it has arrived. The door will open. Oops! The elevator is not there, only the shaft. An expat recently died when this happened to him. He was going on a trip and backed into the elevator so he could maneuver his suitcase in front of him. It wasn't there. He fell to his death. I always look before I get on.

Shopping is not a leisure sport, but a kismet experience. Egyptian saleswomen attach themselves to you like a leech in the Amazon. It doesn't matter if you have specific requirements, they'll try to sell you what's available. Say you're looking through a rack of skirts. You pull one out. It's not your size. No problem. The saleswoman goes into the back room and returns with whatever she has. Too small? Too large? So? What's the problem? To find something you like in your size is a triumph.

Before she left for Maine for the summer, Molly and I browsed through a few shops. I was looking for anything made of cotton, in a color appropriate for my coloring that would reflect the fact that I am indeed still breathing and not being prepared for burial. As an aside, although most women are covered from their heads to their feet, many wear clothing we would consider indecently tight. Everything seems to have Lycra and polyester in it, kind of like wearing a girdle on your whole body leaving no room for the imagination. Anyway, I was delighted to find a pair of soft, light cotton pants in lilac. Cool! They fit me perfectly, so perfectly that I looked like an advertisement for the ladylike benefits of thong underwear! The next size available had to have been two sizes larger. They slid off me. It was not to be.

Now that I've gotten over my aversion for sanitary foods such as bread and my guilt about waste, I've enjoyed stopping by the outdoor bakery around the corner from my building. The bread is usually still warm and incredibly delicious. There's one kind that's like a large, round croissant, another like a huge soft pretzel with sesame seeds. Of course they also sell rolls in several lengths, the squishy kind you'd use to make a sub sandwich. At 1 LE for a bagful, I now understand why Egyptians won't eat bread that's more than a day old. There's no need to and since everything is made without preservatives, they eat a lot of it very quickly. "My" horse, Ramses, likes old bread so I'm saving the stale stuff for him.

Before Molly left, she and Tim were my guests for my first dinner party. They brought me an incredible treat, a bottle of lemon essence vodka, tonic water, and a few beers! We sat out in the garden enjoying our drinks and local white cheese (very similar in taste to feta but with the consistency of firm cream cheese) that I'd mixed with chopped green olives, nuts, and dried cranberries I brought from home. I was able to purchase Ritz crackers. It was very "elegant."

I found an Egyptian cookbook and prepared the favorite dish among Egyptians and many expats, *kusheri*. It's made with rice, brown lentils, and small macaroni, and served with a side of tomato sauce and crisp sautéed onions. The secret is in mixing all the cooked, drained grains together with the leftover oil from the onions and then cooking it for about seven minutes while stirring constantly. It's really delicious.

Garlic is an important ingredient in Egyptian recipes. The cookbook told me how Egyptians prepare garlic in advance. Most women do this at the beginning of the season when the skins are soft and moist. They peel enough to last for several months. I'd seen my bawaab, Mohamed, peeling it for other women in the building so I paid him to peel a kilo (about 2.2 pounds) for me. Once the garlic is skinned, you place about five cloves at a time in a jar and cover them with a teaspoon of salt. You do this in layers until the jar is full. You're not supposed to use a metallic lid, so I put plastic wrap under mine. You don't need to refrigerate it.

Serious stuff. Many Egyptians are reluctant to take responsibility for anything that happens to them. "It's not my fault" could become the national slogan. If something goes wrong, they think someone has put a curse on them or that it's God's will. Sometimes I have to restrain a scream when I hear the word *Inshallah* (God willing). It's used to explain everything, but Egyptians say they use it to thank God for their blessings, or to recognize his hand in everything. I don't see it this way. It's comparable to an American crossing their fingers every time they make plans.

You can't have a conversation without it coming up at least once. The concept of cause and effect is absent. Unless something goes right, many Egyptians see themselves as victims of God's will, not the beneficiaries of his love. There's no sense that we co-create our reality, that we have free choice to ask for the wisdom to overcome life's obstacles, or that what we want may not be what is best for us. "Inshallah, I'll make enough this month to pay the phone bill without working. Inshallah, I'll lose weight without dieting or exercising. Inshallah, there will be peace without working towards understanding. Inshallah, I'll be cured of X disease without modifying my diet or lifestyle. My neighbor will lose everything he has because I don't have what he has. Inshallah, I really can't do it but maybe God will."

Everything is a drama, from the fight going on in the apartment above you to the death of a friend's cousin thirteen times removed. Everyone is expected to join in, whether or not it's any of his or her business. Life is based upon the subconscious fear of loss and a terror of God's vengeance. Yet despite it all, there's still wonderful, hearty laughter, kindness greater than I've ever experienced, and the ability to clearly see that everyone is human and will make mistakes. The pendulum of life swings from light to darkness and back again with each drama, each moment of life. Each utterance of Inshallah impacts everyone, no matter what their nationality.

This week I met the wife of the ambassador from Israel. Susan is a lovely, warm woman with a marvelous sense of humor. She's also an author. I was at the apartment of an acquaintance, Joan, when she stopped by. Joan's maid sells Avon . . . can you believe it! I bought some Skin-So-

Soft to spray on Ramses and me so the flies won't bother him as much. Susan has a driver, but no bodyguard. Why? "Because diplomatic wives are expendable!" As we sat on Joan's balcony, a scream similar to an air-raid siren blew from a factory up the street. Susan's healthy complexion turned to paste. "I'm afraid I'm not comfortable with that sound," she explained with a shudder.

Friday night, Joan and her husband David were at the ambassador's residence for dinner and bridge. Suddenly, the Egyptian cook rushed into the dining room. He'd just heard on the radio that over a thousand people were protesting outside the house. "But no one is there!" he exclaimed incredulously. Susan shrugged her shoulders. They leave in September for Israel and then on to a new assignment, as yet undisclosed.

I brought a spray bottle filled with water and Skin-So-Soft to the stable. I'd already bribed Ramses with carrots, but thought this would send him into ecstasy. Not. The sight of the spray bottle nearly gave him heart failure. I'm not sure he made the connection between terror and a new level of comfort he experienced before reaching the plateau where we sail through the sand.

When you ride in the desert, the flies are terrible, but when you reach a flat, open area and face into the wind, they no longer bother you. It's kind of like life. We don't always have the faith to know that a plateau is just over the next hill; we're too busy dealing with the flies in our face or not looking beyond the illusions that surround us.

While at the Egyptian Museum with a group from England, a European lady began ogling a well-endowed statue. She asked Mo bluntly, "Are all men here that large?" Mo is used to boorish questions posed by some for-eigners. As if seriously considering hers, he gazed at the stature intently and then turned slowly to face her. He allowed a weighty moment to lapse before responding. As if surprised by her ignorance, he retorted with a straight face, "Actually Madame, he's a bit small!" Perhaps this is anoth-er reason why men here seem to be constantly rearranging themselves in public. They're easing the pressure on their ankles.

They think any touching by a woman is sexual . . . like

a pat on the arm. This is why it's a good idea not to let them get physical. They're constantly testing boundaries. They don't understand that Western women can be physical without being sexual, that nonsexual touching is part of our culture.

Although some men are more selective in their preferences than others, many think all women were put on earth to provide a sugar high for their eyes. A man's word here is law. It's not that they set down laws all the time, but there are certain things that his woman is not allowed to do, Western or not. For example, how she dresses. I almost slugged Mo over this.

I was wearing a long dress that buttons from the neck to the middle of my calf. We were getting into a cab. When I sat down, the bottom of my dress opened, exposing some of my thigh. The driver was ogling me through the rearview mirror. Mo reached over and covered my legs and sternly reprimanded the driver. "What are you looking at?" he growled. Being Western and independent, I didn't appreciate his taking on the role of modesty policeman. Big deal. The guy saw part of my thigh. But to Mo it was a big deal. He doesn't want anyone to treat me with disrespect. He was protecting me. He didn't understand why I was offended.

I have a solution to men's concerns. Rather than forcing women to cover themselves, I think men should be required to wear penis holders that can only be unlocked by their mothers or wives. Blinders would be good too. Horses are forced to wear them so they won't be diverted from their work. If men were forced to look straight ahead rather than revolving their heads like someone possessed by the devil, they'd have more time to work and think of ways to improve the world.

God designed the female body so that no matter what a woman wears, the trace of her curves can always be seen. Even when a woman is garbed in an *abbaya* (a long black robe) when she walks or sits, one can see the outline of her legs, bottom, and breasts and a man's imagination is usually fully present.

Why is it a woman's responsibility, rather than a man's to keep his lust and imagination in check? It's his problem. What a concept! Imagine how liberating it would be for women to no longer be forced to take responsibility for how men act.

As a whole, men here don't seem to be as, ah, in control as Western men are. If you smile at them and are kind, they fall in love and are ready for action in less time than it takes to grab a box of milk off the grocery shelf and walk to the checkout line. After a short courtship, like five minutes, they're likely to ask for your hand in marriage. I've learned to inquire as to which wife I would become: one, two, three, or four? Their response certainly keeps one reality based.

Because I rebuffed him, Hussein (my riding instructor) assumed that I don't like men. I've heard that line at home, too. What other reason could there possibly be for my not being willing to ride off in the sunset with him with a crate of live chickens balanced on my head, a cooking pot strapped to my back, and a gag stuck in my mouth? By the way, I just learned that he is not single. He's married and has seven children.

△ △ △

I'm waiting with bated breath to get my last roll of film developed. Said and I stopped along the highway and waited for the sun to fall behind the Pyramids. It's to the right of the Great Pyramid now. As we stood by the side of the highway, a beautiful barefoot boy of about eleven, crossed the road and came to talk to us. Watching him almost gave me heart failure. We're talking about a major highway, but he was as casual as if he were crossing a bike path during a heavy rainstorm.

Apparently he is the son of farmers whose crops of corn dot both sides of the road. He had the face of a nut-brown cherub and a smile that twinkled with sweetness. It radiated his capacity to find delight in every new experience.

He waited with us, watching, listening, and laughing at my antics and facial expression. I took a few pictures of him, which I hope will come out. He was so cute I wanted to put him in my pocket and take him home with me, though I suspect he'd quickly lose some of his charm when he needed his clothes washed, help with his homework, and to be fed.

He asked if I had a pen, *alam*. As luck would have it, I did. He quickly slipped it into his pocket, the one furthest away from me. Many children don't have access to pens. To him it was a precious gift.

We also stopped along a canal that's a tributary to the Nile in Giza. Young boys were frolicking in the polluted water with their horses. They weren't concerned about the mounds of rubbish that floated by or the bobbing bloated carcass of a horse that had been dumped there.

As a reward for cantering several miles without stirrups, Hussein took me to a special place. We came to a small valley, but as we reached the top of a soaring sand dune (actually it's probably a building Egyptologists haven't uncovered yet) I gasped in delight and wonder. Straight ahead was the Great Pyramid, to my right, the Sphinx, and then Cairo. Directly in front and below us was a wide, cavernous *wadi* (a dry riverbed) filled with windswept ridges and culverts of sand. We sat on our horses, the sun and wind in our faces. Tears of gratitude slipped down my face at the beauty of the gift that lay at my feet.

Alas, apparently we weren't supposed to be there because the tourist police came by on their camels and asked Hussein nicely to either have me buy a ticket (to be on the Pyramid grounds) or to get me out of there. He took many pictures. I hope they come out, too.

Because he thinks he's still a stallion, Ramses is a bit high-strung. He doesn't care for camels, donkeys, people on foot, stones, rocks, dogs, or other horses. He's wary and doesn't like to stand where he can't see everything that's going on around him. He kept fidgeting. The pictures may be blurry. Maybe he needs blinders.

Chapter 15

June 2001

I enjoy herbal iced tea with lots of lemon. I've learned to create mixes I can throw together. I make sun tea and, since I don't own a pitcher, I put it in a used water bottle. Next I cook up a batch of sugar water, let it cool then add freshly squeezed lemon juice and mix them together in another recycled bottle. The small *baladi* (local-native) lemons (about the size of a ping-pong ball) are much better than the ones we're used to. They have far more juice and can be purchased by the bag or kilo.

I sometimes make orange juice, too. You have to juice each orange separately and taste it or one bitter one will mess up the whole batch . . . sort of like being selective about the kind of energy you choose to hang around with.

Last week we had about four glorious days of weather: clear skies, warm breeze, sweater evenings, and blanket nights. It lulled me into thinking that perhaps the summer heat wouldn't be as bad as I've been told. It is. Right now it's about 10–15 degrees cooler than the maximum heat we're supposed to experience in the summer.

I'm learning that it's best to run errands in the late afternoon. Since most shops don't open till late morning when the heat begins to peak, I've adjusted my schedule.

I've all but given up on my air conditioners. Since they

were "fixed," their efficiency has steadily declined. The one in my office is so loud my brain can't absorb anything but its jackhammer vibration. The one in my bedroom goes from a whisper to sonic boom at irregular intervals. The one in the living room now only blows hot air.

I've moved my desk into the living room and leave the AC on in the office. It's quieter this way. If I close the doors to my bedroom and the guest room, it stays cool enough in the living area to survive.

I haven't contacted Auntie about this. First of all, when she was here supervising the Three Stooges masquerading as AC repairmen, she let me know that the Korean man who lives upstairs has never complained about his AC; translation, "Next time you pay for it yourself, whiny woman." Secondly, I can't stand the thought of having her, her son, grandchildren, my bawaab, and the Three Stooges here at the same time. They destroy the positive energy I've created by touching everything and leaving dirt and water in their wake. I'm required to entertain the family and to serve refreshments when they come to supervise. By the time the workmen leave, my refrigerator is empty and my apartment looks like a war zone.

Ultimately, this is all for the good, for it's helping me to begin to separate from the security of having created a home in El Maadi. I'm feeling called to move on from Cairo by the end of the summer. Where? Don't know, but it will be within Egypt, wherever it feels right for me to go next to continue the work I've only just begun.

I'm dealing with my fear of starting over where perhaps I will, once again, from scratch, have to develop friendships and find my way around. At least I'm now accustomed to the culture, speak a little of the language, know I can get along by myself, and find it easy to meet people and to choose friends who reflect back to me all the love I have to give. Of course, I can always come back to Cairo to visit my buddies when they return in late August.

We had an earthquake tremor. I was napping and thought perhaps it was my imagination when my bed began to move . . . or wishful thinking. It was small, but having lived through the last big one in San Francisco, it's not a memory I've ever yearned to rekindle.

When I passed the dry cleaner, I learned how they clean rugs. The stores in El Maadi are set back from the street, one step down. The area between the curb and the entrance to the stores is usually covered in tired tiles. Two men had laid out the carpet on the tiles. While one hosed it down (I've never seen a hose with a spray attachment used here), the other vigorously scrubbed it with a long-handled broom. They'd obviously used a lot of soap. It was quite bubbly. I assume they leave it in the sun to dry. It would be too heavy to move. If I were so inclined, I'd take the one from my living room outside to an area of the garden where there are pebbles and do the same thing, but I'm not so inclined. Instead I tackled the furniture in my living room.

I think they once were off-white and pale pink brocade. Now they're faded yellow-beige. Since I never use them, they're no dirtier than when I arrived, but the filth started to get to me. I filled a cooking pot with warm water and light detergent. The couch only took one cleaning, another chair two, but the third *corsi* (chair), after three attempts, was still pretty ugly and will remain so despite much brushing and rinsing. I've begun to see them as an analogy for the work I'm doing on myself.

I too have years of accumulated grime and fear within me. When I look at myself in the sunlight, I often only see the soil that remains, not the areas that are bright and beautiful. I need to constantly remind myself of how far I've come.

I've learned that if I pay attention and really look at what's around me, there's a lesson waiting to be learned. My bathroom is another example. Because it's fiberglass, I thought my bathtub was not just dirty, but stained beyond all hope. Gradually, utilizing different cleaning methods and products (I can't get Western cleanser here), I've discovered that what I thought were permanent stains are indeed removable. So, when I feel a total loss of hope about becoming all I wish to become, I clean the bathtub. As I remove one more flaw I remind myself that there isn't anything I can't bring light and love to within myself if I'm willing to get down on my knees and scrub along with God. The tub will never be perfect, neither will I, but that isn't a reason not to keep scraping away.

Why am I here? I've learned some of the reasons. I'm to continue to clear myself of the garbage I brought with me. With my love, I'm to help heal those I come in contact with, and when my work sells, I'll use the profits to set up a foundation to help the children of developing countries around the world. I believe this is why I've had the opportunity to see so much in such a short time. It's been only three months, but it feels in many ways like a lifetime. I'm sure I'll learn of other challenges I'm to meet, but this is a beginning in understanding my purpose.

I rode bareback again today in bare feet. My bottom may never be the same. The horse (not Ramses) has a spiky spine. Riding her was like trying to balance on the hood ornament of a moving Jaguar sans shock absorbers. I tried to canter, but she had more sense than I and thankfully refused.

Science in each generation has its value and price.

~ Egyptian Proverb

Chapter 16

July 2001

Birth control seems to be widely practiced, but as with everything in Egypt, there's a twist. Kim was telling me about an Egyptian friend who went to see a gynecologist before her wedding. She wanted birth control pills. The doctor explained that since she was a virgin, it would be best for her to wait to begin taking the pill until she was *used* to sex.

Shortly after her wedding she became pregnant. Her new husband was furious. He kicked her out and wants a divorce. I've learned through some USAID people working on family planning that gynecologists don't believe in putting a woman on the pill until they are sure she is fertile. Now they know for sure that one young woman is very fertile! By the way, despite the cultural obsession with virginity, a lot of the young women are not authentic virgins when they marry. For about 300 LE, a plastic surgeon will create a new hymen without her husband or his family learning the truth.

Abortion is not acceptable but it goes on within Egypt the way it did in the 1960s in the U.S. when women went to back alley butchers whose skills often left women still pregnant, sterile, or dead. It's known that at least one million abortions are performed each year. Since these statistics are based upon the number of women who ended up in the hospital with complications from a botched abortion, there are probably far more.

By the way, if a woman explains that she has a *problem*, a euphemism for an unwanted pregnancy, some doctors will perform an abortion and call it something else.

Since Congress passed legislation prohibiting funding of any foreign facility that even mentions abortion as an option, the clinics that most need money for education and birth control to prevent unwanted pregnancies are now unfunded. Hello! If Republicans don't want women to have abortions, why won't they support programs that make them unnecessary?

△△△

At least once a week as I'm walking down Road 9, I see people sitting on the curb with empty propane tanks lined up beside them. They're used as fuel for cooking and hot water. Others sit on bicycles laden with empty tanks. They patiently wait for a long-bed truck to arrive with full ones. In the nicer neighborhoods, a pickup truck goes up and down the street. A guy sits on top of full propane tanks and hits one with a wrench so anyone who needs gas knows they're there to install it.

It's amazing what people carry on bicycles: two propane tanks, animals, potted plants the size of trees, fifty one-gallon cans of olive oil. Their ingenuity and optimism is pastry for the eyes.

There are donkeys everywhere. They're used as transportation and to pull wagons laden with anything from cardboard cartons to watermelons, sugarcane and garlic. As the overloaded carts (depending upon what they're made of, most are dilapidated with wheels that barely have any wood/metal/rubber tread left on them) pass by, the driver (who usually has one or two small children with him) in a singsong voice announces what he's selling. So, if you're indoors you can rush outside to buy his products. An alternative, if you live in a high-rise, is to yell down, and then lower a basket with money in it that is then exchanged for the product the peddler is selling.

It's a hoot to watch a full-grown man ride a donkey. They're quite small (the donkey, not the man). Apparently the correct way to ride one is to sit as far back as possible on its rump with both feet pointing out. Donkeys have a cute, short, bouncy gait that makes its passenger wiggle right along with it.

I pay 4 LE a month for trash service. What I think this means is that Mohamed takes it around the corner and dumps it. The bags are torn open by all the homeless cats and dogs looking for food. Then it's gone through by two children who come along on their cart and pick out recyclables. It would be far easier to sort first, but that hasn't caught on yet. Local street cleaners sweep up the remains. They use handmade brooms made out of some kind of local reed that curls into the shape of an upside-down question mark. The whole thing is tied onto a thick wooden stick that serves as a handle. The brooms appear to be very strong and stiff. The street cleaner uses a piece of cardboard as a dustpan. They really do a nice job. Trashcans are few and far between so they have a lot to do.

There's a young man who lives in El Maadi, probably an American, who roller blades down the street. He's amazingly graceful as he flies by, turns, jumps, and nonchalantly goes on his way. Everyone stops to watch him. We all smile in international harmony. This is one sport I've been longing to try, but I promised my youngest son, Dan, I wouldn't. He's afraid I'll break something or kill myself, so alas I haven't taken it up . . . but. . . .

While on my way to Giza in the daylight, I noticed how lush and green the farmland dotting each side of the road is. The soil looks prosperous. I assume this is a result of the Nile and its tributary's overflowing during the winter rainy season. Right now they're growing sugarcane, corn, and a variety of alfalfa that's fed to livestock. When I first arrived, some were growing rice, garlic, onions, and soybeans. Astutely, farmers seem to constantly rotate their crops.

Speaking of sugarcane, there are outdoor juice stands everywhere that sell a pure sugarcane drink. The stalks are put through a presser and the juice is caught in a glass. Served lukewarm, the customer drinks it very quickly. I understand why. It's the most disgusting thing I've ever tasted, but Egyptians really like it.

I've become accustomed to and grateful for the salt in the native food. In the heat, it's a necessity to increase your salt intake. I can only imagine how much salt the women here have to ingest to survive. One can see perspiration running down their veils and headscarves.

I've always found it fascinating to observe how people adapt to their climate via their food and the colors they surround themselves with. Egypt is no different.

In New England, everything seems to be painted white and the color of trees. In the southwest, the colors of the desert are replicated in the clothing and homes of the people who live there. Here in Cairo, where there is little natural green or desert vegetation, people wear the browns, blacks, and beiges of the desert. It's a contradiction to gangrene green, an Islamic color, many use for trim work. White isn't a good idea. It turns to beige very quickly.

Mo recently escorted a group to Upper Egypt. He said it was so hot they all had their tongues hanging out like a pack of dogs. His description wasn't meant to be unkind, just a colorful way of expressing how bad the heat was. This is the slow season, although Italians and the Spanish seem to like to travel now. Things will begin to pick up in September when it becomes cooler.

As the temperature increases, I see more and more galabayas on the street. They come in a variety of weights. We're into sheer, light fabrics now. The winter version is made of luscious Egyptian cotton flannel. At any time of year, it's great to see small children wearing miniature versions. It's one of the cutest sights imaginable, akin to a toddler wearing Oshkosh overalls or a full-length nightshirt.

Surprisingly, galabayas are not that transparent. Underneath, the men wear sleeveless undershirts and the white cotton boxer-type underwear sold here. How do I know? Because when they're sitting, many men hike them up, and then shake their gowns to cool themselves.

What's really funny is to see what they wear with them, baseball caps, dark Western socks and shoes, sometimes sandals (which seem more appropriate for completing the native look). Women wear galabayas too, but not as often on the street unless they're poor. They're much more ornate, heavier, and come in darker colors than those worn by the men which tend to be white, beige, gray, or pale blue. I'd love to get some light ones for I bet they'll be a lot cooler than my perpetual uniform of denim even if I just wear them around the house.

There are places you can go to have galabayas custom made. You choose the fabric. Eventually I'd like to have one made in purple silk for eveningwear. Unfortunately, many of the dressy ones I've seen are made of polyester that the merchants try to pass off as silk.

There's also been an increase in sightings of men wearing rolls of white fabric on their heads to protect them from the heat.

Speaking of purple, I bought a long cotton skirt. I wore it without a slip until in pantomime some teenage girls were kind enough to tell me they could see through it when I stood in the sunlight. Oops! I went to a lingerie store and bought a cotton slip in a medium. Since I'm a tad on the low side, weight wise, it should have been a little big. It wasn't. Since I was too lazy to return it I wore it anyway. Good thing because I quickly learned that it stretches with the heat. Apparently most women here wear full slips rather than half.

Going to the movies isn't much different than in the States, with a few exceptions. Of course if it's in English, there are Arabic subtitles. The one theatre I've been to (so my expertise is obviously limited) had stadium seating. People were quiet, unlike some of the audiences in D.C. who find it necessary to verbally participate in the on-screen dialog and action. I found it fascinating that as you purchase your ticket, you're required to choose your seat from a seating plan displayed on a monitor facing away from the ticket booth. This is apparently a common practice.

Brick/block walls skimmed with concrete surround most villas and apartment buildings. Embedded in the tops of many walls is an amazing assortment of upwardly pointed shards of glass. I guess it's safe to do this without worrying about being sued by a trespasser who gets injured trying to break into your home as can happen in the U.S. The theory here is that a *harami* (thief) should get what he deserves.

Indeed things are quieter now that expat children are out of school and have gone "home" for the summer.

Americans will celebrate the 4th of July on Friday, July 6, in El Maadi. There's supposed to be a barbecue (pork, I hope) and fireworks. To get in, you have to show your U.S. passport, or be approved in advance if you're not an American. Security, I'm told, will be extremely tight.

I went to the Maadi House (an expat club for embassy and USAID employees and their families) to go swimming. I brought my towel, suntan lotion, hairdryer, and shampoo . . . but forgot my suit. I'll try again tomorrow! I hope these "in your prime moments" don't increase. I don't feel that grown up! Others are less fortunate than I. They may never have the opportunity to joke about their senior moments.

I spent the day with Dr. Mohamed (Dr. M.), my Egyptian friend to whom I've been teaching spiritual basics. He's an ophthalmologist and surgeon. I hope you can keep all the Mohameds in my life straight without creating a flow chart.

His brother, also a physician, lives in California. He's being treated for stomach cancer with lymph node involvement. At Dr. M.'s request, I've been doing absentee healings on him and the prayer group from my church has added him to their list. The tumors in his stomach have begun to shrink. When Dr. M. told his brother of our work, he was surprised by his response. "I felt a new kind of energy coming to me each day. I didn't know why, but I felt as if I had begun to heal."

For those of you who aren't familiar with energy healing, the human "healer" does not do the healing. God does. The energy is merely channeled through the healer to the person who is being treated either in person or at a distance. Prayer does pretty much the same thing; so never underestimate its power. The kinds of modalities I've been trained in are the same as, or similar to the ones that were used in ancient Egypt. In fact, according to the works of Cayce, Melchizedek and many others, Jesus was an initiate of the Sacred Mystery Schools at Giza and was trained in healing at Memphis (not far from Cairo). In ancient times, Memphis was the healing capital of the world.

An ancient papyrus has been discovered that shows, in detail, the ancillary damage caused by a spinal cord injury! Ancient Egyptians used energy, sound, crystals, oils, Reiki, and so on, the same methods just coming out in the West today, but their knowledge far exceeded ours. According to spiritual literature, the root of the word "chemistry" stems from "the science of the Egyptians."

This afternoon, Dr. M. introduced me to the most delightful woman. She exudes love. Her name is Madame B. She has over forty grandchildren and great-grandchildren. In her eighties, the purest light surrounds her. I'm invited to come and stay with her anytime I choose. I'm going to see her next Wednesday. She's anxious to treat me to an authentic Egyptian luncheon and to talk with me about her grandson (he's in his early twenties and lives in England) who has advanced systemic lupus. It does not look good. She called him and we chatted for a few minutes. I felt strongly that a healer will come to him and he should take advantage of the opportunity if he so chooses. He told me he would, but I sense that he won't.

One of the realities a healer must always remember is that not all people who come to them can be, or truly wish to be healed of their illnesses. It may be that their time has come to go. However, we can help to heal their heart and their spirit to make their transition easier; no healing is ever wasted.

△ △ △

It's been a relatively quiet week. The settlement of my property continues to be a major challenge with a purchaser who appears to be playing by his own rules. The building is empty. Not only am I without income, my insurance will be cancelled within thirty days if it remains so.

Yesterday, I rode my first camel—and my last. I'm convinced that Hussein is under the illusion that I'm responsible for supporting his whole family as well as Ramses. It's a long story, but he's always looking for an angle to figure out how to make more money off me. He hasn't had much success. His scheme yesterday was to get me to sign up for camel-riding lessons.

Picture this. Sister, an incredibly repulsive, skeletal, moth-eaten animal on stilts is brought toward me. The owner pulls on a rope and she bends her knees. Her stomach hits the ground with a whack. She's happy. She thinks her workday is over.

I'm supposed to leap onto her back. Slight problem. She's a lot wider than I am. Utilizing a running start like a high jumper, I successfully land somewhere in the middle of her saddle. I straddle her. Fine. I'm sitting upright. Her owner hands me the handmade rope that serves as a rein and tells me to hold onto the pommel of the saddle. I do. The owner pulls on the part of the rope wound around her muzzle and tells Sister, in Arabic, to do something—I assume it was to stand. The camel declines. She rolls onto her side. In the process, my left leg, ankle, and foot become wedged beneath her. Thankfully she is a lean camel. Since my leg was already bent, she doesn't do any damage, but it's a little uncomfortable being pinned by a colossal mix of bones, blankets, and fur.

Hussein goes nuts! He's hysterical! His potential pot of gold is in jeopardy. Maybe he also cares about me. I don't know for sure.

He starts pushing the camel. The owner is pulling on the rope. Stable hands come running from all directions to help. The camel is making the most revolting grunting noises you could only begin to imagine. Her head is swinging back and forth like a giant pendulum; her lips are moving in opposite directions. She's slobbering and spitting. I'm sinking deeper into the sand. Finally, with the help of half the village, they are able to push and lift her enough to free the lower part of my body. Phew!

"Jeanne, get back on," says Hussein in his "Women are dogs. Follow ten steps behind me" tone. I don't think so! I look at him in horror.

Finally, he shames me into it. I get back on. I am not happy. To my surprise, as I pull upward on the rope, the camel unfolds its legs. I now feel as if I'm at eye level with one of the Pyramids . . . the Great one. It's a long way up, especially after having just gotten off Ramses.

Okay. So far, so good. I pull the rein to the right and we do a U-turn. Hussein pulls up beside me on horseback and hands me a riding crop. I don't like crops, but as it turns out the saddle is so big there isn't anything exposed to hit. Hussein says to kick hard. I kick kind of hard. "Kick harder!" he shouts. I do, but she doesn't move. "Kick harder!"

I'm kicking so hard I'm about ready to fall off. Sister responds by pretending to walk. "Kick harder and use the crop!" Hussein demands. I do. Sister's revolting reverberations begin to reach a crescendo. She sounds as if she's trying to give birth while gargling.

We get to the stone underpass that leads to the desert and I'm thinking, before we go down at a rather steep angle, "No way am I going to go out on the desert on this thing," so I pull the emergency brake.

"Hussein. This is not going to work. I'm going back to the stable," I announce in a voice he knows means "Fight with me and I'll eat your liver while you watch."

"You don't want to ride in the desert? You don't want camel lessons?" he asks in his silken honey voice that attracts flies the same way a pile of manure does. I look at him incredulously and reply in a voice coarse with nails, "I don't think so!" Hussein has seen this look before. It's time for him to back off. I do another U-turn.

Before I get off, Hussein insists that I learn how to lower the breathing elevator. It's not quite as easy as hitting the button for a garage door. You pull the rein towards you and down. This is the lower the boom signal. A guy on another camel demonstrates, twice. Okay. I pull and very slowly she goes down. Just as I'm about to dismount, Hussein screams, "Now get her to stand up." I shoot Hussein a look of loathing. Another camel driver demonstrates. You pull up on the rein and back. The camel goes up. Now she's as tall as the Empire State Building. "Now get her to go forward." I do. She's going home. She's happy. "Now get her to go down." I do. As soon as her stomach hits the sand I flip both legs over the side of the saddle as if heading for an emergency exit and walk away as fast as possible without looking back.

I see the colt I met when he was a few hours old. He's with his mother, nursing. Even though she's tied up, I don't get too close. He's grown a lot in just a few weeks. He's going to be a real beauty.

When I arrive back at the stable, as I remove my helmet I notice that my hair is plastered against my head with perspiration. Hussein gets me a Coke. The blacksmith is shoeing a horse. He tells Hussein that Ramses has a fungus

117

infection in his hooves that's spread to his coat. I've been telling Hussein for weeks that Ramses has been a bit touchy and seemed worried about his feet . . . but I'm just a woman. I drink my Coke. Ramses gives me a big kiss. I take a great photo of the blacksmith's rear end as he bends over with the horse's leg between his. I take another photo of Hussein for my dartboard.

What has been gathered by ants in a year, the camel will destroy with his big feet.

~ Egyptian Proverb

Chapter 17

July 2001

Through each opportunity I have to interact with Egyptians, the unwritten rules of their society unfold before me. With one exception, there isn't the sense of personal space that we have. When someone has rung your doorbell, they step back and wait for you to answer. Sometimes they step back so far, after you've opened the door, you need a miner's hat to find them.

If you're trying to get money out of your purse or pocket, an Egyptian will stand as close as possible to see how big a wad you're carrying. They're not embarrassed to make comments either.

When an Egyptian man who is not family or a friend comes by, the front door is left open. If someone else accompanies him, the door can be closed. When the delivery boy brings groceries, he takes his shoes off, carries the order into the kitchen, and puts it down. The front door is wide open. You pay him. He leaves. Pleasantries are okay, but very short. To be too familiar means you have interests other than receiving your groceries. Still, it's greatly appreciated when you treat him as an equal, which apparently some Westerners don't do.

When the FedEx man comes, he stands out in the hallway, but if you have to prepare the package he will stand just inside the opened doorway and wait. Bill collectors, for the gas or electricity, never come in.

On the subway, even if it isn't too crowded, people will stand uncomfortably close to you. If there are no seats available and I have the option, I stand with my back to the car facing toward the interior. This way no one rubs up against me. Some men, as they do in subway systems around the world, do this to get their jollies. The only problem with facing inward is that you see the stares directed your way.

If you offer your seat to a woman who is pregnant or lugging small children, before she can sit down, another woman will pounce upon the seat before the first one has taken a step. Egyptian women are accomplished at using their elbows and hips to push aside anyone who gets in their way.

With the arrival of warm weather, being downwind from some men and women can be distressing. Deodorant is not common among the working class. Even the young women in shops who are helping you have a very strong body odor. They look so clean; you begin to subtly sniff yourself in fear that perhaps you're the source. Of course the odor may also be due in large part to polyester, a lack of laundry facilities, and a wardrobe that doesn't allow for frequent changes.

Men are the protectors. It's their job. To not protect a woman brings shame on him. My driver, Said, sees himself as my driver, my friend, and my protector. While we waited for Dr. M. at his office, an Egyptian man spied me from across the sidewalk and rushed over to talk to me. Said had gone to the car to get a newspaper to place on a wall so I could sit down without getting dirty. I hadn't asked him to do this. He saw the wall was dirty and decided it was his job to protect my clothing. The man was friendly. When Said saw him talking to me, he darted toward me and placed himself between us. Body language speaks volumes. Not a word was spoken. The man left more quickly than he arrived.

On another occasion when I had forgotten to tip the stable boy, I asked Said to stop the cab. I started to get out, but he wouldn't let me. He took the money and brought it to the boy. As I sat in the cab, a woman came up to the window and asked me for money. Said was beyond furious. He rushed over and shooed her away forcefully then shook his head and exclaimed, "Crazy!" Egyptians are seldom politically correct.

As an American, I am ever mindful that my actions may be taken as a reflection of all Americans and how Egyptians perceive us as a whole. Sometimes it's difficult because our television programs reflect the worst parts of our culture rather than the best. I often feel like a one-woman ambassador program. "Warrior Woman" mode isn't good for international relations. I usually keep it in check.

One day while waiting for service at the bank, I saw that I was only one of two women in a line that curved like a serpent from one end of the bank to the other. As has happened before, every few minutes the electricity went off. The employees behind the counter would casually get up and leave their post and then return when the lights began to flash on. Occasionally I would turn my head to look around and catch dozens of male eyes as they suddenly turned towards the ceiling. It became a game. There was nothing else to do. I'd turn quickly and the scene would be repeated. But one man standing in front of me was not as easily thwarted. I think he was Jordanian or Saudi. He turned until he was facing me and leered arrogantly. This was not a wise thing for him to do. I'm an American, not the U.N.

Everything about him made me recoil. He was slight. The top of his shiny head came only to my clavicle. I tried ignoring him. I tried staring him down. I tried giving him a haughty look. Only when I stared back and growled low and deeply did he turn away with a shrug as if to say, "No harm in trying." Growling is good.

This experience reminded me of one I had on Capitol Hill. I was thoroughly enjoying a walk through fresh fallen snow. Two young men disrupted my solitude. When they made a comment about my appearance, I went off. In response one of them shrugged, "Hey lady, you want us to tell you you's ugly, we tell you you's ugly!"

Here, if a man gets too aggressive you can also spit out *Imshi! Imshi!* (Go away) or if you really want to get your point across you scream a choice insult, *Ya kelb!* (You dog).

By the way, this happens to all women, but Western women seem particularly fascinating.

There is a definite class system. Dr. M.'s father was an Islamic judge. He, his two brothers and a sister are all physicians. They don't mingle with the "lower class." Many upper class Egyptians would be horrified if you invited blue-collar workers to a party they attended. It isn't done.

Moopiga is an accountant. One day he took his family to the Cairo Zoo. He found it very upsetting that poor families chose to enjoy an outing while he was there with his family. He didn't think it was appropriate for their children to laugh and play in their bare feet beside his well-shod children. Moopiga gives the impression that everyone else is beneath him, yours truly in particular. I think this means that he really feels he isn't as good as everyone else. I also believe his own little fantasy world is less than, shall we say, pure and sterile. According to Mo, since college days, Moopiga has known far too much about the local prostitutes and their pay scale to be just an "innocent" observer.

If an Egyptian man decides that he's truly attracted to a woman, no power on earth can convince him that it's not appropriate to make plans for their future together. He falls in love in a heartbeat, but doesn't ask how she feels. He studies her, constantly commenting on her positive attributes. He memorizes her movements and facial expressions so he can please her, win her heart, protect her, marry her, and then change her life to suit his.

They're not just into physical beauty. Kindness and gentleness are highly prized qualities. Men are open about their feelings, which is lovely and boring because they push and push to get what they want. If one method doesn't work, they just try another, and another, and another. Tenacity takes on a new meaning. In general, Egyptians never take no for an answer.

Hussein is like this. He still hasn't given up on my coming to dinner! He mentions it each time I see him.

Because men (and women) are allowed to observe the human dramas around them from birth, they are wise and understanding of human behavior. They also use this knowledge to their benefit. A man is supposed to marry a younger woman because then he will be considered wiser than his wife (though he may make an exception for an older Western woman). This is a key, for his word ultimately is law. If he's older, he's wiser; if he's wiser then she will respect and acquiesce to his opinion. So the push/pull of manipulation permeates society.

On the other hand, women know they can get their way, but they can't do so outright. Therefore, they too are masters of manipulation. If she can get his mother's ear, a wife can win. His mother is considered even wiser than he. Some mothers and daughters-in-law team up to outsmart him; others can't stand each other and try to outdo themselves by telling the husband/son how bad the other is.

One way to manipulate (though it isn't seen this way) is for a woman to suddenly become very religious. In some levels of society, there seems to be a deep-seated belief that if she is a good, "pure" Muslim woman, Allah will be on her side, and she can get whatever she wants.

Religious leaders do the same thing here as they do in other religions around the world. By constantly telling people how wise they are and turning human behavior into a guilt trip, they manipulate the people into behaving and not questioning their interpretation of the Bible or the Koran. As the economy worsens, and with satellite television and the influence of the Internet, more and more Egyptians are quietly and not so quietly seeking information from *bara* (outside) to help them find satisfaction in their lives. The Arabic word, *bara*, means "outside/outdoors" or is used to explain that something came from or was purchased outside Egypt.

The great philosopher, leader, teacher, healer, astrologer, and alchemist Hermes (known as the god Thoth in ancient Egypt) said that one of the laws of the Universe is that everything is cyclical; everything is like a circle or a day with a beginning, middle, and end. During his time in Egypt (before 3000 B.C.), the civilization began its peak cycle. Today, Egyptian society may well be at the bottom of the rotation.

Hermes also said that everything would come full circle. When a civilization is at its lowest point, it can only go upward to once again reach its highest point.

Egypt's time has come. It is moving. I see changes happening subtly and quietly. Once they get to know and trust you, Egyptians from every level of society ask questions that show there are seedlings of change sprouting, that all is not lost, that there is hope, that minds and hearts are seeking new answers. There's a spiritual underground that hasn't yet come together, but it's growing and will eventually surface to rekindle that which was lost; to create a new circle to benefit all her people. It's an exciting time to be here.

*If you want to drink milk,
protect your sheep from the wolf.*

~Egyptian Proverb

Chapter 18

July 2001

If a smile does not light someone's eyes, it's not from their heart. Beware!

Hussein rarely smiles. When he does, his eyes don't dance. He wants me to buy medicine for Ramses. I pointed out that Ramses is his horse not mine. He smiled and then suggested that my taxi driver could pick up the medicine to save me the trouble.

I was walking over to Joan's to meet her to go to the *souk* (street market) in old El Maadi. To get to her house from mine, I take a right after leaving my building, walk a half block, cross Road 9, and walk onto what is known as a fly-over, a spiral pedestrian bridge/ramp over the subway track. People on foot, a moped, or astride a donkey usually populate it. From either end, you enter at the lowest point, snake upward to its crest, then downward to street level on the other side.

Yesterday it was empty. As I was descending from the apex, a young man in an undocked bubble-gum colored shirt passed me. As he walked by he said in a perky voice, but without smiling eyes, "Hello. Welcome to Egypt." His greeting was not unusual. Egyptians say this often to foreigners. I replied, "Shokran," and kept walking.

About a minute later I heard someone coming up behind me and instinctively felt they were too close, for when there isn't a crowd, people walk around you on the flyover, leaving a fairly wide space. To let him know that I was aware of his presence, as I have done in similar situations in D.C., I turned and looked him in the eye. It was the pink-shirt guy. He dispassionately walked around me and continued down to where the walkway makes its second to last U-turn before existing onto the street and stopped.

As I approached the bend at a fairly fast clip, I saw that he was trying to unzip his pants. My first thought was, "Oh, he has to go to the bathroom," but my instincts warned otherwise. "Dummy! I don't think so." If I turned around and went back the way I'd come, I couldn't outrun him and he could attack me from behind. However, if I continued towards him, I, not he, held the ace of surprise. He wasn't aware that I knew what he was trying to do.

I quickened my pace. His focus was still upon trying to free his lower brain from his pants. My reflexes were quicker than his zipper. Without breaking stride, as I passed him I screamed menacingly, "Ya kelb!" He was so shocked, he tried to rezip his pants while running in the opposite direction.

With pounding heart, I kept up my pace but turned to see if he was still in the vicinity. He was gone. When I reached the bottom of the ramp, several street sweepers were standing there, obviously poised to come to my rescue if I screamed again. My only regret is that I didn't think to add, "*Mish kiteer!*" (Not a lot).

This story is also a thank you to Camilla. She taught me how to defend myself in Arabic. If he had been caught, he would have been taken directly to the police station, beaten, towed to court, sentenced by the evening, and immediately put in prison. Incidents such as this are unusual and they're not taken lightly.

△ △ △

Dr. M. commented when I brought flowers to the luncheon with his elderly friend Madame B. that he thought Americans prefer plastic ones. He was shocked when I said that wasn't true.

By the way, the luncheon was lovely. Her son, youngest daughter, and three of her grandchildren were there when Dr. M. and I arrived. When we all sat down at the huge, oval table crammed into the dining room, the food was already waiting for us. Generally, when you're invited for a meal, it is served immediately. Everyone else ate with small cock-tail-type forks, but I was given a normal one and told with a laugh to eat all I wanted. "No one will stare at you." Hooray!

I ate a lot, but still Madame filled a second plate and put it next to me with pantomime instructions that I was to eat it too! She didn't expect me to eat it all. The extra plate was there to ensure that I did not leave the table hungry.

She served stuffed grape leaves topped by a thick stew of onions, eggplant, sliced beef, garlic, and tomatoes. The platter was adorned with a fanciful ring of potato chips. Another stew had the same ingredients but also okra. There were sides of rice, garlic/yogurt sauce, and another platter filled with what turned out to be "chicken tenders" surrounded by potato chips for the finicky children's appetites. For dessert we helped ourselves from huge serving bowls of red and green grapes. Everything was delicious!

When I arose to leave, Madame reached up and placed her ripened hands on either side of my face. "I am your mother. You are always welcome here. Come whenever you wish," she smiled in Arabic. I responded, "I am honored to call you my mother. *Ana mus ray-a*" (I am Egyptian). I kissed her goodbye on each cheek (in the Egyptian way) and left with a full stomach, a happy heart, and a smile that lit my eyes.

I believe I'm to move from Cairo to Alexandria, Egypt, on the Mediterranean and it may be difficult to see Madame again. I have no idea why I'm moving, only that I'm to do so for a few months. I'll come back to the U.S. for a visit in September and move when I return to Egypt by the beginning of October.

△ △ △

There are many stories behind the ones I've shared with you; one that's been a heart-stopping challenge almost from the moment I arrived in Egypt has been the sale of my building. Thankfully it's finally behind me, but I have to say, as the now-happy former owner of a multi-unit building, dealing with D.C. and its landlord/tenant laws makes

D.C. the ultimate "third-world" country. I did learn several wonderful lessons from the experience:

If you're honorable in your actions, the time for things to work to your benefit will come. When it does, come from a position of fair strength. God never asks us to be a doormat.

Laws are written to protect people, but they can be used to further the agenda of those they were never designed to protect.

Accept what you cannot change, or drive yourself nuts.

△ △ △

This past weekend I took a mini vacation in Alexandria, Egypt. Until it was over, I had no comprehension of how exhausted I was from the ceaseless drama created by the purchaser's manic eleventh-hour attempts to obstruct settlement. Before he had signed the papers, my agent reported that even his attorneys winced at each reverberation of his nasal whine and unsavory behavior. I was so tired, sleep fled like a refuge from a war zone the minute I closed my eyes.

My friend Rick coaxed me to wash it all away with gorgeous dinners and briny sea air. By tram, we traversed the coast of the city, exploring areas I had never seen. Even our tram rides overflowed with adventure.

On our way to visiting the harbor fort, we found ourselves knee-to-knee with a powerfully built African whose ominous energy was darker than the soil of his homeland. If he'd had an automatic weapon, I felt sure that he would have sprayed the occupants of the tram, beginning with me, until whatever possessed his distaste for humanity was purged.

I was in his direct line of vision. His psychopathic gunmetal eyes flickered with the revulsion of a serial killer when he logs onto a new victim. I could feel his primal rage propelling toward me like searing tar. Momentarily, I felt intimidated. I had no reason to understand his insanity, only to recognize and do all that I could to repel it. Moving to another seat wouldn't diffuse it. It had already permeated the whole car. When I realized what was happening, I decided to take defensive action.

Simultaneously, Rick became aware of the man's energy and mentally prepared himself to defend us.

I leaned toward Rick as if to put my head on his shoulder. In surreptitious shorthand, I asked him to watch the man's reaction.

As if lulled by the rhythm of the tram as it rocked like a boat moored in the harbor riding a wave near saw-toothed rocks, I closed my eyes and willed myself to relax.

Discreetly, I lifted my hands as if to cup my face while positioning my palms outward until they turned toward the foreboding man. I forced all my energy inward until it coupled with my heart. Silently I told the man that I loved him and wished him only peace. As I breathed deeply, I could feel a whirlpool of energy depart my heart and shoot through my hands like a heat-seeking missile of love directed at his heart.

Although my eyes remained closed, I could feel the man's reaction. Instinctively he tried to repel my energy, but it adhered to him like shrink-wrap. Rick said that the man looked everywhere but at me, as if trying to find the source of his discomfort. For not only had I sent him love, I provided a reflection of the darkness of his spirit that bounced back and revolted him. Unable to bear the assault of love, at the next stop, he struggled to his feet and fled. We sighed in relief.

Later in the day, as we waited for yet another tram to take our sweat-soaked bodies home to where a cool drink and air conditioning awaited us, I decided to take photographs of an out-of-the-ordinary looking man who was walking in a small park behind the tram stop.

He seemed ancient, a Biblical figure come to life. Although dressed in a soiled galabaya, his head covered by an equally squalid rag, there was something noble and beautiful about the way he carried himself. He held a long metal pole, which he used as a staff. A filthy canvas bag filled with his possessions hung over his back. It was attached to an elongated fabric handle, which was slung over his forehead to allow him to carry it without using his hands. As we watched, he came closer. Only then did we realize he was blind. To our horror, we saw that he had somehow gotten into the garden area and couldn't get out.

Since the gate of the garden on the street side was pad-locked, we walked around to see if we could help him. Cement urns bordered by barbed wire partitioned the park-like area. At the farthest end, we discovered a crevice hidden by a planter. It was barely large enough for one person to squeeze through. While Rick once again stood ready to intervene if there was a problem, I slipped through the space and approached the man. As I got closer I said soft-ly, "Salaam" (Hello) and reached for his hand. He took it gently and allowed me to lead him out to the main court-yard. Without a sound, when I released his hand, he walked away, up the stairs to a shopping area, and disap-peared. A few minutes later we saw him walking down the other side of the main street. He touched us deeply.

△△△

I took the express train to and from Cairo. Said was sup-posed to meet me when I returned to Cairo, but he wasn't there. As I waited on a concrete island opposite the train station, an average-looking Egyptian woman approached me. In English, she asked if I had any one-pound notes. I didn't. I thought she wanted change. When they saw her talking to me, several cab drivers protectively rushed over and surrounded us. Without warning, she began to scream at them in Arabic. She held her ground and turned back to me, as if nothing had happened, to continue our conversa-tion. I was perplexed. Obviously the taxi drivers knew something I didn't.

Before long, more drivers joined the fray. Horns blared in frustration, but the taxi drivers wouldn't allow any cars to pass until they had moved the woman away from me. They screamed and cursed her. She returned their insults, but retreated.

Though I never felt threatened by her, just curious as to what was really going on, the men were protecting me in case she became aggressive. I hired one of the drivers to take me home. He told me that the woman comes to the station every day asking for one-pound notes. Apparently she is suffering from mental illness.

△ △ △

I went with Joan to once again explore the souk. It's a place where the sights and sounds delight the palate and the spirit.

I bought a rotisserie chicken that was as fragrant and tender as pastry just released from the oven and watched in awe at the sight of a man ironing a pair of blue jeans. He propelled the iron with his foot, not his hand. His ironing board was nearly at ground level. He raised his foot about six inches off the ground and grasped the iron with his toes, impelling it back and forth until the pants were perfectly creased.

On Thursdays, fresh meat is delivered to the market so it's available for the Sabbath feast on Friday. Joan and I watched as the still-warm carcasses were carried from a truck to the outdoor butcher shop where they were hung on hooks the size of a man's fist. After weighing, the heart and remaining organs were removed and the next carcass was set in place. The skinned carcass is striped in red and white like a circus tent. While hairless, hooves and tails are left intact. Flies are provided free of charge with every purchase.

I've noticed that many men wear a wedding ring on their right hand. I asked Mo what this means. He said that engaged men move the ring from the right hand to the left after they're married, but many married men don't wear a ring at all since once they're married their wives don't care. Muslim wedding rings are thick, hand-hammered bands of silver.

The 4th of July celebration hosted by the American embassy was pleasant. It was held on the grounds of the Cairo American College campus here in El Maadi. Tim picked me up. We sat under a massive tent with Joan and her husband David while stuffing ourselves with hot dogs, hamburgers, and Baskin and Robbins ice cream.

There were no pork or fireworks in sight. A band played American music. The grounds were decorated with typical banners making it festive. Different advertisers had booths.

I found one for TWA offering incredible fares to the U.S. Once my property was transferred to the new owner, I wasted no time making plans to come home to visit my children, family, and friends on opposite coasts. Other than that, my only goal is to retrieve some books and clothing from storage, get a real haircut, attend a service at my church, meet with my accountant, and do some shopping. With four stopovers and eight flights in less than ten days, it certainly won't qualify as anyone's version of a vacation.

You'll always feel the wound that's inside your head.

~ Egyptian Proverb

Chapter 19

July 2001

Wonderful news! Dr. M.'s brother received the report from his latest CAT scan. There is no sign of the old tumors or of any new tumor growth, just a thickening of the wall of his stomach! His doctors say it's a miracle. He's allowed to go back to work, but he says he's going to rest for a while before he does. He feels normal again, just tired. I believe his greatest challenge will now be to decide if he wants to live. He's been depressed about his illness and the personal issues associated with it.

Yesterday was another remarkable day filled with the joy of new insights and experiences.

Starting backwards, I rode for the first time in two weeks. My back had been bothering me after a two-hour ride around the Pyramids, so I took some time off. Ramses hadn't been ridden since then so he, like a child cooped-up in the house during a hurricane, was thrilled by the opportunity to leave the stable behind for an hour or so.

Dr. M. had come to spend the afternoon with me to learn additional meditation techniques and to share some fascinating insights about his culture. When we finished our work, I convinced him to join me for a ride in the desert.

Hussein was thrilled to have another potential student. Since Dr. M. is a surgeon, he obviously has to be careful of falling and damaging his hands, arms, or wrists. He and Hussein walked their horses while I went ahead by myself.

Ramses and I cantered for miles. For the first time, I felt in complete synchronicity with him. He acted like a push-button horse, willing and happy to do what I asked. When

I wanted him to go faster, he did. When I wanted him to slow down, he obeyed immediately. While Dr. M. and Hussein walked their horses to the top of the dunes over-looking the Pyramids, Ramses and I went through the desert and circled back to meet them.

It was very hot. By the time I got back to the stables, both Ramses and I were soaked, but happy. I think Dr.M. is hooked. The exercise will really benefit him. Although only forty, he's as larded and bald as a Christmas goose that's just been put in the oven. Unfortunately, his libido is thriving.

I finally had to tell him that since I don't share his ardor, revelations about his romantic feelings for me are not appropriate.

"But Jeanne," he pleaded, "I feel I will die if you move to Alexandria."

"Do you have a will?" I inquired.

"Why?" he responded quizzically.

"Because I am moving to Alexandria. So if you are going to die, you'll need one."

He guffawed appropriately. He thinks I'm playing hard to get. I'm not.

Like most physicians here, his days are like those of an intern in the U.S. In the morning and early afternoon, he visits his hospitalized patients and performs surgery. After the Egyptian four o'clock lunchtime, as well as my bedtime, have become but a memory, he is still working at his clin-ic. He takes only part of Wednesday and most of Friday off.

After we went riding, I prepared lunch at my apartment. As I walked the good doctor to his car, my bawaab glared at me and lowered his head in revulsion. Once again, he assumed we were engaged in horizontal, not upright com-munication. I was annoyed and embarrassed. I struck back the way an Egyptian would.

When I had the opportunity to casually mention to Fatma, Moopiga's wife, how grateful I am to Dr. M. for help-ing me with the research for my book, I knew she'd imme-diately relay this information to her husband and mother-in-law. Like falling dominos, within an hour, the perception of my dirty life took a cleansing bubble bath. The next time I walked by my bawaab, he was all smiles and bathed me in the glow of his customary fatherly warmth. I beat the system, but from my perspective, the victory was empty, merely one of survival.

To clear the air, I used their penchant for gossip, misassumptions, and misjudgment to escape the far-reaching consequences that would impact me wherever I went. If I am perceived to be unclean, I will be treated that way. If I can get them to stop and question, even for a millisecond, their ingrained beliefs about Western women, I perform not only a service for myself, but to every expat woman they will interact with.

All this relates to what Dr. M. wanted to share with me. A woman's sexuality is the central bead of the necklace that adorns not only this culture, but also many others. As it has been throughout history in both Eastern and Western societies, a woman's sexuality is controlled to maintain her purity not only before, but also after marriage. Furthermore, historically it has served to protect royal bloodlines and to ensure a woman's subservience to a man as his chattel.

While virginity and adultery no longer carry the same cultural taboos they once did in the West, they still do in the East for women, but not for men.

Women are assumed to be less hormone-driven than men; therefore by default if a man succeeds in seducing her, she is forced to bear the brunt of society's outrage. This is even true if a woman has been raped (a rare occurrence). Only in recent U.S. history has the burden of the crime fallen upon the rapist, rather than the victim. Today, in some areas of Africa and Middle East, if a man rapes his housekeeper, he is not punished. It is assumed she lured him into an act of depravity that, in some instances, can become her death sentence.

Based upon this mindset, it is not altogether surprising female genital mutilation (FGM) is still practiced around the world, particularly in Egypt, Sudan, and Ethiopia. It's an abhorrent practice designed to ensure a woman's fidelity by physically destroying her ability to enjoy her sexuality.

Supposedly, to keep heat off human rights violations of interest to the U.N. and the West, the Egyptian government passed a law making FGM illegal. Like sodomy laws in the U.S. that are rarely enforced, those who perform FGM are seldom, if ever prosecuted.

I'm sharing with you what I've learned because, although the numbers are lower than they were just a few years ago, and more and more Egyptians refuse to subject their daughters to the procedure, it still exists.

Outrage won't solve the problem. Working within the culture to eradicate it will. I have come to see that only through understanding can we help to change that which hurts another.

To my horror, Dr. M. told me that 50 percent of the young girls who live in the cities here undergo the procedure and nearly a 100 percent in the villages in Upper Egypt are "circumcised."

If there was ever a nice way to describe FGM, it's to call it circumcision. If you did a fair comparison of the same kind of procedure on a man, half his penis would be cut off, not just the foreskin.

It is not a religious custom but a social one that's been practiced for centuries. It probably originated in other parts of Africa. Its purpose is to take away a woman's desire for intercourse so she will remain "pure" for her future husband before and after their marriage. Many cultures believe that marital sex is for the physical pleasure of a man. A woman's reward for enduring his pleasure is to have children. FGM is very effective.

Blood and religious lines flow from the father. If a man can't be certain a child is his, it can cause numerous social problems, thus the emphasis upon virginity and virtue. When it comes to FGM, what's been left out of the equation is she won't desire her husband either; she can bleed to death from the procedure, experience untold complications throughout her life, and it can kill her during childbirth.

But before I go into the details, I need to mention another custom, one in fact that's still practiced in the countryside: the ritual bridal initiation that takes place on her wedding day.

The bride is taken into a room where her new mother-in-law and other women undress her and remove all her body hair. Once she is "clean," except for panties, she is dressed and taken into another room where the groom awaits. The bride is held down; her legs are pried open. While the women hold her still, the groom inserts a finger covered in a white cloth into her vagina and breaks her hymen. If there is blood on the cloth, verifying her "purity," he goes out and parades through the streets waving the bloody cloth while everyone cheers because he is about to marry a virgin. If she does not bleed, her father or brothers whom she shamed may kill her. If she passes the purity test, her husband gets to have sex with her after the ceremony.

There are three variations of FGM. The "worst" is the removal of the clitoris and major and minor vaginal lips. The next "least worst" is the removal of the clitoris and inner vaginal lips (practiced here). The third procedure is the removal of the clitoris. In Sudan and Ethiopia, they do the "worst" procedure and more. They sew the vagina shut so only menstrual fluid can escape through an opening the size of a match head. Just before the girl marries, or when she is alone for the first time with her new husband, her vagina is reopened, usually with a knife and no anesthesia.

The indignity doesn't stop. If her husband plans to be gone for any length of time, he may see to it that she is sewn up again before he leaves.

Dr M. told me about a female doctor who performs ten FGMs per day in Cairo. She thinks she's doing a good thing since "women shouldn't be tempted by their bodily urges." She also knows that if she doesn't do it, a midwife will. They use no anesthesia. The girl is cut with a knife or a broken piece of glass.

Like the penis, blood flows to the clitoris to allow for erection. When it is cut off, blood loss can be extensive. After the procedure, many girls hemorrhage to death. Of course, if they live, they are faced with a lifetime of physical difficulties: painful intercourse, psychological trauma, and complications or death during childbirth.

As Egyptians become more Westernized, there is a growing frustration and desire on the part of men for a healthy, mutually satisfying sexual relationship with their wives. If a woman has undergone FGM, it's not possible. Since mothers are the ones who take their daughters for the procedure, it seems to me that the only way to change the custom is to get men to see what they're missing and to point out that their sons will face the same frustrations when they marry. The practice is too wrapped in the issue of purity for them to see the damage it does to a woman. So, for an anti-FGM campaign to work, the men need to see that to increase their sexual enjoyment, it's in their best interests to stop it. What's so tragic is that a whole new generation of women is being ruined. The consequences will continue to filter down to society for another fifty or more years.

As an aside, Dr. M. believes this is why Egyptian men are so attracted to Western women. Not only do they see us as being without morals, they long for sexual partners who are expressive about their sexuality. This also may be the reason that lower-class Egyptian women stare at us with such loathing and fascination. They're repelled by what they think our culture allows, and perhaps jealous because we have the freedom they'll never experience. We are whole. They can never be.

If you cannot understand a hint then words will not help.

~ Egyptian Proverb

Chapter 20

July 2001

In Egypt, when someone is afraid to express their feelings, they'll say, "I felt shy."

I felt shy this week. Said was kind. I forgot my frozen bottle of water so he insisted on sharing his. I didn't know how to ask if it was bottled water or Nile water without insulting him so I drank it. He also decided to treat Dr. M. and me to a *big* glass of pressed sugarcane juice. I tried to get out of it, but he kept insisting so I felt it was rude to not drink at least part of it. The bottom line, my intestines have been trotting faster than Ramses.

Today when I was running errands, I brought my camera along to take pictures of the people I've come to know: the grocery store owner and his staff, the young woman at the German bakery, the carpenter, and the guys at the produce stand all cooperated. The man at the outdoor bakery asked me not to take his picture so I didn't. Some Muslims don't believe in having their picture taken.

The produce guys were sitting on the sidewalk having breakfast and insisted I join them. I was touched. Due to my intestinal problem, I was also wary.

We sat in a semicircle chatting in Arabic and English. People are so generous; they are always willing to share whatever they have, no matter how little. I explained that my body wasn't happy, so they let me settle for some Sprite and a tiny taste of *tamaya* (bean cake). They insisted on taking a picture of me with them as well.

Farther down the road, a slight, older man who was begging for money let me take his picture, but he was angry when I gave him 2 LE. He thought ten seconds of his life was worth more. I didn't think so. From now on, when someone thinks I haven't been generous enough, I'm going to take the money back, put half in my pocket and give him or her the difference. The reaction should be interesting. I can't wait to pull this on Hussein. We had a rather strong conversation about his constant desire for me to support the village of Giza. He promised he wouldn't do it anymore, but this was after he told me he was "just kidding." I told him he was full of camel dung. His eyes weren't smiling. Now he wants me to buy Ramses. It's tempting, but since my dog died, the boys are grown, and I no longer own a house, I'm not inclined to take on a new dependent. It's incredibly liberating to have freedom to come and go as I choose and not to have to take care of anyone but me for now.

My last ride was interesting. I did the barefoot thing with only a blanket. I rode the bony-spine mare. Unfortunately, the pad kept slipping and some of the hair on her back was rubbed off. I felt terrible about hurting her. I wasn't happy about the parts of my body that got rubbed raw as well. I suggested Hussein use some of the essential oil brew I put together for Ramses' fungus/skin problem. His coat now looks as good as new. Who knows, Hussein may actually listen.

I met Hussein's son, Muhammad. He rode with us. Most of the time I cantered ahead of them, then back. Muhammad is a nice young man. He and Hussein seem close. I was by myself (having left them in the dust) when I stopped to talk to a young boy on a donkey. He spoke good English. We chatted for a few minutes, he in English, and me responding in Arabic. "You don't speak Arabic," he said bluntly. I was crushed.

Because the tourist trade has slowed down, stable hands take two or more horses at a time into the desert for exercise. Unfortunately, they don't wait for the open desert area, but gallop through narrow paths leading to and from the stables in Giza. The only way to protect oneself is to stop your horse and pull over to the side to let them pass. There was a rather bad traffic jam. I'm concerned that a non-equestrian tourist out for a little ride will be hurt when they can't control their horse if it panics. I give them as much room as possible, but since there is a small ravine below most of the narrow areas, it's sometimes impossible to get far enough out of the way.

After my barefoot ride, I switched to Ramses. I was too tired to go back out into the desert and fight the congestion, so we cantered in a small area near where he gets his bath.

Just after we left the stable, a major crime occurred. Apparently a resident of Giza helped himself to a tourist's watch. Half the village chased him. The tourist police's two-way radios were going nuts, whistles were blowing, people were running from every direction to "catch and subdue" the culprit. What happens is the thief is surrounded, beaten up, and then lies quietly in the middle of the circle until the police come and "rescue" him.

I missed most of the drama and had to beg Hussein to give me the details. While the stage show was in full swing, the tourist police wouldn't allow us to go back to the stable so there was another traffic jam of horses, camels, donkeys, and carriages filled with Egyptian families. Most of the women were veiled. Ramses hates crowds so I was relieved when they finally let us through the gate leading to and from the desert.

△ △ △

Egyptian cotton is fabulous but you can't find much of it here. Why? Farmers are growing less and almost all of it is exported. I had visions of treating myself to Egyptian cotton clothes, sheets, and towels. I'll probably have to buy them in the U.S.

I haven't had hot water in my bathroom for a week. At first I thought it was just a temporary problem having to do with the gas supply to my hot water heater. As it turns out, it isn't fueled by regular gas but by propane. The tank was empty. Bawaab Mohamed has to take the empty tank and wait in line for the propane truck to arrive so he can exchange it for a full one. He wasn't in a hurry. The painter, who is redoing Moopiga and Fatma's apartment, helped me to explain to him that this is one problem I'm not flexible about. *"Bod bokra"* (after tomorrow) won't cut it.

Things are falling apart right and left. The lock on my front door has begun to stick, making it difficult at times for me to get out. It was changed about six weeks ago when the tumbler broke. I saw Osama (the carpenter/handyman) on the street and he promised to come by and fix it. My "fixed" overnight bag broke again. I can't decide whether I should give up and buy a new one or ask him to take it back to the shop that repaired it last time. Each time I've gone to Alexandria the handle breaks so I have to carry rather than wheel it. I hope this isn't a message about what my living there will be like!

On Wednesday, Dr. M. is taking me to a mental hospital to...visit and observe. He promised that we could also visit the addiction unit.

Speaking of hospitals, this week Mo's mom had surgery to repair an umbilical hernia that was causing increased pain and the constant concern it would strangulate, requiring emergency surgery. Not a good thing. Top this off with her other health problems—liver disease, heart disease, and the realistic fear of developing a post-op infection—and she's a mess. She's a year older than me, but apparently her body doesn't know it. She had put off the surgery for far too long. Why? She was afraid she'd die from it. Mo was buying into her fear and her health continued to decline.

I did research on the latest surgical procedures for her condition and was able to explain to him exactly what the doctor would do and why. I also told him that if she didn't have the surgery she could die. He used this information to convince her to have it done, but she was in tears of terror. I also prayed a lot and sent them both healing energy.

Mo's mother is very dear to him. He too was a basket case. When I say basket case, I mean he was alternating between crying and folding himself into a pretzel-like fetal position.

Their reaction is typical. There is no confidence in anything Egyptian, in particular medicine and the professionals who practice it. Fear rules the emotional roost. There is also a strong belief that Western drugs can cure anything. If drugs don't heal you, you ignore the problem until it's too late. Inshallah. To my surprise, drugs are actually cheaper here, but as you know the average Egyptian is so poor, they still cost a week or more worth of salary.

I was Mo's "preoperative/postoperative" consultant. Neither he nor his mother has ever had surgery before. I'm an expert surgical patient. I've had so many body parts removed there's little left I wouldn't miss.

Mo and I planned a strategy for preventing, as much as possible, her chance of developing a post-op infection. Hospital beds aren't covered in plastic so they can't be decontaminated between patients. The rooms are filthy. Heaven only knows where the bed linens have been. I instructed him to sponge the bed, to wash everything in the room with a mixture of bleach and scalding water, and to bring bedding from home. Antibacterial soap and ointments aren't readily available, but I had some to give to them. Just before surgery, he promised that his sister would bathe their mother with the antibacterial soap. Anyone who touched her had to wash with it first. Once again, Mary Lewis, your care package was put to good use!

To prevent her from contracting an airborne infection, thanks to my lovely daughter-in-law Adrienne's research, I was able to choose an antibacterial essential oil that could be used on his mom before and after surgery.

She went through surgery fine, but once the anesthesia wore off, she was in agony. Mo called in alarm. "Jeanne. Is it normal for her to be in so much pain?" he asked. Since she'd had abdominal surgery, obviously it was normal. What wasn't normal was the pain management. All the medical professionals told her that she would just have to suffer for twenty-four hours because they couldn't increase her pain medication without complications such as constipation. My assessment is that they don't have enough kinds of pain medication to use, or knowledge about managing side effects. They do the best they can. Sending her healing energy did the trick, at least for a while. How I wish a hospice doc or two would come here to teach pain management, for they know more about it, I believe, than any other category of physician.

When someone is in the hospital, it's another huge drama. The whole family comes and sits in the room with the patient. We're talking aunts, uncles, cousins, children, in-laws, parents—everyone. To decrease the risk of infection and to allow her to rest, I suggested that maybe it would be good to limit her visitors to Mo and his sister. Mo replied that there were only a few who stayed with her all day after she returned to her room . . . five, but while she was in surgery I guesstimate there were nearly thirty people waiting with him! Thankfully, I'm getting a bit smarter about being open to seeing and accepting the cultural differences. I asked if having so many people around made his Mom feel better. Apparently, because she feels loved and validated by everyone's physical presence and the mass hysteria, it does indeed make her feel better. So much for sterile surroundings!

I've recently learned that every person who works with a patient in a hospital expects baksheesh. As you come out of anesthesia they have their hand out.

This afternoon Dr. M. and I went to the public mental hospital. I have an appointment for a tour and meeting next Wednesday with Dr. Mohamed Ghanem, the General Secretary of Mental Health of Egypt. As in the U.S., there's a real concern about negative press coverage. They probably want to sanitize the campus before my visit. They have no way of knowing that I have no desire to harm, only to seek and learn, not to judge. There isn't an institution on earth that has reached a state of perfection and there probably never will be.

I met Dr. Ghanem briefly. He's a well-pressed Greek god in full bloom, a delightful merger of charm, chivalry, and street smarts. He explained that it would be difficult to give me a tour today. "You're like a little parachute that just dropped down from the sky." Can you imagine one of the U.S. cabinet members saying something like that? Of course, you'd never get past his or her flunkies so it's a moot point. I apologized for my unexpected descent and told him I looked forward to meeting with him next week.

I also spoke with Dr. Ahmed el Nahas. A psychiatrist, he's squat with bowed legs, probably from rickets or hip joint problems that cause his swift gait to roll like a shopping cart whose wheels won't turn properly. He's in charge of the female section of the campus. He asked which kinds of cases I was interested in observing. "The worst," I replied without hesitation. "You do not know Jeanne," Dr. M. responded with a jovial chuckle when Dr. el Nahas suggested that my feminine sensitivity might cause me to swoon like a southern belle if I was exposed to the heat of reality.

$$\triangle \triangle \triangle$$

International phone calls from friends and family outside Egypt also keeps me reality-based. My dear friend Philip called from Rhode Island to say hi. He asked how hot it is and if it's humid. I told him it was similar to what a vegetable would feel when placed on a steam table. Curiosity got the better of me. I looked up the weather details on the Internet this morning. It's in the high 90s. The humidity is 78 percent. Where, I wonder, can I find the parchedness of the desert that surrounds me?

I've learned to wait until the mugger disguised as unrelenting sunshine retreats before I run errands. Actually, *run* is an oxymoron. The only thing that comes close to running in this heat are the intestines of tourists foolish enough to drink tap water or to eat food served by street vendors. Walking is difficult enough without a hose held over your head to keep your brain from dehydrating.

Today, as the sun began to shield itself from its own reflection, I ventured out. I had a vital mission. Half the merchants and their young helpers on Road 9 were anxiously waiting for me to accomplish it.

As I strolled by the carpenter shop, the market, the German bakery, and the produce stand, everyone flew from the relative cool of their shops to wave enthusiastically. While I'm well liked, because I don't have a lot of money to spend in general, my long-term value is negligible. Today, however I was a *pasha*!

I was on my way to the Kodak store to retrieve packages of film I had left earlier in the week for developing. Everyone knew I was going there. Soon they would receive copies of pictures I had taken of them. For some, it may have been the first photograph of themselves they have ever owned.

The photos were ready. *"Al hamdulilah"* (Praise God)! As I flipped through a stack, the man who waited on me pointed to one picture and asked if I'd actually eaten the food shown in the picture. He was surprised, even perhaps impressed that I had gotten down on the sidewalk and shared falafel and drinks with the locals. He's a bit priggish. I said yes. This revelation seemed to soften him a tad, but he still oinks. Since it was obvious that everyone expected at least one copy of any photo they were included in, while I was in the store I ordered duplicates and another set for myself.

With the exception of Ramadan, the hawk-faced, galabaya-clad patriarch of the produce stand I frequent, his or her photograph delighted everyone. Ramadan declared the photo of us and half his staff sitting on the sidewalk eating and talking "*Mish kwayyis*" (not good).

Ramadan's antics both annoy and delight me. Like so many things here and in life in general, it's all about the frame you choose to put people and events into. He's endearingly funny, in an eccentric character sort of way— like Scrooge on the verge of an epiphany.

Ramadan is a member of the "follow me immediately, you dog" tribe. He's probably in his fifties, solid like a box of stale brown sugar, and tall for an Egyptian. As I approached, he tried to grab the photos from my hand, but I wouldn't let him. This made his brothers/uncles/cousins smile . . . behind his back. He gently pushed me down onto the sidewalk, handed me a cup of hot tea, and attempted to take a pack of cigarettes from my purse. I slapped his hand away.

Everyone from the produce stand crowded around. Despite his protestations that the photos weren't up to his standards, Ramadan didn't charge me as much for my produce as he usually does. He threw in a beautiful, free tomato.

I didn't bring my camera with me today. I noticed that after receiving his or her photograph, every recipient not so casually checked to see if my mesh, ecologically correct shopping bag was slung over my shoulder. They were disappointed to see that it wasn't. I carry my camera in it. They wanted more pictures taken.

I prefer to think that they were being optimistic rather than greedy. I felt that I had already contributed to every family's daily joy allotment, so I left it at home. Much to my dismay, I missed a great shot.

As I headed home, I saw a cornucopia of tubby unsheared sheep (*khroof*) walking up Road 9. A sheep-herder, the flocks' version of a drum major, marched along-side the parade. A delicate barefoot girl led the way.

Another photo op was a bunch of men lined up in rows on their hands and knees on their prayer rugs for late-afternoon prayer. One of the poses they do while praying is to kneel, then bend over with their backsides in the air. This would have been a great shot, but perhaps a bit dis-respectful and one I will get one day.

Speaking of praying, anyone who enters a mosque to pray, or even those who pray on carpets along the street, must be purified first. This means cleaning all the orifices and extremities of the body with water. For those who drive cabs or work outside, there are special bathrooms in every mosque where they can clean themselves first.

Most public bathrooms and some hotel rooms have neat gadgets, a narrow hose hangs on the wall with a spray attachment for cleaning after going to the bathroom. Some toilets have a curved copper spout inside the toilet you can turn on from a faucet mounted near the side of the toilet. Since everything that goes in the toilet falls on it first, I find the thought of using it beyond revolting.

Speaking of water, throughout Cairo there are little metallic water stands the size and height of a small dress-er with spigots. Tin cups, not disposable ones, are provid-ed for whoever is thirsty. I don't know if the water is clean and I would have to say that the cup isn't, so I've never used one, but they're charming and necessary. Sometimes, rather than a stand, an earthenware jug filled with water, then covered with a piece of wood or a small slab of gran-ite serves the same purpose.

Mo took tourists for a ride in Giza last night and early this morning. I gave him Hussein's phone number. "I won't tell Jeanne you were here," Hussein confided in his well-oiled way. "Why not?" asked Mo indignantly. "She knows I was bringing guests to you. She gave me your phone number."

I think Hussein is afraid I will ask for a kickback. Apparently his Bedouin heritage doesn't allow for the possibility that a person can do nice things for someone else without expecting anything in return.

On Friday I stopped by to see my friend Amin who runs the antique store, but he's in Libya. One of his decorators was faux finishing each room of his shop in a different color and texture. I was very enthusiastic and asked how he had accomplished several effects. He showed me.

His technique requires thick paint that sits in the bottom of a large bucket. On top of the thick paint is a layer of paint (in a different color) the consistency of water. He dips the rag into the bucket, grabs a glob from the bottom and then, starting at the top and working downward, smears the two colors on the wall. Some rooms were more effective than others. I told him about using feathers and sponges to create different effects. It was fun trading information.

I bought a set of coasters to save me from having to constantly clean the glass tops on all the tables in my flat. Just about all the furniture here is covered with glass to protect the wood. Unfortunately, coasters don't work when an Egyptian visits. They're not used to them and think they're for decoration. They push the coaster aside and place their drink directly on the glass. Oh well.

Since Islam does not allow the consumption of liquor by its followers, manufacturers have an interesting way of marketing their wine-based products. I was looking for red wine vinegar. There is no such thing, but there is a product called red "grape" vinegar! Because it has alcohol in it, you can't buy liquid vanilla. It's sold granulated, mixed with sugar in small packages about twice the size of an individual serving of Equal.

Saturday evening Ramses and I had a nice ride by ourselves. I'm going again tomorrow. Dr. M. brought me some medication for my intestinal problem. Thankfully the only one who's running now is Ramses.

Chapter 21

July 2001

Beneath the Pyramids, adjacent to an area where I often go to pray and meditate, a makeshift village has bloomed in the blistering sand. While the residents of Cairo are enjoying the beauty and refreshment of the Mediterranean Coast in Alexandria, others are vacationing for free in the desert.

Sand-washed tents dot the hillside overlooking an archeological site well into the excavation process. It's a summer village created by those seeking relief for their arthritis, a condition that's quite common among Egyptians. They bring the whole family.

There's a makeshift latrine, its backside cleverly positioned against a wall on the other side of the Coptic and Muslim cemeteries that are a stone's throw from the Sphinx. It wears a fabric door, gathered perfectly to preserve privacy. Based upon the dampness of the sand sloping away from it, it's probably used by the whole "village."

Small children run and play in the sand and on top of structures yet to experience an archeologist's trowel. They trudge through the desert carrying recycled bottles filled with water from the village of Giza. Others return with armloads of unwrapped native bread.

While their elders sit in the shade of their tents, their version of a spa, absorbing the heat from the unforgiving desert, the children nestle in the sand by the side of the "road" and sell warm Pepsi or water to thirsty camel and horseback riders. They fight. They laugh. When a foreigner happens by, they wave and shout greetings.

Yesterday I was on foot. I'd arrived at the stable a bit

early. Hussein was not there. Since he has the key to the box protecting my helmet, boots, and insect repellent from theft, there was no reason to ask one of the stable boys to tack Ramses. Instead of waiting, I decided to go by foot to "my grotto" to pray and meditate. I asked Hussein's brother, a rotund version of his younger sibling, to let him know where I had gone and that I would not be riding.

When they're on patrol in the desert, the tourist police in the Pyramids area ride camels. In the streets of Giza, they ride motorcycles. Yesterday they seemed to be everywhere. As I walked under a stone archway leading into the desert, one of them pulled his camel alongside me and stopped. "Do you have a Pyramid ticket?" he asked. "No. I don't believe I need one for I think I am not on the Pyramid grounds," I replied evenly. "*Ana men hena*" (I am from here), I added. "Ah." His was a typical ploy to gain a little extra income from an unsuspecting tourist.

Onward I continued. I reached the grotto, climbed up into its womb, and settled into a corner away from the sunlight, but facing a soft breeze and began to pray and meditate. I could hear camels and horses slipping along the rough, narrow pathway I had taken.

I was rudely jolted back to reality. Tourist police had seen me. Once again, as they shouted to me from the small ravine path above the grotto, I explained that I live here. Even after being told that it was not allowed for me to stay in the grotto, this was my pass to stay. I wanted to ask if it was also not allowed for an Egyptian to come with his prayer rug and to kneel where I sat, but that would not have been wise. Firm friendliness works best.

When I began to walk back to the stable, little girls from the spa village surrounded me and asked if I would kiss them. I did. They responded with smiles, squeals of delight, and major hugs. One, a beautiful, petite child of about eight asked for a "tip." "*Mish baksheesh*" (No tip/bribe), I said with a smile. She followed me for a little while, then waved goodbye. No harm in trying.

Hussein was waiting at the stable. Ramses was tacked. Since I have five rides left on my "group rate," he's anxious for me to use up my credits so I'll sign up for ten more. No harm in trying.

A young man was standing near him. As I approached, Hussein cocked his head in his direction and said in a stage voice the child could not fail to hear, "I told him you were praying. He didn't believe me." I turned to the young man and said, "Yes. I was praying. When you pray you kneel on a rug. When I pray I sit on a rock. Do you think that Allah does not welcome and hear all prayers from the heart no matter where they come from?" I asked. He was surprised by my response. Hussein beamed his sly smile. Neither was convinced of my pipeline to God. Muslims have a set prayer routine. Many believe that the Muslim way of praying is the only one God hears. Although it's said that the choreographed physical movements and the sound of the words they recite do create a high vibrational level, I find their belief and that of many other organized religions an insult to me and to God.

△△△

I went to the mental hospital today. As I suspected, the tour was sanitized, but I made good contacts and learned a lot. I'll share this experience in greater detail in my next chapter.

I started the day early. Said picked me up and we went downtown to the TWA office to pickup my airline tickets. I was in the office for an hour but emerged triumphant. Said, on the other hand, was in the throes of a desperate depression.

He had parked the cab for ten minutes to run an errand. When he returned, he found a 50 LE ticket. It represented the loss of a major part of his income for the day and week. He has five children in private school or college and is constantly trying to earn enough to cover their expenses, an impossibility. He was nearly in tears. His depression was miraculously cured when I told him that since he was waiting for me, I would give him the *faloose* (money) to pay the ticket.

He took me to the hospital, waited until I was finished and then onto Dr. M.'s clinic, where he left me and returned to Cairo. Dr. M. and I visited.

He checked my left eye to see why I was experiencing irritation, gave me some drops and then drove me back to El Maadi where we had a pleasant lunch and our normal in-depth conversation about the Egyptian culture and the world. It's great having my own private physician! Thankfully he's cooled his jets. Now he's talking about what will happen if we marry . . . in ten years.

As we walked down Road 9 toward my apartment, we noticed two scruffy looking boys of ten or eleven. One was "asleep" on the sidewalk, the other "asleep" on the adjacent corner. We put some change under the arm of one and crossed the street to stop at the bakery to buy bread and some locally made coconut cake to have with coffee.

Dr. M. asked the baker about the children. "They are not homeless," he told us. "They sniff things. They are addicts. They beg for money for their addiction." I had heard of this before. As we approached the second child, Dr. M. became suspicious and tried to awaken him. He didn't move. "I think maybe we made a mistake leaving money," he mused. "I think someone gives these children drugs and then leaves them to sleep on the street so they will make sympathy money." We decided to leave what we had left for the first child. We talked about calling the police and asking them to take the children to a foster care facility, but being Egyptian, Dr. M. said he would be viewed with suspicion, and asked many questions. Our inquiry would do more harm than good.

I've thought about this situation. So often in life we try to do the right thing, but oftentimes we don't know what it is. We make judgments based upon the illusion of what we think we see. As a foreigner, I would have gotten more action from the police than Dr. M. without the complications he would have experienced. Given what I know about the culture, nothing is a secret, so I'm certain the police already know what is going on and they do nothing until someone makes waves, but the waves are short-lived, only designed to make it appear as if they care. But this is also a judgment. I have no way of knowing if they care, or what they have done in the past. Is it better to leave money in case the children will use it to buy food? Is it better not to leave money so as not to feed their habit and those who would use them? I find myself without the wisdom to know.

In the U.S., I never give money to those who beg on the street. If someone is hungry, I offer to buy him or her a meal. I was constantly amazed by how many "homeless" people refused a free meal. If the children had been awake, would they too have refused food? I don't know. Please embrace them in your prayers.

A one-eyed man
among blind men is the
one with his eye wide open.

~Egyptian Proverb

*Jail is jail even in
a beautiful garden*

~Egyptian Proverb

Chapter 22

July 2001

The public mental hospital I visited is one of two in Cairo and one of five in Egypt operating under the auspices of the Secretary of Mental Health. There are also private facilities and several other institutions operated by a different branch of the government. The public hospitals house about 10,000 patients; there's a waiting list of equal size.

The one I visited is outside Cairo, about thirty minutes from El Maadi. Originally it was the palace of an Egyptian princess. A century ago she donated it to the people of Egypt. Because the original residence was tinted the color of daffodils in full bloom, it's still called the Yellow Palace.

The grounds of the estate continue to reflect its royal heritage. One can almost see carriage lights bouncing along the Tara-like drive guarded by trees ringed in history, or the laughter of small slippers dancing through flowerbeds nurtured by an army of servants.

The stately drive drifts innocently to a brick building that house the administration of the campus and its residents. Layered like the hooves of a horse, both fresh and restored palace outbuildings speckle the grounds. Two new buildings are home to "private patients," those whose families can afford to pay for their care. The original buildings, the size of small manor houses, serve as quarters for public and special needs patients.

The ambiance of the new buildings is blandly functional, while the original ones, hugged by lazy verandas, beckon for a heart-shaped reed fan, the womb of a rattan chair, and a glass of iced tea on a hot summer's day. I was told that the care each patient receives is identical no matter where they live. I was shown only two buildings; a newer one for men and an older one for men. The women's buildings are located at the bottom corners of a triangle whose highest peak is the administration building.

The men live in dormitories arranged with six to eight beds per room. Everything was fresh and tidy. Contrary to our agreement, I did not see the inside of the women's buildings.

I was told that two of the original structures are secure quarters for patients committed by Egyptian courts and those who have just been admitted for evaluation. My guides hinted that other buildings in the horseshoe accommodate patients who are a danger to themselves or others. I don't know if they treat children. I suspect not.

There's a separate facility for chemical addiction. I was advised that because Islam forbids alcoholic consumption, there is no need for an alcoholic treatment program. Like homosexuality, because it's against the faith, it doesn't exist. I didn't tell my tour guide that Alcoholics Anonymous thrives in El Maadi or of the two Muslim men who helped whisk me through customs in exchange for my semi-annual liquor allotment at Cairo airport's duty free shop. He did say that the primary addiction is heroin, ingested in pill form. When I asked where it comes from, he replied, "I can't talk politics." Later I learned that the killing meadows of poppies are hidden in untamed valleys beyond the mountains abutting Egypt's eastern border with the Red Sea. The only way to reach the crops of the farmers of addiction is by horseback, donkey, or small airplane.

In addition to producing bales of heroin, modern-day farmers cook up cauldrons of ecstasy. Because its use can cause permanent brain damage and psychosis even in the novice user, as in the West, a whole generation of young people is in peril of spending the rest of their natural lives in hearty bodies attached to the brains of a zombie. This import, along with fast food and soft drinks is but another noxious gift from the West.

The ratio of physicians, psychologists, nurses, and social workers to patients is quite impressive. Dr. Tarek, the teakwood-colored psychiatrist who became one of my guides, is the Director of Mental Health Training. Although his position and that of his colleagues places them near the top strata of society, he and his colleagues run their own outpatient clinics to subsidize their income. This means they work a full day (Egyptian, of about six hours), take a break for "lunch" and then see private patients until eleven at night.

After Dr. Tarek (I'm using first names as is the Egyptian custom) and I had chatted for about thirty minutes, Dr. Ghada, a stunning woman on the sweet side of thirty, arrived with her contemporary colleague, Dr. Mohammed. Ghada and Mohammed both trained in Germany. They speak fluent German and English. They were my tour guides for the remainder of my visit although Dr. Tarek kept popping up at each location. Their boss was nowhere to be found.

Dr. Tarek gave me the background of Egypt's mental health system. To its benefit, the system is quite new. I say "benefit" because they're in the process of creating, rather than revising.

About six years ago a man escaped from a public mental hospital. He joined with some friends to destroy an oil facility and its employees in Eastern Upper Egypt. The public outcry resulted in the dismantling of the old system and the creation of a new one.

Dr. Tarek told me that the average female patient has been hospitalized for depression. He said that constant changes in society have made it difficult for women to know what role they play. He was referring to the social changes that have occurred over the last fifty years.

As a woman of the 1960s, I can understand their dilemma. I've often felt as if my feet straddle two different generations, each fighting with the other and the massive social changes that we created to open doors for the women who came behind us. Suddenly nurturing went out of vogue; aggression took over.

Dr. Tarek told me that depression is also caused by spousal abuse, which he believes is rampant. As in the West, when the economy is bad, domestic violence increases. It's apparently an epidemic within the middle and lower classes (the vast majority of the population) but it isn't a stranger to the upper class either. There is a great deal of confusion among followers as to exactly what the Koran says about the treatment of women by their husbands, fathers, and brothers. As with the Bible, depending upon the bias of a particular *sheikh*, the Koran is used as a powerful force to either protect women, or to enslave them.

Since men are wholly responsible for protecting women from danger and the physical or social loss of their virtue, there is a great deal of social stigma associated with female mental illness. To relinquish the care of a woman to an institution brings shame on a man. Therefore, when a woman exhibits symptoms of mental illness, it is often hidden and treatment is delayed. I know of one woman who began taking antidepressants as a teenager. She was upset over the loss of a friend and stayed in her room for several days. Thirty years later, she is still coddled and medicated.

According to my guides, the percentages of major illnesses such as schizophrenia, psychosis, and bipolar disorder are about the same as in the West.

As in the U.S., Egypt tried giving mental patients the right to remain free unless they are a danger to themselves or others. Fortunately, unlike the U.S., the government saw the error of its ways and began to provide treatment whether or not the patient wants it. As a result, you don't see as many mentally ill people living on the street as you do in the U.S.

The goal here is not to keep someone institutionalized, but to treat them, stabilize them, and send them home. Yet Egypt too is faced with the revolving door of mental illness. It is caused in part by a lack of public education and the economic-based requirement that until they fail, patients are given older, less-expensive drugs with atrocious side effects that encourage patients not to take their medication.

They're working on developing halfway houses and mental health visiting programs that focus upon supporting and educating the patients' families about mental illness and the necessity for a patient maintaining their medication. They're also looking for funds to provide newer drugs.

Doctors Ghada and Mohammed told me that their own transition back into the Egyptian culture after medical school was difficult. Dr. Ghada is married to an Egyptian anesthesiologist and has an eighteen-month-old son. Dr. Mohammed is still single, but wants to find a wife who believes in Islam and is as Westernized as he.

I had the chance to interact with two male patients. The second was a young man of about twenty with bad teeth and a bleeding lip he had inadvertently bitten.

When I waved to him, he shyly approached. He looked down at me; tears filled his eyes. "No one visits me," he said. I touched him gently on the arm and said, *"Ana asfa"* (I'm sorry). I wanted to put my arms around him, but I did-not know his medical condition so I refrained. Some touch-ing can be too stimulating or offensive to those suffering from diseases such as schizophrenia. I learned that he's one of the revolving-door patients. He is stabilized, goes home, stops his meds, and comes back. The toll this takes on his family must be heartbreaking as well.

The other patient was as tall and willowy as an obses-sively fertilized sapling. Though controlled, his unlocked pupils broadcast his mania. When he learned that the important visitor to his ward is American, he became agi-tated. In broken English, he begged me to wait until he had retrieved something from his room.

When he returned, like a triumphant child awaiting praise for his work, he waved first one, then another cray-on drawing beneath my nose. They were well executed; so was the subject matter.

I wore my polite, condescending smile, but when I actu-ally looked at his renditions of the world he saw, the papers in my hand began to seethe with the heat of his rage. My expression exploded into one of horror.

The drawings showed an airplane dropping a bomb on a landscape as serene as fields of bluegrass in Kentucky. The missile that propelled downward bore its ownership: U.S.A.

"Why is your government killing good people in the Middle East?" he demanded. "Why are they attacking Libya and Iraq? Why is the United States so powerful? Why do they think they can do anything they want? Why don't the American people do something?" he pleaded. There were no sweet words resonating from my heart. How could I explain or justify that which I oppose?

I left wondering if this young man isn't saner than we are. He was asking questions that we as a people have not, but could ask about the role our government is playing in co-creating the escalating problems in the Middle East and around the world. I've begun to wonder if our democracy is in fact the democracy created by our forefathers. So much goes on behind the scenes that we are not privy to. We become so enmeshed in our daily lives that we fail to take the time to question the PR, the press reports, the sound bites, to dig deeper beneath the illusion and then to tell our elected officials what we want and expect them to do. I fear that we've given up our power as a people. We've bought into the fantasy that the wishes, the kindness of the American people are being extended to those in need around the world. I was too ashamed to tell him this, too proud, too loyal to my heritage, too ashamed of my innocent faith in my government. Until I came here and began to see some of the problems we have created through the eyes of the people of another culture, I too believed the fantasy. But each day, each experience frays more of the blinders that covered my sight. I truly believed that my government mirrored back to the world the love and kindness of her people.

In one second, the last vestige of my innocence was swept away. The young man reflected back to me my stupidity, my arrogance, my self-centeredness, my responsibility, and my naiveté. It really hurt to lose my "patriotic virginity."

A small piece of bread given with love is enough to feed hundreds.

~ Egyptian Proverb

Chapter 23

August 2001

The date palm trees are ready to release the burden of carrying the oozing, dark sweet fruit that hangs on branches beneath their spiked umbrella of leaves. Harvest time is approaching. The dates droop as if encased in orange mesh bags aching to be free from the effort of holding on.

When the time is right, those who own the trees, or have staked claim to them, will shimmy up their trunks like monkeys escaping punishment for throwing one too many coconuts at a sibling.

With the slash of a saber, limbs laden with hundreds of mature dates will be lowered to the ground where they will be loaded into reed baskets, then placed upon the backs of donkeys who will take them to market.

Egyptian mangos and pomegranates are in season. I bought a pomegranate in honor of my son, Bill, who always enjoyed the tangy seeds in fruit salads or by themselves. When you bite into one, it explodes like a rainbow after a sun shower. The local mangos are delicious in any size or variety.

I wash all my produce and eggs in a vinegar/water bath. Since the oranges are dusty, before I make juice, I also wash them with soap and water.

I bought fresh beets. I ate the cooked greens with Egyptian salad dressing. It's delicious and very simple to make. You crush several cloves of garlic in a mortar with salt then add a shallow layer of white vinegar. No oil. That's it. Most Egyptian salads of grilled eggplant, tomatoes, and cucumbers are served with this dressing.

I made yogurt beet soup with the beets. It's very tasty, but I ended up with so much, I would have been smarter to also slice some of the beets for salad. Live and learn. Farmers substitute reeds for rubber bands to keep herbs, beets, carrots, leeks, and green onions together.

I keep forgetting to tell you that I purchased custom-made leather riding boots. They come just below my knees. I have a pair of ankle-length paddock boots, but they don't offer enough protection from the twists and turns of the stirrup holders that leave the inside of my calves black and blue. I've always wanted a long leather pair, but couldn't justify the U.S. cost.

There's a cobbler in the village of Giza who makes them. He came to the stable and diagrammed my foot. He also measured the length and width of my ankle and calf. I did not want the kind that necessitates someone else helping me to take them off, so I had these made with a zipper. The cobbler cleverly placed it in the back of the boot, beginning at the heel. For 150 LE, I can ride in style and comfort. At first the left boot didn't fit as well as the right, but to my surprise it adjusted to my foot and now fits perfectly. They're as soft as whipped cream and as comfortable as slippers.

Yesterday, as I was dismounting Ramses in front of the stable, an Englishman rode by on a camel. *"I say, bang on!"* My gear impressed him.

Yesterday began as what many Egyptians and expats refer to as an "Egyptian morning." This means that it was challenging. Said was supposed to pick me up at 8:00 a.m. to take me to the Meridien Hotel in Giza to meet my friend Rick who was in town from Alexandria to celebrate his birthday, which is the day after mine. He had invited me to come for breakfast and spend the day relaxing by the pool of his hotel.

At 8:15, I called Said's house to ask if he was on his way. His son replied, "He's going to El Maadi," so I thought he would show up soon. When he hadn't arrived by 8:30, I decided that I would look for another cab. I had no way of knowing whether or not he had car trouble or was just running late. As it turns out, I don't think he ever left his house or intended to pick me up.

I interviewed a couple of passing cabbies to see if we could communicate, and finally chose one who I thought knew where I wanted to go. I was pretty clear that I wanted to go to the Meridien Hotel in Giza near Al Ahram, the Pyramids. There was a young man sitting in the front seat. As it turns out he was a passenger, not a friend, so first we went to new El Maadi to drop him. This cost another ten minutes. The cabbie took a route that confused and troubled me. I was right. He ended up taking me to the wrong Meridien. I was furious.

An hour after I left home, we finally arrived. Toward the end of the trip, in an effort to diffuse my displeasure, the cabbie kept hitting his head with the palm of his hand while declaring, "I'm a very bad man!"

Rick and I had a great breakfast, and then headed to the pool where my ashen legs received the benefit of Egyptian sunshine and lots of exercise swimming in the beautiful pool laid out like a cloverleaf with little bridges and a waterfall to swim under. On his way to the train, we shared a cab that dropped me off at the stable.

Our arrival caused more than cursory interest on the part of the stable crew. "Ah. She's with another man!" So far they've met Dr.M., Mo, and Rick.

To my surprise and anguish, Hussein told me that Said had stormed into the stable the previous evening. He was not singing my praises. In fact, he was most unkind. He had showed up at my apartment Friday afternoon. I was cleaning. I thought he was in the neighborhood and had stopped by to pick up the sunglasses he had left at Dr. M.'s. To my surprise, Hussein told me this was not the case. He had come to pick me up to go riding. I had made no such arrangement with him.

As a result of this misunderstanding, word was quickly spreading throughout the village of Giza that I was unkind and not fair. He protested that he had come to get me on many occasions and I had not paid him when I changed my mind. Ugh! It's amazing how quickly I went from being his Nefertiti, the epitome of womanhood, to the daughter of a shoe (a nasty insult).

I was hurt and angry but got over it quickly when I remembered who I want to be. I learned that he was so afraid of not doing the right thing and losing my business, on several occasions he had waited outside my apartment for hours in fear that he had not understood the correct time to come and get me. Instead of asking Hussein or Dr. M. to intercede, his rage turned into a pressure cooker of anger that exploded like a geyser. No matter how generous I was, it could not make up for the shame he felt in not being able to communicate with me. There were many occasions when he was very late or didn't show up, but I always wrote them off as a miscommunication problem and didn't get upset. Unlike him, they didn't cost me anything other than wasted time. He lost income he thought was his.

Apparently, Friday was the day he exploded. He had no intention of showing up Saturday morning. This is too bad for he would have earned a generous round-trip fare to and from Giza, plus another taking Rick to the Ramses train station for his journey back to Alexandria. So, once again I had the opportunity to see the illusion in what I think is going on versus what is really happening.

What ensued is really a gift in disguise. As a special thank you, when I leave Cairo, I had planned to buy Said two new tires for his cab. That's 300 LE I don't have to spend now. I had begun to feel really guilty about his losing the income he obtained from me and was trying to think of ways I could get him other business, but he needs clients who speak better Arabic than I do and will overlook the sad condition of his taxi which is always clean on the inside, but in terrible mechanical shape. So I've been relieved of the responsibility I thought was mine, but was not.

Many of you have probably received the e-mail that's been circulating about the reasons someone comes into our life. It says that every person we meet is brought to us for a "reason, a season, or for a lifetime." I guess my relationship with Said was for a season. I release and bless him with love. I am fond of him and grateful for all he taught me.

△ △ △

Auntie's husband died on my birthday. As is the Muslim custom, after his washed body was taken to their mosque for prayers over it, he was immediately buried in the family mausoleum. Everyone must be buried within a day, two maximum.

The next day I went up to Auntie's apartment to sit with her and to express my condolences. There are three days when this is done. The first day is only for family and close friends. The second and third days are for the preceding group plus others. I'm an "other" so I waited until the second day.

I called Mo and asked what the protocol is. He told me not to bring flowers but to dress up in black if possible. I put on my best black outfit and climbed the stairs to Auntie's fifth-floor apartment. Furniture was arranged around the perimeter of the room. This is very Egyptian. They don't position groupings that spill into the center of the room. Everything embraces the wall. Extra chairs had been rented and inserted between ample examples of "fancy" furniture whose arms were painted bright gold. As I looked around, I could see which pieces would soon be rotated into the furnished apartments in the building.

The front door was wide open. The air conditioning was off and it was stifling inside. What I assume was religious music blared in the background. Egyptian women encased in black robes or clothing and headscarves filled the room where Auntie sat to receive her guests. She was happy to see me. We hugged and kissed. The only words I thought appropriate to say were, "*Ana asfa*" (I'm sorry). A waiter served tea, coffee, and water.

I didn't know how long I was supposed to stay nor what to do when Auntie's eldest granddaughter, Hani, whispered that soon the women would begin to pray. It may have been considered an insult if I had tried to join them.

A short time after I arrived, the women created a line of chairs in the center of the room. Some sat. Others stood in front of the chairs to pray. I was feeling really self-conscious and terrified of making a cultural *faux pas* so I moved to an adjoining room and sat quietly with my hands clasped together and my eyes lowered. I left as soon as I could, like when they finished and before they started all over again.

I've begun to see death and birthdays as a marker not of my age (that would be far too depressing), but of where I've been and where I still wish to go. The good news about my age is, as I told my wonderful D.C. friend Edie, that I'm still here and have the opportunity to grow; the bad news is that I'm still here and I still have to grow!

One of many issues I continue to unravel is my terror of not remaining true to who and what I am. This comes up a lot in my relationships with Egyptians. Everyone wants to help me become more like him or her.

Madame B., my Egyptian mom who had me over for a native lunch, wants me to go to the mosque and become a good Muslim woman. I asked Dr. M. why she would suggest this. "She loves you very much, Jeanne, therefore she wants you to be just like her." "Mohamed, has it ever occurred to her that I don't want to be like her; that I'm happy being who I am?" I inquired. "It is a compliment," he explained. "In Egypt when someone loves another, they want them to become just like them instead of staying who they are. They think this will bring them even closer together." Madame B. wants me to marry an Egyptian, preferably Dr. M., for as with all my Egyptian friends, they don't want me to leave. In the mistaken belief that if my family lives here, I won't leave, Auntie suggested that my children move to Egypt!

Dr. M. laughed very hard when I told him that I thought it would be difficult for an Egyptian man to be married to me.

For example, what would he do the first time he told me that he "forbid" me to do something and I responded by telling him, "I don't think so." Anyway, after a few of these experiences he'd probably wring his hands and call a family conference to help him convince, to no avail, his uncivilized Western bride that her ways are not in harmony with a happy marriage. Of course I could always call my family and friends from the U.S. and ask them to represent me in the family tribunal, to point out that his ways aren't conducive to a happy marriage either, but they'd probably have to move here since the tribunal would meet regularly.

Mo told me that Egyptian men want Western wives. We are considered exotic, highly sexed, and sadly, superior to Egyptian women. They also think that Western women aren't as committed to marriage as their women. If things don't work out, they can divorce us, see that our visas are revoked, and get us kicked out of the country empty handed.

△△△

Several times a day I eagerly sign on to check my e-mail. Thankfully, the new and approved Hotmail has made it possible for junk mail to go immediately to the junk mail box. Unfortunately, I have to check it to make sure something good hasn't gone there by accident. Hotmail allows only 250 blocks. I used them up a long time ago. I wish they'd raise the limit to ten million or so. I can't imagine what people are thinking when they send the stuff they do. How many "Hot Oriental women/Young cheerleaders" do they think I could possibly be interested in seeing up close and personal? One is well beyond my limit and I don't know who Britney Spears is, but she must be sizzling to have so many vying to see naked pictures of her.

There was a story in the *Washington Post* about a recent trial of Egyptian men who were having a gay party on a floating nightclub on the Nile. As you may remember, homosexuality is against Islam so it doesn't exist . . . except this time when a whole crowd got "caught" and are being tried on trumped-up charges as an example to others. Even though homosexuality is not illegal under Egyptian law, apparently the Egyptian government is monitoring gay websites and arranging to meet homosexuals (supposedly the government was involved in the floating nightclub sting) and then putting the fear of public shame into anyone who leans this way by printing their names in the newspaper and trying to put them in prison.

My evil twin wishes the snoops would put their noses into the business of those who send me this e-mail garbage unsolicited. I wonder how many "hot chicks waiting to please" they've met? Heavens! The purveyors of porn could fill every prison here to overflowing with a significant wait list. As much as I deplore cutting back on free speech, the pendulum is swinging so far off center I think they've taken advantage of the Constitution to such an extent that they're stepping on my right to live in a conservative country without being judged by a standard different than the one I've chosen to live by. Egyptians get the same smut from the West, and then assume I'm one of the "hot chicks willing to please." Everything is supposed to eventually balance. I'm waiting with great hope for the return of the pendulum as I ponder one more ethical/moral dilemma.

△ △ △

I'm low on cash. I saw the Egyptian version of an armored truck picking up huge bags of money at the bank I frequent. The doors were wide open as they struggled to carry it from the bank to the truck. Since it has so little value, more of it is used, but apparently not by the people who fill the money machines that have not been working for nearly a week. Maybe they're just sending it out to be washed, spat upon, and ironed.

The young men dressed in white uniforms with black belts and boots who hopefully carry empty rifles and dot every street corner in Cairo (tourist police), like other police forces, work shifts. Huge sky-blue government trucks with convex roofs roll slowly by. The freshly pressed late shift jumps out; the bedraggled, sweat-soaked early shift jumps on. It must take half a shift to switch them all.

Have I explained about horns? They're the most important working part of any vehicle. When a car is coming around a corner its horn is honked to alert other drivers of its presence. If you're walking down the street, taxis honk at you in case you want a ride. I suppose it hasn't occurred to them that if you did want one, you wouldn't be walking up the street in the opposite direction, but standing on the side of the road looking to hail one. Perhaps its just misplaced optimism that they'll be the one to change your mind about walking rather than riding.

Downtown Cairo at any hour of the day or night sounds like New York City. Horns are used to get the driver in front of you to go faster. It doesn't matter if the traffic is bumper to bumper (which it usually is). Patience in this circumstance is not a virtue they practice; yet Egyptians will wait in line much longer than a Westerner would for any other service unless they can use their elbows to get ahead of you. Traffic, due to the heat, is particularly heavy at night, especially Thursday night, the beginning of our weekend. A trip along the Corniche takes twice as long as it does during the day.

Speaking of street corners, prostitution is a healthy industry. Asian, African, women from the former Soviet Union, and yes, Egyptian Muslim women ply their trade from hotels and the street. Since their services are too expensive for the average Egyptian, most of their customers are foreigners (Western and those from other Arab countries).

I smelled gas in my kitchen so I summoned my dear bawaab. Using pantomime, I explained the situation. "Ah!" he exclaimed as he followed me into the kitchen then gestured for a box of matches. First he sniffed the stove, then the surrounding feeder pipes. He struck a match, put his nose even closer to the stove and passed the match slowly over the surface. I stood safely away in the doorway, expecting him to become the cartoon version of a wick for a bomb. My words of caution were met with a wave reserved for shooing away a mosquito.

He found nothing, but the smell continued. A few days later I located its source. It was not gas but the huge jar of preserved garlic he had peeled for me that's sitting on the kitchen counter. I went and got him and showed him what I had discovered. We laughed until tears spilled onto our cheeks, not an unusual occurrence here if one keeps their eyes open to the dance of life being played out on every street corner.

There are animals that roam freely here. A few blocks away, horses owned by the police graze in the early evening in an area with some resemblance to a park, but not much. They have bridles on attached to ropes that brush the ground, but the ropes are not fastened to anything. Perhaps the horses think they're tethered, for I've never seen one cross the street. There's a mare with a baby who's growing by leaps and bounds.

I have five grandchildren. They all have four legs. My son Bill and his wife Adrienne have cats. They started out with

Charcoal, and have adopted others since moving to Phoenix. Dan has a Border collie, Savannah. They're all incredibly bright, beautiful, and funny. I'll show you pictures sometime! Just kidding.

As in other poor countries, house pets are not common in Egypt, but stray cats and dogs are. If you can't feed your family, how can you feed an animal that doesn't share your work burden? Still, many Egyptians put out whatever food scraps they can. Cats and dogs eat chicken bones without ill effects. On the other hand, some people put out poison.

Poison creates a major problem for someone who has a dog as a house pet. It's best to rent a ground floor flat or villa where they can do their business in the safety of their own garden. It's too risky to walk them. There's the poison, but also the wild dogs that run in packs that may become too friendly and scare a domesticated pet. What amazes me is that the wild dogs walk around with a smile on their faces. They truly make the best of their lot in life.

With each fertility season some Egyptians separate the kittens from their mother so they'll die. Well-meaning expats save them, then when they're old enough to survive on their own, release them without having them fixed. Other expats take them in; domesticate them, but when they go home, they may leave them behind. This is particularly true if there is an evacuation. No pets can go with you. In addition, apparently the airlines are making it difficult to transport pets. I don't know if this is due to the long trip, the heat, or what.

You may recall that my friend suckered me into taking home a motherless cranky kitten. I called her Sphinx. I de-flead her, treated her bladder blockage, and nursed her, even took to heating a stone in the oven so she would stay warm. She still cried all the time. I think it was from loneliness. I passed her on to someone with other kittens so she wouldn't be so sad. I'm glad I did for I could have never released her to the "wild" and I didn't want to become attached to her.

Whenever there's a new delivery, my bawaab shows up at my door with a precious kitten for me to hold and coo over before returning it to its mother. At first I thought he was trying to give me one. When I realized he was just bringing them by for a quick visit, I was more receptive.

Speaking of my bawaab, last night he rang my bell. "*Enti kwayyisa?*" he asked (loosely translated, this meant Are you okay). Apparently he was concerned because I didn't go out yesterday. I was working, and the day ended before I knew it so I decided to run my errands this morning instead.

I've made friends with three dogs that run together in my neighborhood. They're a mix with some Border collie, so they seemed to gravitate towards me. They must be related to Savannah.

One is fawn colored. I saw him last night. He's so sweet. One day I noticed that he was itching terribly. Since I happened to have some Skin-So-Soft with me, I lathered him with it to treat his fleas. He hasn't forgotten. This morning he came right up to me and did the "Oh, I'm so happy to see you" butt moving sideways, crying/happy voice, big-smile thing.

Last week while I was waiting in vain for Said to show, he hurt his paw. I tried to remove whatever was lodged there, but didn't want to push the issue since these are wild dogs, and rabies is prevalent. I've been told not to touch these animals, but how can I not? All they want is a little TLC.

The second member of the pack is black with white markings like Savannah, though he doesn't have ears like hers, which, when caught by the wind, threatens to send her airborne like Mary Poppins.

Sometimes he follows me down Road 9. He likes to come up behind me and grab my calf or ankle gently with his mouth. He thinks this is funny. So do the natives. Savannah liked to do the same thing when she was a puppy, but she used her baby-sharp teeth instead of her mouth.

The third dog is mostly black with a little white on his paws. I don't know him well. I enjoy watching them play. They take turns gently putting their heads into each other's mouths. I don't feed them for they shouldn't become dependent upon one food source.

A ten-foot brick wall encased in cement surrounds my backyard. It's topped by pieces of glass that stand ready to damage the hand of anyone foolish enough to try and climb over it. Above the wall and glass is a three-foot-tall metal fence. I do put scraps out in the garden for the cats that use the wall as a runway. They meander over the glass on their way to wherever. The cats are a bit touchier than the dogs. One minute they're asking to be scratched, but if you don't find the perfect spot immediately, they turn around and hiss at you. If they don't want anything, they ignore you. This reminds me "Dogs come when they're called; Cats take a message and get back to you."

I have unwelcome pets who have moved in with me. Ants! We've gone from the teeny sugar ants, to red ones the size of a Corvette. Nope. I'm wrong. As I write this, a medium-sized black ant is crawling across the screen of my laptop. Great. Now they're having a convention.

Last week I found a strange-looking lizard in my living room. It didn't have a long tail and its body was fat instead of slender. I resisted the urge to scream for my bawaab to come and catch it. I chased it with a hand towel, caught it without having to touch it, and released it in my garden. I'm sure we're both happier. I'm afraid I wouldn't have been as brave if it had been a snake. As a matter of fact, I'd have moved immediately in the belief that when there's one, others couldn't be far behind. Ugh! I'd rather come face-to-face with a great white shark in a swimming pool! I'm probably the only mother on earth who waited for her children outside the reptile house at the zoo.

I'd like to share a story. It's about a cat, but specifically about loss and how, if it hasn't been thoroughly grieved, it will eventually resurface when we're faced with another one.

I've been reading a wonderful book for healers, *Hands on Healing*, by Jack Angelo. There are many exercises in it that a designed to help the healer deal with his or her own issues so they won't pass them on to someone else, the old "physician heal thyself" concept.

In my hospice bereavement work, I learned a lot about the theory of loss and its stages from my wonderful teacher, Ginger Blessing, who in every way lives up to her name.

There was a young man in one of our first groups. He

had lost his oldest and best friend. Their friendship went back to childhood. After his beloved friend died, he found that he was afraid to allow anyone else to become close to him. The terror of losing again was too much, but he did not see that he was keeping those who wanted to love him at a distance. I didn't know why, but I felt "called" by a higher source to tell the group the story of the loss of my beloved cat, Shmowie. Later, the young man took me aside and thanked me for sharing my story with the group. He saw how, out of fear of loss, he had been shutting out the opportunity to love again.

The happiest memories of my childhood are of the summers we spent as a family in Connecticut. My father was the director of a boys' camp before buying his own camp in Vermont. My mom was from the area, so we enjoyed many wonderful days with uncles, cousins, and assorted relatives. We spent time at the ocean, explored fields and streams, caught our first non-family adult skinny-dipping, chased horses, milked cows, swam in a pool that was more green with algae than water, and watched television for the first time on a screen the size of a Palm Pilot. We devoured grinders laced with crispy cabbage instead of lettuce and filled our stomachs to bursting with New England seafood, potatoes, and corn steamed in a pit carved in the ground. Our family lived in a cabin apart from everyone else at the camp. It was on top of a hill.

One day my father greeted me with a black-and-gray-striped kitten. For many years she was the world to me; she was my comfort, my confidante, my friend, my playmate. In one small ball of fur, she provided the protection and love I longed for. Most of all, she was mine.

I dressed her in doll clothes, put her in my doll carriage and wheeled her up and down the street. She would lie perfectly still on her back while sucking a doll's bottle filled with milk that she held between her paws. She could jump through hoops and came when she was called. She never had a litter box or an accident. I watched her give birth and care for her babies.

One June on our way to Connecticut for the summer, we pulled into a rest area. I let her out of the car to do her business. She didn't come back. We searched for hours to no avail. Finally we had to leave.

So here I am reading the chapter on loss and I begin to cry my eyes out and I remember the man in the group and how he had closed his heart to those who wanted to be his friend and remembered how after I lost Shmowie, I never ever risked losing my heart to another pet. Over the years I've had dogs, but never another cat. I finished the exercise, sent Shmowie a beautiful pink balloon filled with love and gratitude, and thanked God for yet another insight.

We did a similar exercise on the last night of our bereavement group. Everyone wrote letters to their loved ones. This gave them the opportunity to express their love and to say what had been left unsaid. We went outside. Each member took turns burning their letter; symbolic of sending them directly to the one they lost, and released their balloon.

Bereavement work taught me that when we suffer a loss, in our pain we forget that if we hadn't loved and been loved, we would have no reason to grieve.

The grieving of a loss is a process that offers us the opportunity to face unresolved issues and to heal our pain. It's also an opportunity to express gratitude for what we had and to finish whatever work was not completed. Thank you, Shmowie. You really were my wonder cat.

Chapter 24

August 2001

Rentals. While I'm paying 1,500 LE per month for my furnished flat, Egyptians living in my building are renting theirs unfurnished for 25 LE! Obviously landlords prefer renting their units to Westerners. They make a thousand percent more and can recycle their horrendous used furniture. There's another reason though. It's called rent control for Egyptians! They really need foreign tenants to pay their overhead.

An Egyptian has the right to stay in their flat/villa for life with no increase in rent. If they leave foot-first or by choice, a family member can move in at the same cost. The hitch, in some circumstances, is that the tenants can also kind of "buy" the flat up front for say 20,000 LE (currently about 5,000). Each month's rent is deducted from the "purchase" price until eventually they begin to pay a monthly fee. Needless to say, this kind of deposit is not within the means of the average tenant. I think the "deposit" is a fairly new thing. It's my understanding that when Nasser came to power, rents were fixed without a deposit being required.

Moopiga told Mo that the woman who lives above me receives 8,000 LE per month in child support and alimony. She works full time and pays 25 LE in rent. By Egyptian standards, she's very wealthy. 8,000 LE plus a salary goes a really long way, especially when your housing is so inexpensive.

Expats here under a USAID (and foreign corporations) contract have their rent and sometimes their utilities paid for them as part of their incentive package. As a result, they live in much nicer flats than I. Making this clear, that I'm not a USAID employee, to my next landlord will be interesting since Mo found and negotiated this lease for me. My friend Rick is in the U.S. now. When he returns to Alexandria he'll begin to look for a place for me to move into the end of September/beginning of October. If he finds something great, he'll also negotiate on my behalf. It's far better to have a man do this. I don't plan to be in Alex that long, probably three months then on to the Red Sea area, Luxor, or back to Cairo for the winter. I definitely don't want to be in Upper Egypt in the summer since it's even hotter there than here. I have no idea where I'll go from there.

My bawaab told me today through another Egyptian acquaintance/interpreter that he wants to move to the U.S. and work for me. He doesn't understand that I am no longer a homeowner or that I really don't get a charge out of things like toilets being fixed with plastic bags and used ribbon. Anyway, he was teasing me. So, I asked if that meant he was going to ask me to marry him, if I would become his second wife. Now mind you, Mohamed is older than God. His face lit up with a huge grin as he shook his head and replied. "No. Just work for you." I told him I was insulted. He laughed. I can just see us getting off the plane together; he'd be dressed in a galabaya with a rag on his head, and elbow everyone out of the way to protect me. It would be really fun to watch him try to put my suitcases on his back rather than pulling them. It would almost be worth the extra fare just to have someone follow us with a minicam to record the reaction to my bodyguard at Price Club, Eastern Market, and Value City! How would I explain to the police that he wants to sleep on the front stoop when I stay with friends, that he really isn't homeless, just doing his job as my protector?

He showed me pictures of his three sons. He failed to mention that he also has five daughters! When he reached into the neck of his galabaya, to retrieve the photographs, first he had to remove a kitchen paring knife. I don't think we'd make it through airport security, heaven only knows what else he has stored in there.

Anyway, my bawaab's youngest son is working in Saudi

Arabia. Because he's so far away, this makes him sad.

I will miss Mohamed's toothless grin, but not his snooping. I caught him peering through the living room window from my garden. His face was pasted against the glass. He reminded me of my dog Molly. When I took her to the vet, she hid her face under my arm. She thought no one could see the rest of her! I don't know why he thought I couldn't see him or what he hoped to discover. I was alone.

Now that he's finally gotten used to my Western ways and no longer *always* assumes I'm having an orgy when a man is in my apartment visiting without a chaperone, he has stopped scowling when they leave. On Thursday I had three in a row: Dr. M., the delivery boy who insisted on not allowing me to carry packages even when they weren't from his store (it was this way all along Road 9; my produce guy, Ramadan tried to forcibly take them from me), and last but not least, my friend Ali who runs a wonderful Egyptian gift shop.

My Egyptian male friends say that if I were married to an Egyptian my stream of visitors would not be allowed. Nor would it be acceptable to kiss and hug a man who is not my son or brother . . . even then they tell me they get jealous if their wife shows affection toward any other man. I asked if this meant they don't trust their wives. They kind of sidestepped the question. What they don't understand is that if a woman of any culture loves her husband and feels loved and appreciated, she won't stray unless she has emotional problems.

I've seen the beginning of several Egyptian marriages; weddings. The brides are dressed in traditional, low-cut Western gowns. In fact, one can often see cleavage. They must use the same makeup artist as a certain veteran newswoman. Hers appears to have been applied with a palette knife.

The car the new couple rides in is decorated with real bouquets of flowers. They're attached to the hood of the car and the trunk with tape. Rather than the traditional white flowers we're used to, they use mixed bouquets.

Depending upon the financial means of the family, the reception includes a band or D.J. and a belly dancer . . . no booze. I suppose an Egyptian wedding is something I'll eventually experience. I'd definitely go if they include whirling dervishes, members of the Sufi sect of Islam. They are mystical. Before dancing, they go into a meditative state. As a result, apparently they can twirl for hours. I'd also love to attend a Sufi "meeting" to watch what goes on.

I've begun to pack. Mo and I took a load over to Tim and Molly's last night and we checked Camilla's house too. All is well in both places. I'll move completely out of my apartment by the end of the month and stay with Tim and Molly until I leave for my first visit to the U.S. since moving to Egypt. They have an incredible closet in one of their guest rooms that's large enough to store everything until I head off to Alex.

Things are progressing. I've been cleaning, packing, and showing the apartment to perspective tenants. The process renews my gratitude to my former tenants for all the inconvenience they put up with when my building was for sale.

I have a bunch of bananas growing in my backyard! I check them every day to see if they're ripe and to make sure my bawaab hasn't beaten me to the harvest. I didn't know that they grow on palm-type trees. They're at the top of a tree that's only about ten feet tall. They hang from a stem nearly as thick as my wrist. At the bottom is a mammoth inverted scarlet flower that's gradually opening. Egyptian bananas are about half the size of the Dole variety, but they're sweeter and ripe when you buy them so they need to be eaten quickly.

There are two kinds of dates grown here (maybe more, but I only know of two so far). One is red, the others orange/yellow. I think it's the red ones that become black as they ripen. I can't say I care for either, but at least I tasted them when they were offered to me. Figs have come and gone. I liked them, in small amounts.

Avocados are also in season. They're different from the ones we see in the U.S.: they're bigger; their skin is dimpled; their shape is abstract rather than like a pear; and they don't ripen the same way. If you don't buy them when they're ripe, they often stay hard as rocks and turn black inside. I made a batch of guacamole. It would have come out better if I'd remembered that the hot sauce container doesn't have a sprinkler on it. "Olé" takes on new meaning.

Mo took me to buy a mobile phone. Apparently many come by way of Kuwait and are not quite legit, thus no manufacturer warranty. We went to three shops in downtown Cairo before finding one that was a fair price and had a store warranty.

Getting a mobile is interesting. Auntie's granddaughter, works for Click, one of two mobile companies. She's in charge of buying the line. She needed a copy of my passport. You can either pay by the month, or buy a phone card. Since I don't have a forwarding address yet, I opted for the card. It's actually a tiny computer chip that goes inside the guts of the phone. It's only good for 45 minutes of outgoing calls, 4 months of incoming. Each card costs 110 LE (about $25.00 or $.55 per minute). The good news is you can call any mobile without having to enter a zillion numbers first. It comes with voicemail, but it's cheaper to use your regular phone and a mobile calling card to access messages. Phone service, housing, cars, and cleaning products are about the most expensive things here.

For nearly six months, Cairo has been a wonderful home. To leave behind all the people (and animals) who greet me on the street each day and my wonderful Egyptian and expat friends feels pretty daunting. I've become a part of many different families. In Egypt, if an Egyptian decides that they like you, they adopt you. There isn't enough money on earth to buy their love and there isn't anything they wouldn't do to help you. Each time I pass my bawaab, he shakes his head sadly and says, "Madame *kwayyisa awi*." (very nice). He's asked me to send him a letter from the U.S.

The expat community is the same. We never know how long we'll be here so friendships begin and deepen more quickly than they normally would. Need to borrow something? No problem. Need a stamp? You've got it. Need advice on how to handle situations, where to buy something? It's there in a flash.

Dear Camilla is back! She called right away! I can't wait to see her. Molly and Tim are due back very soon. It will be wonderful having the midlife chicks together again.

Soon I'll be closing this chapter on Cairo and opening another in Alexandria.

Many people have told me that they admire my courage for coming here. I see my adventure in a different light.

I've been blessed with an opportunity that has more facets than a human-size, cut-glass vase, an opportunity most will never have. I'm glad I seized the moment and found the faith (some would say mental instability) to just do it.

At times it's been far harder than I ever thought possible, but not only have I survived, I've blossomed. Each part of me sparkles and catches the light in ways I think would have been impossible if I hadn't embraced the possibilities. People tell me I glow.

I'm moving on to Alexandria with the same quivering stomach I arrived in Egypt with. Yet I now know more of the language, I understand the culture and rules, I have an incredible support system in place, and most of all I know if I can do it once, I can do it again. I have no doubt, when I move on from Alexandria to wherever I'm supposed to go next, I'll leave enriched with the same gifts of friendship and wisdom I found in Cairo.

My incredible niece and goddaughter, Christine, recently asked if there are products I really miss. Hellmann's mayo still tops the list.

I sure was guided when I packed my four suitcases for there's little I brought that I haven't used. There's also little in the material sense that I've needed that I can't find here or, with a little imagination, create an alternative for.

I've come to enjoy living simply, without attachment to things or to the outcome of events and situations. If I lost everything I came with (my computer and e-mail would be pushing it) and all my stuff that's in storage in the U.S., it wouldn't matter. It can be replaced. What can't be replaced are my perfect health, my family, and friends at home and here.

I've learned to be flexible and more patient. I've begun to see that when things are blocked, it's usually for a good reason. More and more I just say, "Okay God. You've got all the pieces to the picture. You handle it, please." He's never failed me.

Yesterday while I was waiting for Ramses to be tacked, Hussein's brother asked if I was married. I bring this up because my reply surprised me. Despite what the fortune teller told me, I've been wondering if perhaps I'm afraid of commitment or if its more about knowing that there's far more I need to experience on my own, to learn about life and about myself before settling down.

Spirituality teaches that we attract what we are; this is a great reason to keep growing. I don't want to repeat the relationship mistakes I've made in the past! No one can do my growing for me. So, my reply surprised and pleased me. I spoke rather flippantly, but from truth.

"Nope," I replied nonchalantly.

"Why not?" he asked.

"I think it's been easier for me not having a husband," I said. "I have the freedom I need to do my work." I didn't go into detail.

"But are you looking?" he insisted.

I laughed and said, "Always! If the right man is supposed to come into my life, he will."

"Ah," he said. I could almost hear his silent thought, "This is one strange woman." I think he was also putting in a plug for Hussein.

I'm healthy. I'm at peace. Life is fantastic!

If you're without loved ones, only dogs and cats will visit you.

~ Egyptian Proverb

If a flower dies it will keep its good smell.

~ Egyptian Proverb

Chapter 25

August 2001

This summer, about once a week Tim and I went by Camilla and Yosef's garden to ensure their Egyptian care-taker was tending it. Actually, it's Yosef's garden.

Our arrival usually coincided with the cave-like illumi-nation of a house shuttered from breath-stealing heat. It's the same time of day when those on foot quicken their steps to arrive at their destination before they become road kill.

Through fingers of light, I could still discern the subtle changes waiting to be unveiled: the grape arbor that cre-ates an intimate oasis from the sun, the blossoms of fruit trees that change overnight into miracles of sustenance, and bulbs switched on to illuminate filigreed lampshades handpainted with fields of buds that can only hint at their full potential.

In observing his garden and the meticulous care he had taken in planning and creating it, I felt that I already knew Yosef. It reflects his soul.

When we finally met, it was as if I had known him all my life. We curled up in the womb of their villa and talked about many things, feasted on gourmet hamburgers, and delicious drinks permeated with fresh limejuice while being serenaded by ecstatic frogs mating in the baby pond hid-den behind their villa. I couldn't have felt more at home than if I had been in my own living room. As with Molly and Tim, it's a joy to inhale the love that radiates between Camilla and Yosef, to be integrated into their lives like a beloved sister, a natural part of the family.

When I returned to my own flat, I felt the peace I've created here and will soon leave, but I also realized I'd let a few things slide that I shouldn't have.

In hiring my bawaab to water my garden this summer, I've missed seeing the surprises it holds. I saw them in Yosef's garden, but not in my own.

Since becoming an avid gardener, I've discovered that whether it is deep in slumber, just awakening, or showered and dressed to greet the day, a garden is an analogy of life, a mirror of Thoth/Hermes' universal law that says everything has an opposite polarity; where there is constant sunshine (as in Egypt) there will be a lack of water; where there is death there is life; where there is color there is an absence of or many hues of the same color.

When I'm digging in the soil, cutting back old growth, cleaning up the small debris that floats from tiny hands and the wind, I have the opportunity to connect to the truths of life, to see the whole garden, not just what has faded, but that which is in the process of being created.

This summer, due to heat that threatens to buckle my knees, I've watched my garden from a window. I became separated from it, an observer rather than a co-creator. I no longer appreciated its potential, but focused upon the burden. I didn't get close enough to see what was hidden above and beneath it.

Auntie has been trying to rent my apartment. Last night, the early evening air began to stir with the temptation of a breeze. I decided to work outside for a little while to spruce things up to the standards a potential Western tenant would expect.

I broke off the dead tops of the annuals and cut back the spent leaves on the perennials. I pulled weeds, gathered together an assortment of unsolicited gifts from the wind and placed them in rubbish bags.

Although they were still green and hard, I decided to harvest the bottom layer of bananas I hoped with some ingenuity would be within my reach.

I positioned a wicker garden chair beneath the palm, climbed up onto its arms and stretched like one of Snow White's dwarfs standing at a carryout window until the tips of my fingers connected with hard flesh. With a twist of my

184

wrist, I was able to free a tiny bundle from the master stem.

Glistening with exertion and victory, as I climbed down from my dangerous ladder and looked around at what I had accomplished, I was pleased to discover how quickly my efforts had returned the garden to one that looked cared for. I was also delighted to observe that despite the desert heat, new growth was sprouting like notes from a piano as it's being dusted.

As the sun began to set and visions of a cool drink and shower tempted me to return inside, the lacy foliage of a small tree directly opposite my office window beckoned. I moved beneath the canopy, remembering how as a child the leaves of summer had transported me into a world hidden from a reality I longed to escape. This tree was too delicate to climb; there was no limb to sit upon while resting against and inhaling the energy and strength of its bark. Still, we were joined together. Her branches, like the arms of a small child weighed down by handfuls of candy spearmint leaves, bumped against my head. To my surprise, I felt something dislodge and rudely bounce off my crown before landing at my feet.

Concealed discretely in the colors of the forest, globes of limes, half the size of a newborn kitten's head, revealed their hiding place. But amongst the bounty were tiny thorns. To get to the fruit, I had to risk being pricked. It was worth it.

I reached up, grabbed a branch and began to fill my grimy upturned t-shirt with my harvest. Instantly the air and my fingers took on their tart fragrance.

I cradled my booty and carried it inside. After each perfect ball had been washed, I sliced a few to embellish a glass of homemade lemonade. They were perfectly ripe, bursting with sharpness. Perhaps if I'd discovered the secret of the tree earlier, I'd have been impatient and picked them before they had reached their full potential, but they wouldn't have yielded as much juice, and I would not have appreciated and enjoyed them the way I did last night.

I guess, like a garden, the trick in life is to not allow the darkness nor the sunshine to obstruct our vision, to do the work we need to do to create what we desire and to be patient and confident that if we nourish our dreams, the time will come to harvest them when nature decides the time is ripe. Thank you, Yosef. Your garden is a wonderful reminder!

*If you plant well you
will get a good harvest.*

~ Egyptian Proverb

Chapter 26

August 2001

Everyone I know here and back in the U.S. seems to be clinging to the same vessel that materializes and vigorously bounces us through the currents of life.

One of the major accomplishments I've achieved since settling in Egypt has been to slow down, to not always let the storms around me create leaks in my boat. This week I allowed myself to become swamped, but thankfully I've been bailing fast and my boat has stabilized.

As the time comes closer to coming back to the U.S. to visit, I feel myself becoming repressurized, as if my mind is preparing me for reverse cultural shock by handing me lots of little challenges from both sides of the Atlantic.

They say when you get pulled into a riptide you need to let it take you where it wants to go, then when the opportunity presents itself, to swim parallel to the shore rather than fighting against it. I think letting go and letting God handle the details is the same concept.

After cleaning my apartment with a toothbrush, washing all the bed linen and getting one more layer of grime off the surface of the bathtub, I went to see Auntie to let her know I was ready for her to perform a landlord-tenant walk-through before she returned the majority of my security deposit. I had just paid the gas and electric invoices, but since phone bills are only delivered every six months, I knew part of my deposit would need to remain with her until a final audit was completed. I was exhausted.

When I went upstairs to her flat, although she was expecting me, she was on the telephone. Since she wasn't happy with the photograph I had already given her (which she asked for), I brought her a new one and a box of beautiful chocolates as a farewell gift. As it turns out, rather than requesting the photo to remember me by, she probably wanted it for her "Expats Moopiga and I've Taken to the Cleaners" album.

Two of her teenage granddaughters were sitting with her, listening to their grandmother's animated conversation. As it turns out, they were there to translate if Auntie needed their help. New marble floors were being installed in the apartments of several family members. I thought perhaps Auntie was upset with the performance of the workmen and was reaming them out.

Our bawaab padded silently into the living room. He began to gravely walk around in circles, occasionally offering a tidbit of advice that Auntie repeated to whomever she was talking to. I was beginning to feel insulted by her behavior.

Via taxi, I'd just returned from taking the last of my belongings to Tim and Molly's. I wanted to say goodbye with love and go on my way. I still had to go to the market to buy staples and ingredients for some meals I planned to make for them when they arrived home from Maine. Their refrigerator was empty.

To my horror, Auntie abruptly handed the phone to me. She'd kept me waiting for close to an hour. She'd been talking to Mo! I was beyond furious. I was apoplectic! Her intent flew over me like a bird about to squirt the contents of its intestines directly onto my face.

Mo was beside himself. Since I use the Internet, Auntie and Moopiga were *concerned* that my phone bill and unbilled utilities would exceed my 1,500 LE deposit. They planned to keep it all. They hadn't bothered to go to the phone exchange to obtain a bill. I certainly had no intention of sticking them, but as a good faith gesture, I wanted at least part of my deposit refunded. On the off chance that I would owe more, Mo had told Auntie he would be responsible.

It wasn't the money that concerned me; it's my aversion to being used as a sucker. I'd already learned from other expats that Egyptian landlords rarely return what is due

188

the tenant. They use security deposits to earn an extra month's rent, or, as in Auntie's case, pay for new marble floors. I'd already been cautioned not to take it personally if my deposit wasn't returned, but I did. So did Mo.

Since he'd found me the apartment and was friends with Auntie and Moopiga, Mo felt responsible for my loss. I'd told him from the beginning I didn't trust Moopiga, but he always replied, "He's very kind." Worst of all was the knowledge that my relationship with them had been an illusion. They didn't care about me, only what they could take from me.

I asked Auntie to accompany me to my apartment. She refused. I insisted until she acquiesced. As we were doing the walk-through I realized that she'd already gone through it while I was taking the last load to Molly and Tim's. The place hadn't been that clean since it was built. She didn't care how honorable I had been and she didn't acknowledge my Herculean efforts.

It's a good thing my Arabic is meager for I was so angry I would have shared a little story about Moopiga with his mother.

While work was being completed on his apartment, Moopiga tried to make a major pass. Unbeknownst to me, his wife and children were staying with her mother until the work was finished. When I went upstairs to bring something to his wife, he invited me in. Ugh! He called her from their bedroom phone so I could talk to her. I felt really uncomfortable about being alone with him in their bedroom so I stood in the doorway, but he kept patting the bed and motioning for me to come sit beside him. Yeah! Right! I made the conversation as short as possible and beat a hasty retreat. Within this society, his actions were an insult to his wife, his religion, and me.

My inability to communicate this information was a blessing. What good would it have served? I was right about Moopiga all along. I was wrong about Auntie. I know everything we do to another, whether it is kind or not, comes back to us. The not-so-nice part of me takes great comfort in the fact they will get back what they've dished out.

I have been going through all my stuff, reorganizing,

consolidating boxes, and trying to figure out how little I can bring back to the U.S. with me so I'll have room for the stuff I need to buy and lug back without spending more than I saved by paying exorbitant excessive baggage charges.

Tim and Molly live in a high-rise. The view from their balcony is primarily one of an amazing assortment of satellite dishes and a few penthouse apartments with rooftop gardens. Their apartment is lovely. I feel as if I've moved from the Comfort Inn to the Four Seasons!

When I lived off Road 9, there were several mosques, but none in direct line with my building. This was good because they're all equipped with loudspeakers that blast not only five times a day for call to prayer, but during the Friday Sabbath service as well. Molly and Tim aren't as fortunate. Their apartment is in direct line with a mosque whose speakers are facing them.

Friday afternoon I was nearly blown off the balcony by the decibel level of the message being broadcast throughout the neighborhood. Though I didn't understand 98 percent of what was being said, I picked up enough to know that the speaker was outraged about the conflict between Israel and Palestine and the role the U.S. is playing in it. In case some sheikh works everybody up during Friday service, the U.S. Embassy has told us that we shouldn't be out and about between 11:00 a.m. and 3:00 p.m. on Fridays.

I never feel in danger, nor has anyone ever expressed a negative opinion about my specific nationality (except the mental patient), but even he did not attack me personally. Egyptians are kind, Westerners are important to the economy and everyone knows me so they're protective of me.

I had a lovely dinner with Camilla and Yosef at their home Friday night. Instead of coming directly back to Molly's, I had the cab take me back to Road 9 to buy fresh baked bread. Molly loves Egyptian bread. I wanted to surprise her. But on the way back to their apartment, I was overcome with grief when the lights of my taxi illuminated the broken body of a dog on the side of the road. It was what remained of the little dog who had enjoyed following me up and down Road 9 while playfully nipping at my heels. My exhaustion from the week's events and my encounter with Auntie, mingled with the shock that his sweetness had been extinguished as quickly as a candle at bedtime, exposed my fragility. The dam of my self-control exploded in waves of tears and sobs of rage. To the dismay of the taxi driver who became unglued by my hysteria, I cried for the rest of my journey and long after I'd climbed into bed begging for sleep to bring me back to the light of morning refreshed and able to go forward with all that awaited me.

Apparently the outdoor bakery on Road 9 has become the circus tent for a hotbed of live animal antics. One day I saw two young water buffalo trying to reach the street from an area behind it. Joan told me that the following morning, a horse wandered off from its owner and tried to help itself to bread cooling outdoors on huge metal racks.

I need to find the manual for my mobile. When I carry it the buttons get pushed and I end up making calls. This means going through boxes again as well as doing several more suitcase "sorts" before I'm ready to leave for the air-port tomorrow night. I can use your prayers. I've scheduled far too much in a short period of time. My travel agent got a migraine just reading my itinerary. Since this is my first trip back, I guess I'll learn a lot from it . . . about what to try and do and what not to try and do.

This will probably be the last chapter I'll write until I return from the U.S. on September 17.

The fig tree is not full of raisins.

~ Egyptian Proverb

The good Muslim will not hurt others by his hand or tongue.

~ Prophet Mohammed

Chapter 27

September 2001

I think this is the hardest chapter I've written. I have so much to say, yet each time I sit down to write, to express all that I've felt and experienced since leaving Egypt to visit the U.S., the words flow backwards like the Nile. I see this as a reflection of the turmoil, the range of emotions that clog my mind. After 9/11, our world will never be the same.

I had hoped to be sitting on Tim and Molly's balcony while I wrote this, but due to the horrific events of September 11, subsequent airline cancellations, and a major injury to my knee, I'm writing from the patio of my son and daughter-in-law's home in Phoenix. I hurt myself during a yoga class while in L.A. with my son Dan. I overextended my knee. It locked, went out, and tore a bunch of ligaments.

I expected that I would share with you the joy I rediscovered on my journey from Cairo to D.C., of how my family and friends drove hours to spend precious time with me, of the kindness of my children on the West Coast and Denny and Cini McGrann and Paul and Fran Byers who took me into their homes and spoiled me with their love and endless generosity on the East Coast.

I wanted you to know that just hours before the flight bound for L.A. was hijacked and used as a bomb against the Pentagon, God brought me, via the same route, safely to L.A. to visit with my youngest son, Dan.

The turmoil created by my love for both Egypt and the U.S. has caused a war within myself. I have grieved for the victims of terror, their families, their friends, our nation and the world. I've grieved just as deeply for the terrible backlash that has spilled over onto those who, by virtue of their religion and cultural heritage, have become silent victims of hatred by otherwise decent Americans. That they may die a senseless death at the hands of an American is too terrible to contemplate.

I've vacillated between my deep faith and inner knowing that everything happens for a higher purpose and the bubbling rage and fear that, for a time, have threatened to drown me.

I've received the gift of extra time to connect with my incredible children who have cared for my heart and my body for far longer than they had planned.

Over and over I've waited for the American public to ask, "Why are we so hated?" and for those of the Islamic faith who live the goodness of the Prophet Mohammed to rise up against the fundamentalists who mock it.

As an American, I want George W. Bush to know that I do not believe a violent response is the answer. If it hasn't worked in Israel or Ireland, why would it work now? I want to ask world leaders to get down on their knees and pray to the God they say they serve, to ask for the wisdom to find a way to provide the highest good to all the people of the world without concern for religious, cultural, economic, or racial differences. I would ask that they set aside their egos, for it is their egos that are the most dangerous of all terrorists.

Two days after 9/11, I flew from L.A. to Phoenix. Due to the injury to my knee, I was given special treatment by the airlines, but not by all the airline employees. This surprised me, for during a time of crisis people tend to be kinder.

When I arrived at the terminal on crutches, idle baggage handlers turned their backs upon me. Dan had gotten me as far as the roadblocks leading to the terminal, but the guard refused to let him through. The reason? "She does not have a permanent handicap!" So, being a very clever man, Dan hailed a cab. There was no way I could be dropped off at the satellite area and manage to get on a bus with my luggage. Somehow the government's logic is that terrorists don't take or drive cabs! The driver was able to take me directly to the terminal, but since he couldn't leave his cab, he had to drop my baggage and me at the curb where I was left to fend for myself. He was Middle Eastern.

There I stood. I couldn't pull my stuff and walk on crutches. I was helpless. I waited patiently for a stranger to show kindness. I asked my angels for help.

Eventually a baggage handler approached and carried my bags to the ticket counter. The woman who waited on me assigned me a seat in the middle of the plane and told me to take my carryon luggage to another area where I was to wait for a wheelchair. Once again I waited and prayed quietly for kindness to rear its head. It finally did.

When I reached the boarding gate (via wheelchair), I saw a family of Indian Sikhs huddled together. They were under the armed protection of airport security guards. The women were crying. A teenage boy and his sister tried to act like nonchalant adolescents. Only later did I learn that an American man tried to even the 9/11 score by murdering a Sikh from Phoenix. I think the family was on their way to Phoenix to attend his funeral.

I didn't know if they were Americans. I don't care. They're human beings. If we are the "land of the free" why did they need to be protected from an American? Palestinians who danced in the street outraged us. Why aren't we as outraged by the fact that innocent people are in danger even though they did nothing to bring it upon themselves? The fact that Sikhs aren't Muslim makes the murder even more surreal.

I've been waited on hand and foot by Dan, now by Bill and Adrienne. I have a knee brace that goes from my ankle nearly to my hip. I "walk" with spiffy aluminum crutches. I'm in limbo about my travel plans. Obviously the universe wants me to stay put. I'm safe. I'm being taken care of with love and compassion. My leg hurts like hell sometimes, but not as much as my heart.

Recently a friend told me that she'd read about someone's near-death experience. The person looked down from heaven and asked what the beautiful golden rays of light were that flowed upward from earth. "Oh, they're prayers," an angel replied. I send you and the world beams of them.

When you come back
from traveling bring
even a stone as a gift.

~ Egyptian Proverb

Chapter 28

September 2001

My return to Egypt has been a whirlwind of activity, albeit at a slower pace since I'm definitely still in healing mode and more immobile than mobile. The good news is that my fancy aluminum crutches have been put into storage, but I'm still wearing a brace to support the torn ligaments at the top and inside of my knee. Thankfully, although an MRI and x-rays showed a fractured kneecap and nasty damage to the ligaments on the top and inside of my left knee, physical therapy, not surgery, was indicated.

There's a lot to be said for traveling as a temporarily handicapped person. Airline personnel treated me royally. They whisked me through security checkpoints (though I did have to take my knee brace off at one point so security could check to make sure I didn't have an Uzi hidden in it). With the exception of one suitcase that cried uncle and began to spew its contents all over Cairo baggage claim, everything went beautifully. Since TWA immediately stopped flying here after 9/11, I was transferred to British Air. This meant I could fly directly from L.A. to London, rather than having to go through N.Y.C. On both flights (from L.A. to London and London to Cairo), I was able to obtain three seats across. This made it easy to keep my knee elevated and to rest most of the way. The flight crew even provided me with ice packs.

Dear Mo was waiting at the airport, and when we reached Molly and Tim's, their bawaabs brought my luggage upstairs. Since it was nearly 1:00 a.m. by the time I reached El Maadi, Molly and Tim were fast asleep, but a beautiful sign, "Welcome Home Cutie," graced their front door.

My young friends, Mohamed and Amyl, who wait on me at the local market, were very worried about me. They knew I was due home on the seventeenth, so when I didn't come by, they were terrified that I had been hurt or killed in the terrorist attacks. They greeted me with hugs and kisses, but with shock when I exited the cab on crutches. They thought I had suffered a "war" injury. A week later, only Camilla's intervention in Arabic helped to dispel their fears and the rumors that must have flown from one end of Cairo to the next.

While I was gone, my friend Rick bought a used car. He's waiting for his Egyptian driver's license to clear. Hopefully he will move me this week. He has a lead on an apartment. I'm looking forward to settling in Alex and beginning my next adventure.

Before I left Cairo for the U.S., I was asked to apply for a position as an independent editor for a company working under a USAID environmental contract. While I was gone, I was approved. The first document I'm to work on was delivered to Tim and Molly's Thursday morning. Although I was told that it needed "limited editing," I quickly discovered that this was a bit optimistic. It's interesting trying to rewrite a report that uses the same adjectives ten times in a short paragraph. The pay, in dollars, is good. I can work from home and transmit data via e-mail. I'm also grateful that engineers find it difficult to write in their native tongue.

Rick wasn't available to move me last week so I jumped upon the opportunity to join Tim and Molly for the weekend in the Sinai resort of Sharm el Sheikh. We left El Maadi Thursday afternoon and caravanned with friends for the six-hour drive. With the exception of sideswiping a donkey (thankfully only stunning it) that had wandered onto the highway, it was a lovely trip by moonlight.

As we approached the Suez Canal, a full moon the color of an egg yolk began to climb the distant mountains. As it scrambled higher, it softened until it glowed like sweet butter, then just as suddenly transformed itself into a round crystal to light our way.

We spent the last three days snorkeling on reefs that begin just a few feet from shore. Since I'm still recovering, I opted not to go out on a dive boat. It's been six years since I became a certified diver. I didn't feel physically or mentally up to the challenge.

The snorkeling in shallow areas was worth the trip. I wore my knee brace and had no problems. Many of the fish are similar to those I've seen in the Caribbean and Grand Cayman, but there were some that made me gasp. My favorite is the Picasso triggerfish. Most of its body is yellow, but its diamond-shaped head is encased with a periwinkle necklace. Its eyes are framed by sunset orange. As a matter of fact, most of the fish appeared to have been decorated in every spectrum of color imaginable and in startling combinations. Only nature could conspire to create combinations man hasn't even considered. Perhaps decorators should take up diving to expand their repertoire.

Tiny black-and-white fish darted about like chocolate bonbons in search of a mouth. Schools of fish in every hue and size reminded me of freshly bathed and groomed commuters of different races and cultures on their way to work. But unlike their human counterparts, they seemed to be in perfect harmony with each other.

The mood in Egypt is one of anxiety. Egyptians and expats join together in trepidation as we wait for the U.S. to drop a "shoe" on Afghanistan. On the positive side, I'm thankful that the plight of the Afghan people under the Taliban has finally reached the ears of the average American.

As I traveled around the U.S. and back to Cairo, I had the opportunity to speak candidly with people from around the world. The consensus of citizens from Korea to Europe seems to be that the arrogance of the U.S. government has brought terrorism to our doorstep. The people I spoke with were not without sadness for what happened, only aware of the possible cause for the attack. I don't believe that those who danced in the streets upon hearing of the horror were celebrating the violence and loss of life. Rather I think they were celebrating the fact that America is no longer immune to the same suffering others have experienced, in some cases, for half a century. The more I see the differences between cultures, the more I see and appreciate our similarities. I continue to pray that all people will begin to know that we are truly one, no matter how much water separates us.

Security is tight everywhere, but in particular along the Sinai. We went through numerous checkpoints. The landscape of Sharm is totally different from Cairo and Alexandria. Mountains and desert surround the Red Sea. I'm looking forward to seeing it in the daylight. Apparently the greatest danger we face on our return trip will be from the wild camels that sometimes cross the road like deer. There are even "camel crossing" signs to alert drivers to the potential danger, something you don't see in the more populated areas of Egypt like Alexandria. I moved there yesterday.

I took the train up Saturday morning. Rick and his lovely British friend Suzanne met me at the station. While they went off to do their thing, I spent the afternoon looking at apartments with Ahmed, an Egyptian Realtor Rick found for me. Ahmed was available to help me on short notice, not surprising given how few foreigners are moving here now. His fee is 10 percent of the total lease amount. Since I'm only looking to rent for two and one-half months, I'm not exactly a moneymaking machine. By the way, his version of our multiple-listing service (MLS) consists of a notebook and an incredible memory.

Sunday morning Rick and I drove round-trip from Alexandria to Cairo to gather my belongings from Tim and Molly's. Dear Molly had purchased a beautiful Egyptian meal to take back with us. Since events unfolded a bit differently than we had envisioned, it was wonderful to have a dinner we could pop in the microwave that night.

Rick has a roof rack on his four-wheel-drive vehicle. We were able to take everything in one load. I'm amazed by how much I've accumulated. Molly and Tim's bawaabs made quick work of hauling things downstairs.

Alexandria is an ancient city that kisses the southern end of the Mediterranean Sea. Originally known as the village of Rhakotis, it was used by Phoenician mariners as a trading center. In 332 B.C., Alexander the Great came here and began to create the city that still bears his name.

Before the Christian Romans burned it, Alex's library was renowned as the world center of mysticism and philosophy. A new library is nearly finished, but alas the majority of ancient manuscripts and sacred text it once contained may have been lost for eternity.

The landscape, even the feel of the city, is very different from Cairo. In addition to being hilly, it's cooler, greener, and damper. The main boulevards overflow with shops and offices. The narrow side streets are strewn with trash and packed with high-rise apartments.

I'm told that a French firm has been hired to come to Alex to clean it up and to educate her citizens about proper trash disposal. People do recycle here, but it's limited to reusing garbage bags. They empty the contents on street corners (not unlike D.C. where residents think alleys are dumping grounds), take the bag home and refill it.

Sitting high up in the front passenger seat of Rick's car, I was amazed to discover that Alexandrians take ten times as many "insane pedestrian pills" as the citizens of Cairo. They're totally fearless. Perhaps because the streets in Cairo are wider than they are in Alex, it makes them seem more dangerous. I marveled at Rick's ability to dodge scores of pedestrians while avoiding vehicles driven by kamikaze pilots maneuvering what they seem to think are bumper cars. If I ever buy a car, I want someone to glue mattresses to its perimeter so pedestrians can bounce off.

Since the streets and sidewalks are hopelessly broken, it's an adventure going anywhere on foot. The concept of pedestrian right-of-way doesn't exist. Want to cross the street? Suffer the consequences. Because my knee is still a bit unstable, it makes things even more interesting, and, since I can't "show" the brace on my leg, drivers can't see that I'll be a bit slower crossing the street than the average person. Today, I talked a tourist police officer into acting as my crossing guard.

Apartment hunting is an adventure. In my price range, a water view is available, but you can only see it by risking life and limb to hang half your body off the side of a small balcony. Actually, I think when you tell an agent what you're willing to spend, every vacant, mediocre flat suddenly falls into the budget you set. Rents certainly have nothing to do with a property's rental value.

Ahmed showed me four apartments. One was a possibility, but it had three bedrooms and felt like a cave. It did have a wedge of a view of the ocean from the living room and easy access to the tram system.

Today, at Mo's suggestion, I looked in an area a bit further away from downtown Alex but still only a 10 LE taxi ride away. It's called Maamora. It's a resort area in summer but a quiet seaside community in fall, winter, and spring. This afternoon I found a sort-of-charming two-bedroom apartment. I say "sort of" because the furniture, furnishings, and basic maintenance are as unattractive as what I left in Cairo; but once again I'm blessed with a private garden and two patios. It's overpriced to the point of thievery. It's a short walk to the ocean without having to cross any major streets. I'm thinking about buying a bike once my knee is stronger.

I plan to move in on Wednesday. I hope this relocation will be less colorful than unloading Rick's car Sunday night. When we arrived from Cairo, we discovered that the elevator in his building wasn't working. In retaliation for tenants not paying their electric bills, the electric company turned off the electricity to the elevator. It was a sad sight to watch two bawaabs carry my things up *nine* flights of stairs in the dark! Seeing me climb the same stairs wasn't a pretty sight either. Apparently the bills have been settled because the electricity came back on this afternoon.

Last night I was feeling really sad about leaving my wonderful friends in Cairo and starting from scratch in Alex. I'm blessed to have Rick here, but the roadblocks that began to pop up while I was in the U.S. and continued after I arrived back in Cairo were beginning to get to me.

Last night I had a talk with God. I said something along the lines of, "Okay. You asked me to do this. I'm doing it, but I could sure use some help. Please find me an apartment. Please also give me a sign even I can recognize that confirms I'm on the right track!"

This afternoon when Ahmed was showing me the apartment I just leased in Maamora, he called to me from the master bedroom. "Jeanne, there's something you must see!" he exclaimed. Normally when a man uses that line, I head for the front door. However, since we were with the owner of the unit, I followed his voice. As I entered the master bedroom and looked towards the left, I stared straight into the sweet, loving eyes of a figure mounted on the wall. It was a poster. The subject was the Virgin Mary.

Ahmed and the owner of the apartment (a retired pharmacist married to a charming Greek/Egyptian woman) were a bit unsettled when I burst into tears. They didn't understand why I was so "upset." By the way, the apartment has never been rented before. Ahmed just "happened" to call the doctor to ask if he'd rent it to me for a few months for a sum two to three times its value. It's their summer home. I'm their first tenant. I hope your signs and blessing are as numerous as mine.

If it was good
the bird would have kept it.

~ Egyptian Proverb

Good morning neighbor.
Mind your business
and I'll mind mine.

~ Egyptian Proverb

Chapter 29

October 2001

The past week has overflowed with opportunities to seek out and then pounce upon any ray of optimism to be found between here and the Atlantic Ocean.

The sunbeam infused, celluloid waters of the Mediterranean crinkle and stretch as if seeking a sandbar it can hold onto, if only for a blessed second. The horizon, beckoning of Italy, Greece, and Malta reminds me of a world far larger than the tiny village of Maamora on the furthermost Eastern edge of Alexandria where I have settled. While I am before her, my spirit floats upon her buoyancy.

With the exception of my bedroom, the interior of my new home is as inhospitable as a snake-infested cave on a moonless night. Since I am on the ground floor, the apartments above, trees older than I, and shutters stronger than any wayward sunlight foolish enough to try and penetrate their thick slats, coat everything in shadows. The streets appear as empty as those in Dallas during the Super Bowl when the Cowboys are contenders. Yet eyes stealthily peer through the planks of the privacy shutters protecting my jail. Upside down and sideways, they rotate bravely, their lashes fluttering against decades of grime to fill their lens with the secrets of the strange rituals they assume I perform whenever I am alone.

Since there is a door that can be unshuttered, bathing my bedroom and the Virgin in immaculate light, I've set up my office there, directly beneath her picture. My landlord provided me with a small table; the circumference is so

minute it holds only my laptop and telephone. I've
rearranged everything, even filed the papers I'd tossed, like
unfinished memories, into the corners of suitcases and dis-
integrating Siwa water boxes. Yet I feel no closure, only a
sense of aloneness recently discovered.

At night, "rich" teenagers use the street in front of my
building to drag race. They tune their engines into
testosterone screaming trumpets while echoing the
uncertainty of their manhood with screeching tires and
horns that blast and reverberate. Thankfully they have yet
to discover how obscenely massive speakers can cause a
vehicle to buck like a cowboy on a feral bronco.

When the roads are silent, my new bawaab's one-room
house that's adjacent to my apartment takes on the
ambiance of a live soccer match. When he and the children
of Maamora are asleep, construction on the other side of
my bedroom awakens me to the sound of bulldozers. I
think Maamora is paradise lost.

My landlord tells me that in the summer, small flats
such as mine are rented to families of twenty or more. No
wonder they opt to spend only the spring here, then retreat
to Canada for the rental season.

I've been adopted by what I think is a pregnant cat. If
she isn't, though she's barely passed the time when she
would have been weaned, she needs an aerobics class and
a forklift bra. Because she has seven circles on her tail, and
there are seven major energy centers in the human body,
I've named her Chakra. She's a silver classic tabby with
eyes the size and color of tarnished copper coins rescued
from the bottom of the ocean. At first she came to me only
in the evening while I sat outside observing Maamora from
the shadows of my patio.

Yesterday, I discovered why. While I was at the fish market, I saw her and her friends assisting the man who cleans
fish. They help him by ingesting anything that hits the
floor, thus saving him from cleaning up after a long day
brandishing a sharp knife. By the way, the fish is incredible. You can take it home and cook it or have the fish man
grill it on the spot. I've done both with mouth-watering success.

Chakra moved in bag and baggage last night. She hasn't

206

left my side. I made friends with the local roasted chicken guy. His name is Hassin. He's probably in his thirties, roly-poly around the middle; the dumbest-looking glasses I've ever seen decorate his face. They're blue-black metallic with myopic lenses, straight out of the 1950s.

I told him that I'd like to buy or rent a bike. No problem. His "friend" who rents bikes turned out to be his father. This afternoon I went to negotiate. After they'd adjusted the seat and handlebars on a girl's bike (not as easily available as a boy's bike and I don't believe I've ever seen an Egyptian girl riding any bike) we got down to business. He says he gets 5 LE per day for a bike rental but is willing to rent me one for two months for 200 LE. I don't think so. At that price, I'd rather spend a bit more and buy a used one I can then give to Mo's son or to one of the children in the neighborhood when I leave. Anyway, I thanked him for his time and said I felt that 100 LE is more within my budget.

Hassin asked my nationality. I've decided not to hide and say I'm Canadian. I am what I am. He asked what I thought of the U.S. actions in Afghanistan. I seemed to pass the litmus test when I replied, "I am very sad. Violence does not heal violence."

People I've spoken to in Alexandria about our invasion seem to fall into two categories. The more educated Egyptians think Bin Laden and the Taliban are getting what they deserve, but the average citizen feels that the loss of the lives of U.S. soldiers is a payback for its disregard for human rights violations in Palestine and Afghanistan. Until things are settled equitably between Israel and Palestine, peace in the Middle East cannot be achieved. It really is the cornerstone to everything that is happening in the U.S. and around the world. It's also a major reason that another generation of terrorists is being created. Without a resolution that saves face for everyone involved, Americans will be hated more each day.

I read the *Washington Post* and listen to BBC and VOA on the radio. I try to understand the local news shows. The perverse part of me had a good chuckle over our "humanitarian" drops of dried food, peanut butter, and crackers over Afghanistan. Please! Are they going to cook it over a campfire or does Bush think they all carry microwaves? I

suppose on the upside they'll be bigger targets and health-
ier when they're blown up.

I think we could show our humanitarianism by seeking
solutions that don't require killing innocent people who are
already at their physical, mental, and spiritual limit. I
wonder what would happen if every person on earth
stopped what they were doing for one minute each day and
prayed for Bin Laden and every terrorist around the world?

I've had many discussions with my Egyptian friends
about the responsibility of the leaders of Islam to set the
record straight about what they believe and to stand
together before the world against terrorism. For the record,
most Muslims do not believe in terrorism. However, I see
clearly in the lower class that Bin Laden is making inroads
in his campaign to justify terrorist violence by inciting the
fear that the West's hidden agenda is to eliminate Islam
from the world.

The people of the Middle East have long memories. They
remember that it was our CIA that funded renegade troops
who fought the Soviet Union, we did not lead the moral
charge to stop the atrocities the Taliban has committed
against the Afghan people, women in particular, or that
England has refused to extradite terrorists, or to support,
for the last ten years, Egypt in her desire for a conference
on terrorism.

The good news is the people of the West are beginning to
understand why we are so hated and hopefully come to see
the average Muslim is no different from any other decent
human being.

This has been a hard time for all of us, but perhaps
some good will come of it if we begin to see ourselves not as
Americans or Westerners, but citizens of a large world.
From my perspective, with all the terrible things that are
happening, we cannot do anything else. Everyone on earth
is in the same boat. We're like rats caught in a maze we co-
created. The fact we from the West are living in fear is an
interesting one, for I think this is how most of the world
has lived for generations. They're not necessarily in fear of
only war or terrorism; what they fear most is the lack of a
roof over their heads and not being able to feed their families or themselves.

We can choose to live in fear, or we can choose to put it aside and seek to live in peace by getting to know, understand, accept, love, and take care of each other.

Thankfully, I've had some funny experiences in the last week, too. Before I moved to Maamora, since Rick kindly stored me and my things in his guest room, I felt it was appropriate to cook and do the laundry.

There are local markets close to his apartment. I made the mistake of walking into one that turned out to be a fresh poultry/rabbit stand. By "fresh" I mean that live animals in cages sat on shelves. To my horror, I realized too late when you order a chicken, it's taken from a cage, killed and plucked before your eyes. Yuck! It's still warm when they hand it to you. I swear the one I carried home quivered all the way to Rick's front door!

Rick had an Egyptian moment. He stopped and got gas for his new used car that's adorned with a male hormone enhanced cowcatcher. A few yards down the road it stopped cold.. It turns out the gas guy filled it with diesel instead of regular gas. It had to be towed, the engine and tank drained. Rick has sworn off *Misr* (the Egyptian gas station chain—*Misr* means Egypt in Arabic) and has vowed to only frequent Exxon or Esso, but I think their pumps are in Arabic, too, and of course the attendants are Egyptian.

I'm going to venture into downtown Alexandria this week. There's an English-speaking Women's Association and an American Community Center. The representative from our embassy will be there Sunday to do embassy stuff like ripping off Americans on notary fees. I guess I'll reregister so they can contact me in an emergency, not that I'm optimistic it will do any good. I registered in Cairo but as yet I have not received any of their "alerts" via e-mail. The new ambassador, from what I've heard, seems to be a good guy with diplomatic level-headedness, so perhaps he'll get things organized.

While I'm basking in clear skies, sunshine, and temperatures in the low 80s, my friends in Cairo are encased in a dome of pollution, heavier than normal. The burning of rice fields causes it. The burning of rice fields is illegal, but no one seems to care enough to do anything about it.

I finished the first draft of the USAID report I was editing. I learned a lot about the *normal* sources of pollution in Cairo. In addition to millions of cars and thousands of factories, garbage burning heads the nasty list. It's a problem in Alexandria, too, but thankfully not in Maamora. The burning of the rice fields could very well cause a health crisis in Cairo identical to the one they had in the fall of 1999 when record pollution caused lung and heart problems for an astounding number of Cairo's residents.

As always, help finds its way to my door in the form of an Egyptian or expat angel. I found the local supermarket. I don't know what it's like in season, but off-season it has the potential of serving as the main source for bubonic plague.

When I arrived home with the few items I thought safe to purchase, I tried to explain to my bawaab that I needed another store where I could buy dairy, fruit, vegetables, and fish. He took me down the street to meet another bawaab who speaks some English. No problem. He hailed a cab and instructed his two young daughters to take me to the nice, big supermarket near King Farouk's old palace. On the way home, the girls showed me where the produce and fish stands in Maamora are located. The kindness of the girls and their father, while not unusual, continues to amaze and awe me. I wish that it happened everywhere.

As I watch the Mediterranean turn from lapis to turquoise to churning white and ebony, then to a painter's palette encompassing every color imaginable, I wonder if it is only the cooler weather, gentle storms, and the wind that is affecting it, or is it a byproduct of the unrest, the agitated emotions of fear, dread, uncertainty, and disillusionment we are all projecting in the wake of 9/11?

We seem to have turned inward like turtles buried beneath a fine layer of sand. The problem is that the winds of life and the tide keep uncovering us, forcing us to deal with the realities of not just a new world, but the mundane stresses of life we'd much rather ignore.

My life too has been filled with turbulence, unexpected problems, and many gifts. Most of last week I felt like Rambo engaged in a constant battle to protect myself from being taken advantage of. Within forty-eight hours I ticked off my bawaab, Saza, his young nephew Islam, Dr. M., a taxi driver, the fruit market guy, the bike rental owner, even Chakra.

Chakra is seeing red because I brought a homeless kitten home. Her ears turned sideways like the vibrating wings of an airplane. She hissed in indignation and left in a huff. The kitten is a Bombay. She's black with rusty markings around her ears that will turn ebony as she matures. In Egypt, black cats are considered to be evil spirits, ghosts.

She has eyes the color of sapphires that will turn to copper and a sweet, smart disposition. I've named her Om, which loosely translated is the universal sound of love and peace. I estimate that she's about ten days old.

On my way to the beach I heard her crying. I looked down and there she was, wobbly and bowlegged like an Irish grandmother who, after having a bit too much of the drink, left her walker behind at the local pub and determinedly tried to cross the street.

I looked around for her mother. She was nowhere to be found. I thought about leaving her until I retraced my steps from the beach. I couldn't. The risk of her being hit by a car or bicycle was too great. So I picked her up, turned around, and brought her home.

I emptied a squeeze eye drop bottle, fed her some milk, put her in a box with an old T-shirt to keep her warm, and then went to the beach. I didn't stay long. In less than an hour, the weather turned from sunny 80s to chilly 60s.

Dr. M. is annoyed because I told him that if he wants to come see me he has to keep his hands to himself. "But of course," he replied. Yeah, and I'm an All-Star pitcher.

My bawaab, Saza, is mad because I wouldn't fall for his pity party. He wanted me to advance him a few pounds because "he hurt his foot." He limps well, but selectively. I offered him my crutches. He declined.

Saza, although it's his job, sends Islam to pick up my trash each morning, for a fee. Islam has become a pest. Not content to ring the doorbell, which sounds like the agony of a donkey whose cart has turned over while he's still attached to it, he also bangs upon the door ten times a day until I gave up and let him in. He's an angelic looking, honey-colored child with the heart of Machiavelli. I think he's related to Moopiga. He has a beautiful smile, but it never touches his eyes or heart. I was getting really bad vibes from him. He pretends that he doesn't have a mother so he can con me into becoming the Egyptian version of a fairy godmother. This means that he expects me to fulfill all his dreams in the first week (a new bike, Nike sandals, a Playstation . . .) while casing my place to find out what he can snatch and sell in a hurry. Although only about nine years old, it isn't beneath him to cop a feel. He doesn't go to school.

One has to deal with these situations promptly before everyone in Alexandria labels me as a sucker. I'm a Westerner, therefore I am "rich," therefore I am available to support everyone. The only way out of the situation is to be tough and to have all my Egyptian friends call Saza to set him straight. The phone lines have been scorched. I think we're now in respect mode.

What's really interesting is that you cannot buy love or respect. In the end, it's street smarts, then kindness that opens hearts. Being tough and hard right now to develop a level of understanding and respect is difficult for me. It fights with my desire to be kind and generous. I don't want to close my heart to anyone, but at the moment I feel like a lone bicyclist being chased by hungry lions. I successfully went through this training exercise in El Maadi. It's a pain in the behind to have to do it again for it saps my energy, yet, since I lack a husband to "protect me," it's part of the equation.

I often ask why I'm here, not just in Egypt, but also on earth. Sometimes I think I know, but most of the time the answer is, "It's not for you to know; go with the flow."

One of my dear teachers, Reverend Marcus Capone, once told me that as much as I may want to understand everything now, I can't and won't until I'm in the arms of God. Marcus also advised me to trust where I am, that everything I'm experiencing is for a reason. In every moment of life, we are where we're supposed to be. It is neither good nor bad; it just is. The trick is to stop long enough to see the lesson in each experience.

How someone else chooses to act is up to him or her. The

only control I have is over my own actions. Marcus used to always remind me, "It's the journey that's important, not the destination." So, the challenge has been to not shut down my natural kindness, to not judge Islam or Saza, but to treat them both with love while being true to myself. It might be easier playing quarterback for the Redskins.

The economic situation continues to deteriorate at an alarming rate. Egypt's main source of revenue is the Suez Canal. Since those who issue insurance for maritime cargo have arbitrarily declared Egypt a "war" zone, rates have skyrocketed and fewer ships are venturing this way.

Their second source of revenue, tourism, has virtually come to a halt. Many hotels are empty. The economic fall-out impacts tour guides like Mo, restaurants, even the aggressive, often nasty-acting hawkers and camel owners who try to twist you into a pretzel to sell services and goods no one wants or needs. They will become even more aggressively cunning. This really makes me shudder! With Ramadan coming up from the middle of November till mid-December, food establishments will take an even bigger bite, no pun intended. Because Muslims fast from sunrise to sundown during this holy month, daytime patrons will be nonexistent.

My knee is doing really well. I can almost sit in my favorite cross-legged yoga pose, not quite, but getting there. I've promised myself that when the weather cools a bit I'd go back to Giza and ride Ramses to the outskirts of Sakkara where Zoser's step pyramid is located. I think it may be closer to December before I can do this. I want my leg to be as strong as possible for the ten-mile-or-so ride each way.

Hussein, my riding instructor, will be so happy to see me, actually, not me, but my money. I can hear him now, "You haven't called. Did you bring me any shoes from America?" If you looked up "whine" in the dictionary, you'd see Hussein's picture plastered next to the definition.

The chicken guy is hitting on me. I played dumb when he asked, "What do you do at night?"

I feel as safe, or safer here than anywhere in the world. I think unless we do something really stupid, Egypt will remain safe for expats. The real danger is from extremists who think Egypt isn't religious enough. Egypt thinks it's doing just fine, but by recent Western standards, any Muslim country is too religious.

I've made a wonderful new friend. Her name is Carla. She's a Bolivian diplomat on leave for four years because her partner, a British executive whom she met while they were both stationed in Israel, was transferred to Egypt. Carla is a petite dynamo. Part Inca, she's served in posts around the world. She speaks five languages and is working on learning a sixth.

We're taking an intensive Arabic class at Alexandria University. She's "diplomatic" while I am not, so she's handling a few problems that have cropped up with instructors and the administration. We both want to learn to speak the language, not to read or write it at this time.

The trouble is we've had two instructors and they teach in different styles. We've been asked to choose one. We don't feel we should be put in this position, but we do prefer Zizi rather than the woman who taught us today. Zizi isn't a "linguist" who bores us to tears with her love of the root of languages. We want to learn colloquial (street) Arabic, not classical. They keep trying to teach us how to read, too. Since there's no written street language, we'd have to learn to speak classical Arabic and the shop people we interact with the most won't be able to understand us. Classical Arabic, I'm told, is similar to speaking in Shakespearian English.

Dear Camilla asked a friend who came to Alex to visit relatives to contact me. We hit it off immediately. Mary is probably in her sixties, very kind, wise, and spiritual. She leaves for Cairo this afternoon. I was fortunate to have the opportunity to spend many hours with her over the weekend.

So, the sea of life changes in a moment from happy to sad, to angry, to joyous, then to peace and love. I spend a lot of time praying for world harmony and for the strength and wisdom to hold a space of positive thought that will enable me to see the joy and lesson in each moment, for the moment is all any of us really has.

I too have been like the turtle hiding from the turbulence rather than overcoming it. I ask God's help with everything.

Recently, I've requested assistance in overcoming my penchant for making invalid assumptions.

I find it striking how the obvious is so often clouded by my failure to see what is right in front of my face. Instead of looking for simple answers, I constantly conjure up complicated ones that push the truth further away. I'm reading a wonderful book, *Communion with God*, by Neale Donald Walsch. It deals with this issue.

Buddhists say, "When the student is ready the teacher will appear." Teachers surround me, from the cab drivers that think they can take advantage of me, to the head of the language program who is incapable of speaking the truth about any issue, to Chakra and Om.

Because Chakra makes threatening noises when she eats, now that she's begun to eat solid food, Om has taken to replicating the menacing sounds. Imagine a tiny kitten growling threateningly like a full-grown lion protecting its kill! It's comical and sad; comical because anyone hearing her from another room would be intimidated, sad that she thinks she needs to be so forceful. In her actions, Om has shown me that we make the choice to see and react through the veil of our fearful experiences.

I observed that many men in Alexandria have round "birthmarks" in the center of their forehead. Since intermarriage in families was the norm until the general population experienced firsthand the biological consequences of children born to cousins, I wondered if all these "marked" people were related. I finally asked Mandore, Carla's driver. Duh! The mark is actually a bruise caused by hitting one's head on the ground five times each day while praying. I guess they miss the prayer rug that separates them from the ground or pavement. Since so many men wear the mark, one has to wonder if they're clumsy like a *khroof* (lamb) or if they think it's a symbol of "devotion" they wear to impress the brethren. Obviously one could choose to pray a tad more carefully. I also wonder if any neurologist has thought of studying the long-range implications of constantly jarring one's brain in this way.

Last week Om suffered from projectile diarrhea, thankfully in the kitchen. I was afraid that she'd eaten something off the floor. It turns out that since the propane tank to my hot water heater was empty and I couldn't heat her bottle, the cold milk gave her a bit of a stomachache. This was her only accident. Cats are far easier to potty train than humans. She now uses a litter box. I made one by cutting a water bottle carton in half. I filled it with sand, which there is an abundance of at the construction site next door, but the sand isn't as effective in masking the odor as litter is.

My landlord came by last week to solve the newly escalating Islam/Saza problem. I want them both to leave me alone, Islam in particular. The child's boldness unnerves me. My efforts to ask him not to bother me have failed. I lost it when, after answering his knock, I asked him to go away. As I tried to close the door, he pushed against it. I went nuts.

While he was visiting with me, my landlord was not pleased to see a very pregnant Chakra walking in and out, or my caring for Om. He used the bathroom. Hopefully he was doubly relieved to see that I do not allow the cats to use his flat as a litter box.

Saza is awake at all hours of the night. Several times this week, usually at 3:30 a.m., I could hear him screaming at someone. His hut-like house adjoins my flat. I asked Ahmed, my real estate agent, if perhaps something fishy was going on. He patiently reminded me that Egyptians do not sleep regular hours. One more assumption propelled to the hot place!

Arabic class is difficult. On Monday, Carla and I joined the regular class. They've been studying since September 9. We had eight hours of lessons to play catch-up before joining them. We're now dealing with plurals and masculine/feminine nouns. There's a slight problem. There are rules, but so many exceptions it can make your head spin. I'm so overwhelmed I don't care at this point whether or not I get that part right. My biggest challenge is remembering and using the mountain of vocabulary we get each day. We do not have a workbook. Thus far I've not experienced the total joyful abandon of learning that Om does when she practices her leaps. Each class is but another midlife moment. As they say in Egypt, I'm "a little bit shy" about making an ass out of myself. The good news is that I seem to have a good ear for duplicating the various sounds, even the "a" that requires one to fully open one's mouth like a hungry lion while projecting the sound in a whisper, or the "k" which requires one to imagine that they're trying to remove a mass from the back of the throat without covering the person they're talking to with spittle. Our three classmates hail from Japan, Korea, and Greece.

Carla is so kind. After class, which ends at 1:30, we run errands. More often than not she sends me home via her driver. The sight of me being whisked along the Corniche in a black Mercedes sedan as long as a camel is impressive. I tried to sit in the front seat, but the driver won't let me. He prefers the illusion that I'm important and that he is my driver and protector. Sometimes I practice the royal wave; I pretend I'm rich or have a jar of gourmet mustard ready to share with the driver of the car stopped next to us.

We do hope to visit a few museums. Last week we went to a special preview of the new Alexandria Library. They don't have many books, but I was thrilled to observe that the shelves contain some that have been donated on the subject of spirituality. This is incredible for two reasons. First of all, the original library contained renowned metaphysical works. Secondly, reading material is strictly censored here. Spirituality, which is seen as a religion, is considered by some as a threat to Islam and thinking outside the Islamic box is not encouraged.

There are little things I keep forgetting to explain like sheets and shower curtains. In Egyptian homes they only use an unfitted bottom sheet on their beds. I don't know if there is a reason other than economics; two cost more than one.

Most Egyptians do not use a shower curtain. The tub is open. There's a drain on the bathroom floor that eventually eliminates the water that hits the floor. It also emits nasty sewer smells.

Dinner plates are the size of the ones we use for salads, dessert or lunch. Egyptians have ingenious ways of dealing with household problems. The washing machine in my flat drains via a hose that hangs directly into my bathtub. Rick's drains onto his bathroom floor.

Since he lives in a high-rise without a balcony, his maid

dries his clothes on a rack indoors. I hang mine on the line or on a rack indoors if the weather is iffy. Not many places come with a dryer. Things dried very quickly in Cairo, but since Alex is humid, it can take several days inside.

I've experienced my first rain in eight months. I love it when it rains late at night. As I snuggle under a warm blanket, it feels like a big hug. This is an illusion I have no desire to change!

What doesn't feel great are the ants in my apartment. They have now found their way into my bed! "Ants in her pants" is no longer merely an expression, but a real-life experience. I had never considered that our expressions come from real life experiences.

Because it rarely rains, and usually only in the winter, like Arizona, the roads aren't able to handle much of it. After a storm, which generally lasts less than an hour, the streets are flooded. This makes it difficult to walk, as well as for drivers to negotiate waves of water and people crossing in the middle of the street. Then of course there are the other cars whose drivers lean into whichever lane they wish without using a turn signal or looking first.

The city of Alexandria is looking a lot better since the French firm hired to clean the streets began to work. You can almost walk down a side street without stepping over garbage. Another firm is creating charming narrow sidewalks where none existed.

Alexandria is really quite different from Cairo, El Maadi in particular. It's hard to find what you need unless you ask someone, there are few major roads that are easy to cross on foot, the streets are much narrower, and to my surprise, the people I've met are candid about their greed. Many are also not very nice to interact with. I've discovered that not only Egyptian cats have sharp claws.

On one hand I made a mistake leasing a flat thirty minutes from school, on the other, it's nice to be able to walk along the beach, breathe the salt air and sit outside in relative peace without too many cars and street noises. I do feel like a commuter, however.

My real estate agent, Ahmed, gave me a bicycle. It belonged to one of his sons who outgrew it. Though it's a child's bike, it's fine for me. Rick calls it my "clown bike."

In exchange for my doing some letter writing for a member of his staff, he also fixed the brakes. This addressed the illusion that writing is not a tangible commodity worthy of remuneration. Carla's driver, Mandore, drove my rusty treasure home for me. It will be nice to expand my exploration of Maamora. Perhaps the exercise will remove the upside-down happy faces I see on my thighs each time I look down. They, unfortunately, are not an illusion.

Although I'm finding it difficult to adjust to Alex, my inner peace and happiness continue to expand. Sometimes I feel lonely, but just as quickly I remind myself that even if I cannot physically touch and see the people I love, we are joined together in magical ways that transcends the illusion of separateness. Perhaps the hugging night rains are but a gentle reminder that being alone is also only an illusion.

*Only your nail will
scratch your skin right.*

~ Egyptian Proverb

*The wise man will get it by
an eye sign, but the unwise
will need a kick to understand.*

~ Egyptian Proverb

Chapter 30

November 2001

Animals are amazingly useful. In addition to creating
enough ammonia for the whole village of Maamora, Om and
Chakra serve as early warning devices when something is
amiss. Chakra alerts me by hissing at the door or window
when young Islam is close by. This enables me to yell
through the slats of the window, *"Walad! Imshi! Imshi!"*
(Boy go away). Since he knows I can't see him, this puts the
fear of God into him and he runs away. He has no idea how
I know he's there! My mother didn't have Chakra, but for
many years she had us convinced that she had eyes in the
back of her head.

Tonight as I was washing dishes, until Chakra and Om
started running in circles around my feet, I didn't notice
that the drain had backed up on the kitchen floor. No harm
done. With any luck, a byproduct of the mess may be that
a few million ants drowned.

Ramadan will probably start tomorrow. This is all pred-
icated upon a new moon that signals its beginning. For
about a month, from sunrise to sunset, Muslims fast (no
food, drink, sex, or tobacco during daylight hours). By the
way, I recently learned that the correct pronunciation of
Muslim is: "Mus-*lamb*" not "Mus-*lum*."

My professor, Zizi, who is fast becoming a dear friend,
explained the daylight fast originated as a reminder to the
faithful how poor people feel when they are hungry.
Unfortunately, she observed, many Muslims have forgotten
the purpose and binge all night long to prepare for the next
day's fast while ingesting enough calories to exceed what

they would have normally eaten during the day.

It's traditional for families and friends to gather together at dawn and sunset to pray and eat together. In the evening they begin with soup and sweets. I'm told that not much gets done during the day and people are cranky.

Markets are carrying a variety of dried fruits and imported nuts. Unfortunately for the merchants, the economy is so bad most Egyptians are not buying these expensive delicacies, which are normally eaten plain, stewed, or cooked in cakes and entrees.

In celebration of Ramadan, Egypt is decorated with brightly colored lanterns of many sizes. Some hold candles, others are powered by electricity. Batteries are needed for the small, cheap plastic ones made in China.

Last weekend, Rick took me to the local street market. We had a fabulous dinner at a Korean restaurant and shopped in alleyways filled with outdoor stalls. I bought a Ramadan lantern. Its glass is purple and red. The base is made of tin. Someday, if I can get it back to the U.S. in one piece, it may become an entrance light. For now, it's a small way to join in the celebration. There's no switch on it so I have to turn it on and off by plugging and unplugging it.

I've thought about fasting, too. I can go without food for ten hours, but liquids are another story. We'll see.

A large part of the tradition of Ramadan is to make an extra effort to give more to the poor. As you may recall, a tenet of the faith is to give away a small percentage of one's salary each month. Ramadan goes beyond that. So, when I saw three beggars on the street on my way home from school, I found the coincidence interesting. Since I've been in Egypt, other than those who affect a limp and look pathetic as they try to sell boxes of tissues to motorists and pedestrians, or the small children who are drugged and left to sleep on the sidewalk so people will leave money around their dozing forms, I've seen few beggars. I asked Mo if perhaps a few Egyptians were planning to take advantage of the spirit of the holiday. He confirmed my suspicion. One guy would have shamed the "homeless" drug addicts who hang out on Pennsylvania Avenue, S.E. He was dressed in the remains of an overcoat. He wore only one sneaker. A hand and unshod foot painted black to look as if they were ready to fall off peeked from beneath his torn overcoat and one-legged pajamas. He was so convincing I almost rolled down the window of my taxi to hand him some money. Fortunately, the light changed before I could delve into the bottom of my handbag.

On Monday, Carla invited me to join her to meet a prominent Egyptian woman for tea at one of the local country clubs. It was like an exquisite private city that houses an Olympic-size swimming pool, a polo field, and a golf course. Even if I were planning on staying here, the decadence was far more than I could handle. I'd rather give the monthly fee to one of the fake beggars on the off chance they really are hungry.

Over tea, I had a wonderful opportunity to sit and talk with a handful of Egyptian matrons. Coincidentally, as we chatted in English and Arabic, we heard of the plane crash in N.Y.C. Our reaction was the same, total horror and fear that terrorism had struck again. We all spoke of our desire for peace. Everyone but I felt we could do nothing to make it happen.

This got me thinking. If Christ founded Christianity and blessed those who crucified him, how come we think one person and forgiveness can't make a difference?

I received an e-mail about a woman who created an open field of 50,000 daffodils that anyone can experience each spring. She did it one bulb at a time.

A garden is created one plant at a time; a wall is built one brick at a time; an invention begins with one idea, hate begins with one thought that's passed along to another and another, but so are love and peace. So why can't each and every one of us be the "one" to show love and kindness and lead the way towards peace?

My experiences in Egypt have taught me that when we open ourselves to understanding our differences, it is impossible to hate. When we understand why we are different, when we see the world from a perspective totally opposite ours and accept that our way is not necessarily the right way, just different, then we can begin to see that our diversity really doesn't matter and we can embrace and love what makes us all the same: our humanness. We can not hate that which we know; in knowing, love grows. In loving one person at a time, peace is created. We are not powerless unless we choose to be so.

I plan to return to my beloved Cairo after my last class in December. I don't know what I was/am to accomplish here, but believe that my mission will have been completed by then. Rick has agreed to move me, again! I'll be going to Cairo in a few weeks to find a flat, then move and spend part of the Christmas season with my dear friend, Mary Lewis, who's flying from Maryland to meet me in Malta. How long will I stay in Egypt? What will I do? Who knows? I sure don't. Remember, "It's the journey, not the destination." If I can "get it," control freak that I've been, anyone can! I'll keep you posted.

$$\triangle \triangle \triangle$$

Today I witnessed a miracle, actually four! I had no role in creating any of them. Three came in the form of Chakra's litter. She awakened me this morning to inform me that she was in labor. I prepared a box for her and sat beside it as she went through labor then delivery, another delivery, and another.

Nature is fascinating. She had just enough time between births to clean the newborn, consume the afterbirth, sever the umbilical cord, clean herself, and allow the new arrival to begin to nurse before the contractions for the next birth began. Her body quivered gently, then harder. Within an hour, she was finished. At one point she gave me a woman-to-woman gaze that seemed to say, "You did this too? Are we nuts or what?" "Better you than me," I replied.

Later, as her brood was crying and fighting over a single nipple, she looked at me as if to ask, "Now what do I do?" I laughed in sympathy. One screaming infant is a challenge, three . . . good heaven!

She allows me to pet her and each kitten. I'm not sure of their sex. Each has the coloring of a russet-patched calico topped by a miniature monkey face. Chakra ate a hearty dinner tonight. Needless to say she's exhausted.

The other miracle has to do with Chakra taking on the role of mother to Om. Just as she went into labor, nature must have detonated a maternal bomb in her bloodstream. As I was feeding Om her morning bottle, Chakra jumped into my lap and, rather than trying to jealously knock her off, began kissing her! Om nearly had heart failure.

Since I brought Om home, I've been appealing to Chakra to be kind to her and to love her. As I write this, Chakra is nursing her brood while Om jumps on her head and nibbles her ears. You may recall that when I brought Om home, Chakra had a major temper tantrum. It did not abate until this morning. Each time Om passed her, if Chakra thought I wasn't looking, she took a swipe at Om.

I guess it's payback time. Om is pushing the envelope, but her "new mother" is taking it with a grain of salt and Om is as happy as a small child surrounded by adoring grandparents as she stands on her rear legs like a kangaroo and practices her leaps on Chakra's head.

How lucky I was that I "happened" not to have class today and had planned to spend it studying at my desk in my bedroom (also known as the delivery room, nursery, and ant farm). I would have missed not only the miracle of birth, but maternal love. May you see both as clearly in your lives.

The best favor is to rescue the one most in need.

~ Egyptian Proverb

When you are hungry
you lose your mind.

~ Egyptian Proverb

Chapter 31

November, 2001

From the perspective of a non-Muslim, Ramadan is both a major inconvenience and an interesting religious custom to observe. It's a pain because one quickly learns that nothing happens up to two hours before sunset and for a few hours after while everyone is enjoying *iftar*, the evening meal, which translated means "breakfast," or "break fast."

"Nothing happens" means everything closes. If you need to get through customs, forget it. If you need a taxi, you're out of luck. Need food? Stores are closed from about 4:00–7:30 p.m., but they don't open early in the morning either so you have to really plan everything in advance. If you're on the tram when the call to end the fast sounds, it will stop with you on it. You just have to wait until the engineer has eaten, which could be quite a while. If you're staying in a hotel, as ridiculous as it sounds, there's a strong possibility that breakfast and lunch may not be available.

From a religious perspective, I find Ramadan very confusing. The purpose of fasting is to serve as a reminder of what it is like for those who are truly hungry. My understanding is that it's also an opportunity to seek forgiveness for the sins committed over the year. Prayers and good deeds rack up double "karmic bonus points" during Ramadan. Therefore, the fact that everyone gorges himself or herself after sunset doesn't make a lot of sense to me from a religious, or for that matter, a health perspective.

People spend far more on food during Ramadan than any other time of the year. In addition, everyone works shorter hours to help them get through the day. People leave work, go home, take a nap, eat at sunset, eat all night long, stay up for most of the night, eat before sunrise, go back to sleep for a few hours, go to work late, and then get off early. I'm told that the Prophet Mohamed wanted people to live their lives normally when they fasted. I guess a lot of people have forgotten.

Ramadan is a bit easier for people to deal with in the winter when days are shorter. Even with all the concessions, apparently summer is horrible, especially since one cannot drink any liquids. I can only imagine the health crises this causes from dehydration. I wonder if anyone has performed any studies linking Ramadan with heart and liver disease. Twenty-eight percent of the population suffers from high blood pressure, 25 percent from diabetes. Egyptians eat tons of sugar and fat in the form of *ghee* (clarified butter), but they double their consumption during Ramadan.

In the quest to get rid of the dates that have flooded the market for Ramadan, merchants have "named" them. The cheapest are called "George Bush," the most expensive, "Bin Laden." Interesting marketing strategy. It makes people laugh, but they're still not buying.

Ramadan will end with several days of feasting. Children get new clothes; fathers will supervise the slaughter of a goat, lamb, or sheep, or do it themselves. The concept of giving more to those less fortunate during Ramadan will culminate with part of each animal being shared with family, friends, and the poor. But most of all, Ramadan seems to be about families and friends spending even more time together, as we do in the West during Thanksgiving and Christmas when we also gorge ourselves and spend too much money and forget the real reason we're celebrating.

My Thanksgiving was quite simple. I ate part of a small roasted chicken. I shared it with Om and Chakra while working furiously at trying not to feel sorry for myself. Tears and roast chicken don't, and didn't, mix very well.

The highlight of my day was phone calls to my children. Knowing that they are healthy, happy, and sharing the day with friends made the day much easier for me. And, as my youngest son, Dan, said, "It really isn't a holiday unless we're together. It's just another day."

He's right. If I'm to be really honest with myself, I have to say that I really don't like holidays and haven't since the boys went off to live their own lives. I seem to end up feeling full of food, but empty in the really important ways when I can't look across the table and see my children looking back at me. Don't get me wrong, I've had many beautiful holidays with wonderful friends and now that my children are on limited diets or vegetarian, cooking for the holidays is a major challenge; I'm delighted to turn it over to someone else.

For me, like Ramadan, our holidays get confused with commercialism and "shoulds." I can't remember the last time I looked at a Thanksgiving turkey and thought of, and really felt, what it was like for someone else to be hungry or lonely, or for that matter, what my forebears went through just to procure one, let alone cook it! We're taught to be generous and kind during November and December. Why don't we consider every day to be a holiday of giving and thinking of how others feel? Why do we need holidays?

An expat asked me what Thanksgiving means. I didn't talk about the bounty of a good harvest, of being thankful for family, friends, and good food, but found myself instead talking about how to me it's really a celebration of freedom, of the incredible wisdom of the founding fathers that created our democracy. Living in Egypt and in the Middle East is an opportunity to experience what freedom means each day there and here.

I've come to clearly see the weaknesses of our government, of how we as a people have allowed it to do things in our name we don't even know about. But I've also seen, up close and personal, what it means to be able to freely practice my faith in whatever way I choose. In the U.S., I can be a Christian one day, a Jew the next, a Buddhist the next, and a Muslim on Friday. People might find me strange (if they don't already) but no one has the right to tell me what I can and can't believe, even those irritating souls who peddle their religion door to door, for I also have the right to shut that door in their face.

I think most foreigners know that our currency says "In God We Trust," but I doubt if they know that we are also required to say "So help me God" when we swear to tell the truth and "under God" in our Pledge of Allegiance. That we put God on our money is probably seen as a reflection of our materialistic society asking God to protect our assets. I think they would be surprised by the other two.

While many Muslims see us as "godless" perhaps they don't understand that while some of our citizens don't believe in God or don't practice one faith, our country was founded on the belief in one God and our right to choose to worship him as we see fit.

Thankfully the holiday weekend is about over. On one level it was a truly miserable one, but on another, it's been the most enlightening I've ever experienced for I will never again take Thanksgiving for granted. That's a fantastic gift. Every day really is an opportunity for thanksgiving and all the really important, non-caloric intangibles that go with it. I'd like to believe that this is the real legacy the pilgrims hoped to leave with us.

A very small flat with good air and sunshine is better than a dark, damp palace.

~ Egyptian Proverb

Chapter 32

December 2001

Things in North Africa (I say this rather than Egypt because I often forget that I'm living on the continent of Africa and thought you might appreciate a reminder as well) are, shall we say, no longer filled with dull moments.

Thursday night I returned to Cairo to search for a new home. It was an amazing trip. My friend Carla decided to join me. Via Cairo airport, she was going to Israel for the weekend to visit some of her diplomatic friends. What a luxury it was to be delivered to the train by her driver and then to be picked up by another in Cairo. This, I could get used to! Carla doesn't do anything second-class. Because she comes from a wealthy family, she has had servants and perhaps drivers all her life. She trains them well and is not shy about communicating her displeasure when they don't do things the way she expects.

In between visits to some of the most revolting rental units available on earth (complete with bugs and furniture that cringed with shame), I visited with my merchant friends along Road 9. On two of the three mornings I was there, I passed up the free, pathetic hotel breakfast and enjoyed the sunshine as I sat outside the German bakery reading several newspapers and sipping a cup of freshly brewed European coffee. The Egyptian version is either thick Turkish coffee, which I really like, or instant Nescafé, which I find repulsive. It was fun watching the action and antics of my friends at the produce market next door. It felt so good to come home.

Friday afternoon I joined my friend's salon at his antique store. Everyone else drank Bloody Marys (I opted for a virgin version) and talked with other expats about evacuation and our fears of what will happen next. I met several lovely people, one of whom (Sue) was kind enough to show me a flat in her building. She's a terrific free spirit who's lived in Cairo for fourteen years. The flat was terrible (a seven-floor walk-up!), but she made us a lovely light lunch and we got to know each other. She'll be traveling until February. I look forward to reconnecting with her then.

On Saturday, Mo hauled me all over El Maadi to look at apartments. I more fully appreciate his doing the dirty work for me last spring! When I arrived in Egypt, all I had to do was move in.

We looked at a tiny enchanted cottage situated on an old estate in old El Maadi. The owner, a European married to an Egyptian, and I hit it off immediately. The property has a stream and an orchard! Because high walls guard property from prying eyes, I never knew such things existed here! The rental unit is probably a converted carriage house. I was in pig heaven until Mo gently asked if the rent was 1,500 LE (my budget) or $1,500.00. Sob! It was dollars. She was willing to come down to $1,000.00 but I couldn't justify the expense. I really hate it when Mo bursts my reality bubble by being so smart!

Friday night I had dinner out with my wonderful friend Jennifer. Since I lived primarily on cheese and fish in Alex, I decided to order what turned out to be a close replica of a filet mignon. I've never had it served cut up before, nor do I look forward to it being served that way again. It was terribly overcooked. I did have an authentic vodka and tonic that I thoroughly enjoyed.

Saturday night I attended an iftar feast with some of the merchants (who are also Ali's relatives) whose stores are adjacent to his shop. There is a small, covered alley runs between them. This is where we ate. Ali created a narrow table out of low stools that were then covered with newspaper and platters of incredible homemade Egyptian food. Surrounded by eight Egyptian men of various ages and sizes, I gorged on diminutive Egyptian sausages sautéed with onions, beef kofta, chicken stew with chickpeas and vegetables, the Egyptian staple salad of tomatoes and cucumbers, hummus, yogurt salad, macaroni with ground beef and béchamel sauce, and fresh bread. Since there were no dinner plates or utensils, eating bread, which I rarely do, was a requirement. You break off a piece and scoop up food from one of the platters. Each dish was more delicious than the last. After "breakfast" I wandered up the street to the produce stand. The guys there were waiting for me to join them for post-iftar tea. I'd been invited to join them for their feast, but since I'd already accepted Ali's invitation, we settled on my coming for tea *(shay)*.

My flat hunting culminated in my signing a lease with the owner's representative, Egypt's former ambassador to Hong Kong (he's served around the world). We sealed the deal over tea in his Chinese furniture store. The ambassador is a delightful man with candid insights into the U.S./Middle East mess. He fears that George W. Bush has only begun his campaign to control the majority of the world's oil supply by using Bin Laden and terrorism as an excuse to remove the leaders of other countries. Any country that doesn't agree with his take on terrorism is fair game . . . Iraq, Jordan, Iran. . . . If Bush's agenda becomes reality, the rage will be so great in this part of the world, terrorism will become a way of life worldwide.

We also talked about the apparent suspension of the Constitution, the right to a public trial of those who have been "detained" by the U.S. government, and the actions of the U.S. Congress changing the rules pertaining to privacy, unlawful seizure, and detainment. The ambassador's reaction really shocked me. In Egypt, people are detained all the time, yet he was horrified that the U.S. would turn away from the democratic process. He truly believes that the U.S. government is committed to eliminating Islam from the world. This is a cultured, brilliant man. If he feels this way, it's just the tip of the iceberg!

The weekend whizzed by. Molly had been in Maine and didn't arrive home until Saturday afternoon. I was delighted to have a few hours to spend with her before catching the 2:00 p.m. express train back to Alex on Sunday. She sent me off with a ham salad sandwich, which I discreetly wolfed down as soon as I got in a taxi.

Dear Rick performed the yeoman deed of caring for Om, Chakra, and her kittens. He lives thirty minutes away, but each evening (twice on Friday) he drove to Maamora to feed and play with them. Fortunately, since they were locked in the kitchen with all their amenities, Chakra hadn't found it necessary to perform her door-opening trick. She stands on a counter in the kitchen and jumps onto the pull down handle on the inside of the door until it springs open.

My new flat is modern and sunny! It's on the seventh floor of a two-year-old building with two elevators. It has two huge bedrooms, two full baths, a decent kitchen, two balconies, a living room/dining room combination, and pretty blue and gold furniture. The owner has agreed to provide a desk and to clean the flat before Rick moves me in on the night of December 13. Best of all, it's right around the corner from Tim and Molly, spitting distance to Camilla and Yosef's, and costs exactly what I've been paying since I arrived here. Based upon the other stuff I saw that was both disgusting and more expensive, I got a great deal.

There was a drama associated with my lease after I returned to Alex. I'll fill in the details later, but for now everything is fine.

I took a six-month lease with the option of extending for another six months at the same rent. At this point I'm beginning to look at the possibility of returning to the U.S. in March to buy a home in Rhode Island. I'd return to Egypt until it's time to settle (probably end of May early June). In any case, I caution that nothing is settled for I'm still going by the seat of my pants.

I've picked up a few more writing assignments so I'm extremely busy right now, and of course I have to pack. I've decided to quit my current Arabic class at the university. Molly and I will take one in El Maadi in January that's more basic. Hopefully what I've learned will enable me to move more quickly than I have been. Carla and I really got ripped off. I was never able to catch up with the other students who had been studying Arabic sixteen hours a week for nearly six weeks. Live and learn.

As I work at my computer, Om has taken to sleeping like a purring muff on my neck or shoulder. When I arise, she stays attached like a parrot. This makes it difficult to bend over the refrigerator without propelling her into it, to cook over the stove and avoid the potential of her becoming the main protein source, or even to go to the bathroom for fear of accidentally drowning her. I feel like one of the Egyptian women I see walking down the street with an overflowing container balanced upon her head while trying to hold onto the hand of one or more small children.

Since it's cold in Alex, her sweet baby breath and downy fur warm my body. However, to climb the Mount Everest of her adopted mother, she uses her baby claws. They're sharper than a spanking new surgical knife. Her climbing used to be confined to my legs. Now my back and neck, along with my legs look as if I've spent the past month rolling in barbed wire.

But there are other times when a simple leap will do, like when I read. She either bends her body in half on my lap or climbs up under my chin until she's transformed into a vibrating muffler. Such are the joys and hidden perils of human/animal motherhood.

The other day Chakra and I watched in amusement as Om tried to move a kitten half her size. It had ventured out of its nursery box onto the kitchen floor. In alarm, Om pushed and pulled until the little one was scooted across the floor, over the lip of the box and securely home with its siblings.

Chakra has reverted to her pattern of jealousy, but apparently for different reasons. If I'm "nursing" Om, she swipes at me so I'll put her down. She's now jealous because Om won't nurse with her kittens.

We've had heavy rainstorms. My yellow ducky slicker and rubber gardening shoes I found in storage when I was in D.C. have come in quite handy, though the puddles are often as high as my ankles. Saturday night, Rick bought me a yellow umbrella. When it's open, a large orange bill and massive oval duck eyes pop out. I think it's totally cool!

In his continuous effort to fatten me up, Rick took me to an Egyptian fish restaurant near the place where we saw the blind man who couldn't get out of the park. We arrived at the end of iftar. As sated Egyptians followed behind their overflowing bellies, stacks of plates were being removed from about a hundred tables. We were the only Westerners.

When you arrive, you stop at the "fish counter" at the restaurant's entrance and choose your dinner. We ordered a half-kilo (a kilo is 2.2 pounds) each of calamari, prawns the size of my hand and silky baby sole. After we were seated, a basket of native bread appeared, then soup and a buffet of salads (mezzas) that threatened to collapse the table. When our grilled fish course was brought to the table, we had to stack plates to make room. As always, we had a wonderful time talking, eating delicious food and laughing. On the way home we stopped at two grocery stores to pick up items I can't find in Maamora.

I'll really miss Rick. He's been kind in so many ways and has helped me to keep my sanity during my time in Alex. As a Western man he understands the unique problems a Western woman faces. He helps by letting me vent. As an employer of Egyptians, his perspective of the culture is different in some ways from mine. It's fun to share information that often fills in the gaps for each of us.

We talked a lot about what we would consider to be a cultural lack of honesty. People don't take responsibility for their actions, nor will they admit when they've made a mistake. Instead, they create intricate webs of fabrication to cover the truth. If they get caught, they blame the problem on someone else. "Not my fault" is a common expression.

I think dishonesty, as we from the West would label it, is based upon our cultural norms. It begins with Egyptian mothers who, due to their status, cannot ask for anything in an up-front way. Since they aren't usually allowed to approach their husbands directly, they go around the bush, the mountain, the ocean, and their village to get what they want. Their children see at an early age how well manipulation and deception, rather than the truth, works.

If a man wants a woman, he'll stop at nothing to convince her that she should succumb to his charm by marrying him. I've experienced this with a few of the Egyptian men I thought were just friends, Dr. M. in particular. Over and over when he made a pass at me I'd explain that I wan't interested in anything more than a friendship. "But of course," he'd reply as if I were the village idiot who did not "understand" his "kind" intentions. The next week we'd go through the same drill.

When sweet words didn't work, he tried unkind manipulation. He suggested I have plastic surgery to unwrinkle my neck and, while I was at it, have my breasts lifted and enlarged. I told him that I'm very happy with how God made me and I'm really glad I can look over my breasts and see my feet and truly, I have no desire to look like a Barbie doll version of Joan Rivers. Really! In any case, I was kind in my restraint. I didn't mention that he could use a major hair transplant and liposuction to remove about 20 kilos from around his stomach! Only by being what a Westerner would consider rude, did he finally stop, but stopping meant he has retreated from our friendship. Subtle doesn't make it here.

Speaking of looks, most Egyptians think I'm far too thin. To them my slenderness is comparable to someone in the West who looks like Twiggy or suffers from anorexia. In reference to this, Zizi, my professor, tried to reassure me of my attractiveness by saying, "Jeanne, don't worry about your body. You have a pretty face." I laughed for days.

Lying in business is really confusing to a Westerner. At home, business is business. If a friendship develops, it's done slowly. People help each other out through the "old boy's/girl's network" with the understanding that it will eventually pay off, but you also have to do a good job. In Egypt, any business kindness means you're supposed to pay. If someone gives someone else a referral, they expect something in return—cash. They don't see that what goes around comes around. Everything is about instant gratification, not long-term building.

Egyptian business people work really hard to convince you that they're your friend. If they're your friend, it's not business. They're doing you a favor. So, if they do a terrible job, tough. They're so good at playing out the drama you fall for it. You actually begin to believe that they care about you as a person, not just your money and fall into the trap of being too forgiving for the inadequacies of their product or service. When an Egyptian tells me not to worry about the cost of something, I then begin to worry. They're trying to decide just how much they can overcharge and get away with.

My Realtor here in Alex, Ahmed, is a perfect example. I

referred Carla to him. I expected nothing in return. She's been looking to rent a villa in the range of $5,000.00 U.S. per month for four years! The commission on this rental is worth about a year's income to him. I even counseled him on how to handle the situation, but he wouldn't listen to me and will probably get gouged by the woman who has the listing. Ahmed was too "busy" to go with the listing "agent" and Carla to look at the property. Now he has no relationship with Carla and the "listing" agent is squeezing him out. The truth is he was lazy and didn't do his job. He wants me to run interference to ensure that he'll be paid. I don't think so. Carla owes him nothing.

My bawaab tried to tell me that I hadn't paid his "fee" for October and November. I had, of course. When I wasn't here on December 1 and returned from Cairo on December 2, he saw the lights on in my flat and turned off my electricity. This was his not-so-subtle way of reminding me to pay up! What's funny is that at the exact moment he turned off the lights, I was going out the door to pay him! So, when the lights went out, instead of calling for his immediate help, I lit some candles and waited a few hours. I'm sure he didn't know what to do next to "get me."

Egyptians think they work much harder than Westerners. Those who work for themselves do work really hard, like the guys at the produce stand who start at dawn and leave late at night. But employees who work for someone else often don't. They "work" longer hours because so many have two jobs, but half the time they're taking up space on the phone, visiting with coworkers, and gossiping. This is the norm. They remind me of D.C. government employees under Marion Barry.

Back to Ahmed. He whined a lot about my leaving Alex. "Please stay. I'll miss you so much," yadda, yadda. Turns out at the same time he's been calling my landlord to tell him that he's been trying to talk me into staying and to remind him that if I extend my lease he's due an additional commission! On top of that, when I rented this overpriced hellhole, he told me that my landlord wouldn't pay any commission. I ended up paying the "whole" commission, 400 LE. Last week my landlord told me he also paid 400 LE so Ahmed made 800 LE for about three hours of work, an enormous sum. To teach Ahmed a lesson and to get me to stay, my landlord offered to let me extend my lease and to drop my rent from 1,500 LE to 150 LE per month! Thanks, but no thanks.

Jealousy is quite prevalent, so is vicious gossip. Black magic is often used to bring down anyone who has more than another. More can be defined as anything someone else wants and doesn't have. People actually go to "witches" to have spells cast and pray for harm to come to their enemies. As the economy continues to worsen since 9/11, I imagine the witches are making a fortune.

Fortunately, I've also been blessed with Egyptian friends who are about as kind and decent as any human being I have ever known. The problem is, as Rick observed, I've had to develop a suspicious, defensive attitude when dealing with anyone new, particularly a taxi driver or a merchant. It's sad, but true. I'm working hard to regain my balance, to not take things personally and to go with the flow. Thankfully my sense of humor is still intact, but there are times when one more attempt at snookering me or an overt sexual remark or touch will bring me and other Western women to the edge of sanity. We become warrior women.

Rick's friend Suzanne is even more of a fireball than I. She reached her limit when they were walking down a narrow side street in Alex and a taxi passed them with only inches to spare. As he drove by, the driver pinched Suzanne on her bottom. She lost it. In a rage she picked up a brick and threw it at the taxi. She has great aim. She eliminated the rear window. The driver was foolish enough to step out of his cab to yell at her. He probably learned words he didn't know existed and was in jeopardy of having his skull crushed.

This week, Karen and I seemed to be on the same wavelength as Suzanne. In different incidents, we raised bloody hell. Karen was walking down the street when a man coming in the other direction said, "I love you!" He was shocked by her response that was something along the lines of "You idiot. What do you mean you love me? You pig, go away!"

When I took a taxi from Maamora to Carla's villa, and the driver saw where I was going, he tried to up the fare. I went berserk. He had no way of knowing that after a week of greedy drivers, his protests sent me over the edge.

By the way, please remember that I share these stories because they're part of my experience, not as a negative judgment of the Egyptian people who have far more to cope with in one week than we do in a year. People are no better or worse here than anywhere else in the world; they have different ways and cultural norms that "work" for them in their attempt to cope with life. The biggest mistake I've made has been to take things personally and to think that I have the right to judge them. I don't. Unfortunately, when I reach my limit, I forget.

My apartment is freezing. I do have a portable heater, but it's not enough. This addresses Mo's query as to why Westerners who are used to far colder climates feel as if they're freezing during the winter here. The answer is quite simple. There's no blasted central heat!

I've been busy writing, packing, and saying goodbye to the friends I've made in Alex before I leave for Cairo. My phone has been out, my electricity off more than on (after my bawaab's little game and lots of rain and high winds).

I forgot to tell you that it's not a good idea to drive along the Corniche during a heavy windstorm. Satellite dishes have been known to fly toward the sea!

Tonight I'm invited to the home of an Egyptian friend. Monday night my Danish friend Karen is coming to dinner with her Italian fiancé Berhan (he owns a sock factory). Tuesday night I'm having dinner at the home of another Egyptian friend, and Wednesday my landlord is coming by to return my security deposit . . . I hope!

It should be an interesting, busy week. I've written two articles for the USAID contract's E-news and have one more to finish if I can get the background from an employee who was out sick last week.

I'm looking forward to moving into my new flat. In some ways I suppose I've "sold out." It's okay with me! I've lived like a middle-class native for nine months. It's not that I'll be moving into luxury, but it certainly will be closer to Western standards, and quite frankly, I'm ready for a toilet not held together by a plastic bag, heat and AC that don't sound like a runway when they're turned on, no ants in my bed, a phone with more sound than static, and a sink that doesn't flood the floor from the bottom. Of course, I'll have to contend with elevator problems and electricity, phones and water that go out without notice, and the local mosque blaring the news that sunrise is just an hour away.

I continue to be grateful for my health, the wonderful people I've met, and the harsh, as well as the gentle, lessons I'm exposed to each day. My street smarts are now international!

I've had such an interesting week. I want to share the details before I forget anything.

In the following accounts, as I've done throughout when I thought it appropriate to do so, I've changed the names of the people whose life stories I'm about to share with you.

I had a delightful evening with Sheree, her husband Osman, and their two lovely daughters. Osman was in and out most of the evening or on the phone gossiping with his friends.

Their oldest daughter died of leukemia when she was five. Sheree took her to London for treatment and she died there. So she wouldn't upset her family even more by bringing her body home, she chose to have her daughter buried in England, a decision she greatly regrets.

Sheree and Osman are professionals. They're devout Muslims. She is a gentle, loving, insightful soul. He is a prick in any language.

Sheree is having a really difficult time dealing with his tyrannical rules. He expects her to get up each morning to feed their children, drive them to school, work a full day, come home and prepare "lunch," and then help them with their homework. At the end of the day she's exhausted.

Since he doesn't believe in adhering to a schedule, including being on time for work, each morning he sleeps in. At night he wants her to stay up to keep him company.

She recently learned that she's pregnant. She's forty-two. He's thrilled. She isn't. He wanted another child. She was happy that their children are able to function more independently and looked forward to a little more time for herself. He brags to their friends, family, and colleagues that he "had nothing to do one night so he made a baby." I think he's insecure and impregnating his wife in midlife has really pumped up his ego. I nearly swallowed my tongue in my effort to hold it.

Sheree is one of those women who are sick for nine months. She's sad, exhausted, and trying her best to welcome the new life that's growing inside her. She wants to have a C-section, but confided that she will have to get her doctor to tell her husband that she must have one. Why? Because her husband is in charge of her body, not her.

Sheree has been candid and willing to talk about her role as a woman in Egyptian society. It's a difficult role to play, perhaps even more so for someone as well educated as she. She was raised to obey her husband and does so even when she wants to strangle him. It takes a toll, but her experience, she would readily say, is nothing compared to her mother's. By the way, Osman thinks that women in Egypt have all the freedom they need. He made his case by comparing them to the women of Saudi Arabia. I didn't hold my tongue. I told him that comparing the life of an Egyptian woman to that of a Saudi woman is similar to comparing a prisoner in a minimum-security prison to one on death row who will never be executed. Imprisonment is often a matter of degree.

Sheree's mother gave birth to six children. One day her husband announced that he was taking his secretary, a beautiful eighteen-year-old woman, as his second wife. To prepare for the wedding, Sheree's mother was required to make a mattress and pillows for the new bride and her husband's marriage bed.

After the mattress and pillows were finished, the sight in her right eye began to fail. Eventually, it was completely lost. Over the years, as he took more wives, her left eye began to fail. She is now blind.

At one point her husband told her that he had hated her from the beginning of their marriage. He said that he had married her because he was pressured by his family to do so. When asked why he had six children with her, he confided, "It was my lot in life."

His second wife had three more children. He was never interested in raising any of them, only making them.

He didn't stop with one additional wife. He married a third time (a woman who was unattractive but quiet and happily willing to obey him, unlike the first two), then a fourth, but he quickly divorced her because she was "after his money." What's funny is that even today, all the wives meet to complain and to plot against him. Sheree's mother has not spoken to him in decades; she stays within herself, mourning her terrible life and loving her six children.

Sheree also told me that as recently as seven years ago, a woman was physically afraid to stand up to her husband. He could murder her, cut her body into pieces, and scatter them. He'd probably get away with it, too. Now it has more to do with economics. Older women who are not professionals are stuck, just like women around the world, and a good woman "obeys" her husband, as the culture and religion requires. These days if a wife mouths off, more than likely he'll retaliate by taking a second wife or divorcing her. This is why she puts up with so much from her husband.

Sheree had an insightful observation about her fellow citizens. She said that Egyptians are so busy watching and judging the lives of everyone else around them that they don't take the time to go inward, to work on their own weaknesses. This is true for many, but certainly not for those who have so generously allowed me into their lives and spoken candidly about the pros and cons of their society and culture. I am indeed privileged and honored by their trust.

Last night, my Danish friend Karen and her fiancé Berhan came for dinner. Berhan is Italian, but was raised in Turkey. Due to the pressure to conform to the rules of the Islamic society we Westerners live in, they, like Carla and her partner, pretend to be married.

We had such a grand time that they didn't leave until this morning! They're totally in love and devoted to each other. It's wonderful to see.

This evening, another Egyptian friend treated me to a beautiful home-cooked fish dinner. I met Lily's eldest daughter. She's studying to become a pharmacist. Today is her twenty-third birthday. She, like many other Egyptians, is fascinated by my desire to learn as much as I can about the culture. She liked that I seemed to have "gotten it."

A few years ago, Lily's husband, a college professor, left her for one of his students, a Muslim. This is a terrible cultural shame for her, but it also created a religious crisis. They're both Coptic.

By leaving her, Lily's husband has "ruined the lives of his children." I still don't understand why (only that it's religious), but as long as their parents are not living together, her daughters will have trouble marrying a Coptic man of a higher or the same social status. I gather the other family won't accept a daughter-in-law who comes from a broken home. Divorce is not usually allowed in the Coptic faith, but there are exceptions. By the way, Coptic means "Egyptian." A Coptic Christian is an Egyptian Christian.

I asked what would happen if one of her girls wanted to marry a Muslim? She replied without blinking, "I would have to kill her!" When I realized that she was serious, I nearly fell off my chair!

Since his father left, Lily's fifteen-year-old son has become a major problem. He recently found out from a schoolmate that his father is living with another woman, a Muslim. He wants to kill them both! On top of this, Lily thinks he's on drugs. He skips school and the tutoring sessions she gives him cash to pay for. He stays out all night. When he comes home he sleeps the day away. There are few programs available to help her. She wants him to go live with his father, but he says, "The children are your problem." She has no family in the area and can't talk to her Egyptian friends because they would gossip about her problems and make things worse for her. She's living in a box and everyone is sitting on the lid, but the pain her children are experiencing fuels the anguish of her soul.

The more I talk to Egyptians, the more I have come to believe there's a great deal of animosity and misunderstanding between members of Islam and Coptic faiths. Contrary to some of the teachings of the Prophet Mohammed, who believed "good" people of other faiths should be considered equal to a good Muslim, Copts are discriminated against by the Muslim-dominated society in which they live and many Copts think Islam is unworthy of their respect.

This all reminds me of a song written by gifted lyricist, Tom Lehrer, famous for his social parodies. Over thirty years ago, in his song "National Brotherhood Week," he lampooned members of the world's major religions for their intolerance of others. All the bickering in His name must drive God nuts!

My chapter in Maamora is coming to a close. Tim, Molly, Joan, and her husband David were in town overnight. We met for breakfast this morning and I joined them on a private guided tour of the new library. It was so great being with my Cairo family. I look forward to more adventures together in El Maadi.

I'll visit the ocean tomorrow to say goodbye and watch as taxi drivers use the three fountains that form roundabouts along the main drag as a water source to wash their cars. I'll go by the fish market to buy some fresh fish to freeze to take with me, say goodbye to the guys at the little market who patiently worked with me as I practiced my Arabic when buying groceries, the chicken stand stud, and the newspaper man. Since we'll be moving during iftar and he'll be busy eating, I hope to avoid seeing Saza, my bawaab. He taught me many lessons about tolerance, temper, and non-judgment. Some I learned and overcame; others I didn't. The sight of his oily smile still knots my intestines.

Not all of our teachers are kind and gentle, yet their value is priceless. Every time we see a part of ourselves in need of healing reflected back to us by the traits we don't like in someone else, we're given a magnificent opportunity to change. I leave Alex and Maamora in gratitude for the lessons and for the wonderful friends I've made whom I'll carry in my heart wherever I go.

Yes, I hope the rest of my journey is less challenging, but if it isn't, I've learned not to ask that the challenges be eliminated, only that I continue to be provided with the strength and wisdom to learn from each one and to keep myself balanced so I don't miss the miracles I know await me.

Many of you have written to express your outrage about how women are treated here and to ask how I cope with it. My response is a complicated one.

When I first came to Egypt, the culture made me nuts. Sometimes it still does, but that happens when I try to project my values and culture onto one that's totally different from mine. I've learned that if I want to understand

Egypt and her people, I need to see it as a whole, to not separate it out in bits and pieces.

From this perspective, I've come to the conclusion that how women are treated is a by-product of the economy, the lack of freedom of speech, and the men's feeling of worthlessness. I discussed this a long time ago in an earlier chapter. My theory is that when men feel they don't have any power over their lives, they take it out on their women. Historically, and in 80 percent of the world today, women are treated as second-class citizens. If you look back to the 1960s in the U.S., you'll see the same pattern. We were second-class citizens, perhaps not to the same extent, but we sure didn't have the freedom we have come to see as our right today. In many ways, Egypt is about thirty years behind the U.S., in male-female equality in particular.

Egypt is not a democracy. It's not quite a dictatorship either, but there is no freedom of speech, freedom of the press, or right to demonstrate. The economy has been ghastly for many years. Men work two jobs and barely survive. Wages are kept low, perhaps artificially so by the government to keep men so busy and exhausted they don't have time to look at what's happening, how they're controlled by the government and their religion. They don't see that they have choices. They think the way things are is the way they'll always be. They feel powerless outside the home. When men are frustrated, they pick on women. An example of this around the world (and in the U.S.) is domestic violence which we know increases as an economy weakens.

Islam is used as another way to control men and, by default, their women. Each time the call to prayer sounds, they are reminded of how "impure and imperfect" they are. This is not the basis of Islam, but it's how it has evolved and is often used to control others by those with power agendas. Ninety-five percent of the population doesn't understand how the holy book, the Koran relates to life so they rely upon religious authority figures to interpret it for them. This is similar to how the Bible, and religion in general is used by conservative religious groups to control people in the West.

Here, women work really hard to be "pure." Perhaps this

is their way of thinking that if they're "good" enough they'll be given more power and receive what they most want: respect, validation, and love. To compound things, those who aren't Muslim face discrimination. It's interesting that on average, Copts make more money than Muslims, but their women, by Western standards, are second-class citizens, too.

What no one seems to understand is that when half the human race is enslaved, society as a whole suffers. Female energy balances male energy by curbing aggression and providing creative, nurturing energy. A civilization that is not balanced with both energies cannot grow and prosper. So, in effect, Egypt's future may very well be directly linked to how it treats its women. But for women to become equal and to embrace their nurturing nature, men have to feel powerful inside themselves. It's a cycle that can only be broken by those who live it.

Two questions can still raise my hackles. The first is, "Is it true that Americans don't believe in God?" The second is, "Why did America create Bin Laden?"

Second and third-world people really believe that we live like the characters they see in our movies and television programs. They don't know this is all fantasy. They don't know that we have people who live on the street, who have no home, food, or shelter. They think everyone is rich. They really believe that we go to the office for a few hours a day and make huge amounts of money. They believe we all have everything material we could ever dream of. They think our lives are easy, that we have no problems. They've bought the "dream," and it makes them furious that they can't live it, too. They delude themselves into pretending that they're superior to us by buying into the perception that we're godless, sex-crazed, pleasure-oriented, alcoholic, drug addicts who carry guns.

They know they're not superior economically, but they take comfort in believing that they're superior in their morals and relationship with God. This is why it's so difficult being a Western woman in this culture. Until people get to know you, they assume you're impure. It's not nice, but it's reality. And the filth that comes over the Internet only reinforces the perception. Yet, when they get to know

Western women like Molly and me, their perceptions are shot to hell. In a small way we are the ambassadors who give them the opportunity to question what they thought was the truth. For me, living in this society, sometimes causes conflict between showing respect for the culture and remaining true to who I am. I've worked too hard to become the woman I am today to lose myself.

I keep my legs covered, but I refuse to wear my shirts out or to put on long-sleeved tops in the summer. Everything I wear does have sleeves, but short ones. I do entertain men in my apartment without a chaperone. I have male friends. I couldn't be happy without their energy and perspective.

In my new place, I'll have to go through the process all over again with the new bawaabs. Some of my male friends may stay overnight in the guest room as well as unmarried couples. This should really enliven the lives of those who will keep an eye on me. Who knows, as the fortune teller predicted, I may meet a wonderful man and have a relationship with him. This is really taboo, but I don't give a flying farthing. I know who I am. I will not stop smiling or being friendly to the Egyptian men I meet or stop hugging my male friends in greeting in public.

But in being true to whom I choose to be, I also know I have to suffer the consequences. It's a constant battle, but one I willingly participate in. Because I love Egypt and her people, I continue to seek to know and respect her culture and religion.

I get angry when people tell me we "created" Bin Laden. Hello! He has free will. He decided to become who he has become. Since the Egyptian culture doesn't factor in free will, they blame the man Bin Laden chose to become on the U.S. We are seen as having everything they want; yet at the same time they're afraid that our morals are contagious. They don't really believe in free will, in changing their lives themselves. I think in the West we often suffer from the same inability to take responsibility for who and what we choose to become. How old does one need to be before we let the mistakes of our parents go and begin to take responsibility for being an adult?

I had a truly beautiful Christmas with my Cairo family, Tim, Molly, and their daughter Liz who's visiting from

Boston. We cooked together, laughed, served a beautiful dinner to many friends and relaxed. The only thing that would have made it better would have been to have my children here to share it with us.

Sometimes things happen here that make you laugh so hard your tear ducts begin to fill and spill over. Today was such a day. I spent a good part of the morning running errands.

I have three bawaabs. They work shifts at my building. Someone is on duty twenty-four hours a day. They all seem really nice. This morning, Ramadan (the day man) grabbed the bag of garbage I brought down in the elevator with me. I missed morning pickup. Since it was full of dirty cat litter, I decided not to wait to put it out tonight. Ramadan sweetly asked if I needed a taxi. I did. Within seconds a cab pulled up.

Ramadan, with great ceremony, put me in the back seat, and then to my surprise placed the bag of garbage on the front seat next to the driver. I thought this strange but figured perhaps the taxi driver was supposed to dispose of it for him. Unfortunately, as he put the bag into the cab it broke. Dirty kitty litter began to fill the front seat then pour onto the floor of the taxi.

Ramadan raced back into the building for another bag. He returned and began to transfer my garbage into it. I saw that the cleanup process could go on forever so I got out of the cab, gently shooed him away and tied a knot in the part of the bag that had split. "Ah!" they exclaimed. "S*hartra!*" (very clever).

As the driver removed the bag from the taxi and began to scoop out the litter that remained behind, Ramadan continued to go through the bag asking with each handful, "Rubbish?" "*Aywa*" (yes), I replied again and again.

The taxi driver kept shaking his head in dismay but was amazingly easygoing about the mess Ramadan had made. We left the bag with him. As we drove away, I finally "got it!" Ramadan thought the bag contained good stuff. Being helpful, he put it in the cab for me to take with me!

Apparently my driver came to the same conclusion at the very same moment. We laughed until we cried, enjoying a human moment in pidgin English and Arabic. In

appreciation for his kindness I doubled his fare. As I exited the cab he said, "Merry Christmas," and waved goodbye.
A smile of universal joy at having truly connected once
again in laughter with another human being slid across his
face and mine. It made my day.

*Walk with glory,
not with a big belly.*

~ Egyptian Proverb

Chapter 33

December 2001

When I arrived home from Malta, predawn Christmas Eve, a lovely wreath on my front door twinkled. Molly had been at work. Since she has a key, she even decorated the inside of my apartment.

Many flights leaving Cairo are scheduled to leave somewhere between 3:00 and 5:00 a.m. and arrive at the same miserable hours. In addition to allowing for the connection of international flights through Europe, I've been told that the predawn flights from here allow carriers to park their planes overnight in Egypt, rather than in Europe, at a much lower rate. I've wondered if local hotels have something to do with this schedule. When a tourist arrives in the middle of the night, they're likely to book a hotel room for another night rather than waiting for a late afternoon check-in.

Upon entering Egyptian customs, I was not pleased to discover that the last Egyptian employee to extend my visa hadn't matched the dates with my ability to leave or reenter the country. I had to pay extra dollars and then deal with questions about "what my husband does." When I figured out that the customs guy was hitting on me, it was a lot easier to pay the fee and charm him rather than fight.

Mo wasn't at the airport. He had called Malta Air to confirm my flight and was told it would arrive Monday afternoon rather than Monday morning. This was just as well. He had to work that day and would have been up all night. Of course, industrious taxi drivers looking for a tourist to overcharge swarmed me at the curb.

I ended up negotiating with one driver and off we went, sort of. Just outside the airport exit, his cab stalled and he had to jump it by pushing it down a hill. Ah, home at last! How quickly I manage to forget the "rules" here.

Malta is a volcanic island located about sixty miles south of Sicily, and several hundred above Libya and Egypt on the north side of the Mediterranean. It's terraced to allow for maximum usage of its limited land. Ancient worn steps and roads rival San Francisco in their slope from the waterfront to the towns and villages above.

I stayed in Valletta. Malta is about the size of Washington D.C., very old, and quite beautiful. In the countryside, diminutive farms are separated by narrow rectangles of walls created from uncovered stones.

I had arranged for a driver to meet me at the airport. John is a typical Maltese. The top of his head came to my chest. The Maltese people seem to descend from several bloodlines. John is from the munchkin fork, others, since their noses look as if they had been crushed in a prizefight could be identified as coming from a long line of gladiators who lost. The women are either round as a column or their torsos rest upon elongated thin legs that end at surprisingly high fannies destined to spread over time. All the women have long, black hair. As in Egypt, I think I was the only woman on the island with gray in hers. I keep forgetting to buy stock in henna!

I quickly arrived at my plain hotel and was pleased my arrangements for an early morning check-in had been honored. The man at the reception desk (it turns out it's a family business) motioned for the smallest adult human being I've ever seen to take me to my room. I'm still not totally sure of my guide's gender; androgynous comes to mind. S/he didn't speak or carry my luggage. I followed behind to the lift. Although my room number was 124, we stopped on the fifth floor.

We took a right and a sharp left into a hallway as big as a minute. It was barely wide enough for me and my luggage to pass through. The lock on my door was at my knee level. S/he opened the door and I entered. With no pretext of showing me how to work the shower or heater, s/he just nodded with a greedy awareness as I reached into my pocket to give her/him some money.

The lira is currently worth 2.5 U.S. dollars. This took some getting used to since the Egyptian pound is now 4.55 to one U.S. dollar. The room was like a cell with a bathroom fashioned out of a closet that still retained a sliding plywood door. The accommodations were more like those of a prison or a religious order than a hotel. I fully expected Mother Superior to bang harshly on my door, hand me a bucket and brush, and then demand that I clean the stone floors before mass and a breakfast of bread and water.

The saving grace was a view of the harbor from the single, leaking window in my room. It was magnificent. I could see an ancient fort and many cliffs. Sunlight streamed from a holy-card sky decorated with fingers of light that joined heaven and earth.

Unfortunately, it was freezing outside! Even with four layers of clothing, I was chilled to the bone by the wind and dampness.

There are only two flights per week from Cairo to Malta so I arrived the day before dear Mary, my friend from Maryland. Mary worked for my ex-husband. We became fast friends. She's an amazingly talented woman, an incredible cook, and an expert in real estate settlements. She had my power of attorney to handle the sale and settlement of my building. As kind as she is, she's equally strong in her "no nonsense, don't mess with me" attitude. She's an animal lover who took care of my dog Molly when I traveled. She's also the most generous, thoughtful person I've ever known.

Normally, when she travels she takes only a carry-on, but this trip she checked her baggage. As a surprise, friends from my Monday night spiritual group had gotten together and prepared a love package of gifts, cards, and letters. Mary graciously agreed to bring the contents to Malta along with the odds and ends from the shopping list I had given her. She carried my things in her carry-on! Her luggage was lost for twenty-four hours. For some reason, any time she travels, baggage handlers target Mary. On her return trip her luggage was lost, too. Customs doesn't like her either; they must think that she fits the profile of a smuggler or terrorist. They search her bags so thoroughly they take the lining of her suitcase apart, even her ball-point pens! I wonder what they thought of the Barbie bike horn my friends sent me.

I ate breakfast in the hotel dining room. A group of men from Jordan were awaiting the arrival of a ship. It was fun to eavesdrop on their Arabic conversation. I met several guests who were either there as tourists or came to Malta to escape the cold London winter. Malta was freezing. With the exception of the Arctic, I can't imagine that Europe could be much worse.

Traveling alone has its downside, but the benefit is that I've been forced to reach out to strangers. As a result, I've met some interesting people from every corner of the world. I immediately hooked up with an Iranian eye surgeon who lives in London. We had some fascinating conversations about the differences between the East and West. She was about my age, but very much into the overdone look often favored by Middle Eastern women when they travel or live abroad: skin-tight clothing, low-cut tops assisted by up-and-at-you bras, high heels, long, henna-dyed hair, and theatrical makeup. Next to her I looked like Mary Poppins.

Breakfast, which came with the room, was interesting. Instant coffee disguised as the real thing, fake orange juice, incredibly delicious, heavily crusted peasant bread, a local cheese that was both strong and delicate, and slices of delectable salami. The rest of the week they served sliced ham. It was good, but by the end of the week since so many Muslims were staying in the hotel and didn't eat it, it began to turn a pale shade of green. After Mary arrived, we thought of emptying the platter and taking it outside to give to the cats so we wouldn't have to see it again. Our plans must have gotten back to the kitchen. The next morning it was gone.

Mary has trouble with her knees and hips so we hired John to take us around. This was a wise choice. He was efficient and saved her many steps. He also developed a crush on her.

We spent one day at a "craft village" and saw cathedrals, ancient ruins, and several museums. We didn't try to do everything, but focused on what we absolutely wanted to see. The museums were bland, but the magnificent cathedrals and the ancient sites of rock formations (advertised as predating the pyramids) that I imagine are similar to Stonehenge, were filled with miraculous energy I lapped up.

Most days we enjoyed a long lunch in a local restaurant. The food was good. We gorged on lots of pasta and beautiful pastries. I usually ate more in one meal than I do in an entire day at home. I tried the "native" dishes of stuffed green peppers and also rabbit stew . . . mediocre.

The Maltese language is an interesting one. Since Malta is located in a strategic position between Europe and Africa, like Egypt, it's been occupied by most of the world. The Arabic influence is still prevalent in their language, so is Greek and Italian. English is the second official language of the island.

It's a Catholic country dedicated to the apostle St. Paul who landed there and healed many. The Virgin Mary is everywhere. Throughout the cities and villages small shrines can be seen carved in rock walls dedicated to her. Church bells chime on the hour.

After living in a Muslim country, I found it interesting to be in one that's super Catholic. Non-Catholics in Malta must feel as left out of society as Copts do in Egypt and Muslims and Christians in Israel.

Over and over I wondered if God likes so many opulent churches and cathedrals that dot every village as mosques do each street corner in Egypt. I wonder if, throughout history, he wouldn't have preferred that we use our resources to build homes for the poor and homeless in honor of him rather than filling places of worship with gold and silver.

Tourism, then agriculture, are Malta's major industries. As with the rest of the world, their economy is suffering from the lack of tourists brought about by 9/11 and, as in Egypt, taxi drivers try to rip you off.

We spent part of each day sightseeing. On our last day, Mary stayed in to prepare for her trip home. I took the ferry to Gozo, a neighboring island. My excursion was uneventful. I saw a few caves and more ancient stone sights I suspect were used for initiations similar to those performed at the Great Pyramid in Giza. We had wanted to take a boat to Sicily for a day, but our hosts argued against it. He told us that the weather is too unpredictable during the winter and we could be stuck there. As it turns out, the day we had planned to go, there were squalls near Sicily and we couldn't have gotten back. They had snow! Since becoming adjusted to a desert climate, "snow" has become a four-letter word.

Located literally around the corner from Molly and Tim's, I live on the seventh floor of a high-rise. My apartment has two huge bedrooms, two baths, a modern kitchen, and a living room/dining room combination.

Although the building is quite new, the white ceramic floors with a raised design in the living areas have been badly trashed by the former tenant's ground-in dirt as well as leftover construction debris. They weren't cleaned to my standards before I moved in. I've discovered that really hot water, gallons of ammonia and industrial-strength cleaner applied with a brush will remove most of it. I'm doing a section at a time and working really hard at not allowing the balance of the mess to drive me nuts.

I have two balconies. One is large enough for four people to sit on; the other is tiny, designed for hanging laundry.

I haven't met my landlady yet. She's supposed to come tomorrow to meet me and to discuss the list of things that need to be repaired: the broken glass top on the dining room table, phone outlets that don't work, a toilet seat that's strategically cracked, a running toilet, and doors that lock and can't be opened. She also needs to provide a desk and patio furniture. I was smart enough to put these additions in my lease. I really don't want to continue to use the dining room table as my desk. There is a nice, small built-in one that's part of an armoire in the guest room, but the phone outlet there doesn't work, I'd be facing away from the sunshine, and there's no place to put my printer. I've rearranged the living room to create an area for the television and my desk, and a separate area for entertaining.

My biggest challenge is to keep the cats from destroying the decent furniture. Hooray, it's blue—not brown or sepia-colored.

I bought a scratching pad but they won't use it! I'm thinking of hiding the kittens in Mo's car during her visit.

If I were she, I wouldn't be pleased to see them, though I will tell her they'll be gone as soon as they're weaned.

With the exception of my office space, I'm settled in. I'm delighted to be back home in Cairo. Molly suggested we take a belly dancing class. I'm thinking about this. Who knows, perhaps it will offer the opportunity for a second career. When I told Mo, he couldn't stop laughing. Ha! Wait until he sees the pile of money that comes my way!

*Some people eat a date
and others throw its stones.*

~ Egyptian Proverb

Talk without thinking is like hunting without aiming.

~ Egyptian Proverb

Chapter 34

December 2001

People here are really clever. Yesterday I saw a guy riding a bike. It had a huge basket mounted over the front
tire. It used to be a desk drawer. I could use one for my
bike. He was going by too quickly for me to see how he
attached it.

I awakened this morning with a new revelation about a
part of myself that needs a whole lot of work—my attitude.
It wasn't a very nice reflection, but I've learned to welcome
each one that comes my way, for if I don't see what's looking back at me in the mirror, I can't change it. I'm also of
the opinion that in recognizing what needs to be changed,
50 percent of the work is already completed.

I got out of bed feeling cranky. Chakra talks a lot! She's
gotten into the habit of doing so when I'm deep in sleep.
She does this high-pitched whine thing to let me know
when something isn't right: her litter box isn't pristine
clean, she wants food, or a kitten has escaped and is
trapped in the bathtub. I'm ready to kill her. I lock her and
company in the guest bath at night, but she's figured out
how to open the door by jumping onto the washing
machine and then hitting the door handle with her paw.

I was grumbling about how arrogant she is to think that
my life revolves completely around her needs when I realized that cats are like that, but alas, so are people.

Her attitude got me thinking about how often I expect
the world to revolve around me, how easily I fall into thinking that just because I'm an American things should be

done the way I'm used to and how snotty I become when they're done the Egyptian way. "Hello, Jeanne. You are living in Egypt. If you want things done the American way, go back to America!"

Mo and I had a rather tepid discussion about customs officials. I was telling him about the latest problem I had at the airport when coming home from Malta. He was quiet, but I could tell he was a bit miffed that my nose was out of joint about being quizzed about my marital status, etc. Mo is a lot like my beloved friends Philip Smith and Fran and Paul Byers. They know me so well. They understand that when my brain is attached to the rear end of a horse, the best way for me to see the truth is to gently slide it under the door rather than delivering it on a videotape accompanied by a life-sized viewing screen. Eventually I'll get it.

You can say a lot about the inefficiency of the Egyptian government when it comes to providing services you *want*, yet they're first-class in tracking tourists and expats. They know everything about you: where you live, what you do, where you've been, and they're really good at confirming the information to make sure you're who you say you are. They track your bank business. They also tap your phones and sometimes make it impossible to make or receive international calls. I know this because a friend works with the Egyptian phone company. Based upon the number of clicks he heard on his home phone, he decided to "drop" some misinformation during a conversation. Sure enough, within a short time the misinformation came back to him. The big joke amongst expats is that when a call is disconnected in midconversation, the guy monitoring it had to go to the bathroom or out to pray. Before you start getting puffed up, you should know that our government and possibly one of our allies also closely scrutinize us. When you take a cab from the airport, you have to stop at a booth and provide your name and the address where the taxi is taking you. It doesn't matter that you've already given this information verbally and in writing in customs. Egypt doesn't tolerate terrorism; it has set up a system of checks and balances to prevent it. It works well. They may be "third-world developmentally," but I don't think what happened to us on 9/11 could happen here.

So, Mo listened to me rant and rave. Then he shared his experience with U.S. immigration and customs when he came to the U.S. to visit me last winter. He was flying through Holland. Before he could get on his connecting flight to the U.S., he had a private "interview" with a U.S. customs official. He had a valid visa and had already been interviewed at the U.S. Embassy and provided all the information they requested, including copies of his bank statements before his visa was issued!

Apparently the last "interview" took on new meaning. What he found particularly disturbing was when the official gave him a hard time because his signature doesn't match the one on his passport. There's a simple explanation for this, one the customs official should have known. In Egypt, your passport isn't signed by you, but by the person who issues it. This may not make sense to us, but that's how things are done. Every question he was asked made him feel like a fugitive from a terrorist camp or that he's not "good" enough to visit our great country. Mind you, this was before 9/11. On top of this, because his name is so common, he goes through the same interview process with Egyptian customs when he comes home. At no time could he say, "It's none of your business."

I bought contact lenses the other day. The doctor who sold them to me told me he has a visa to the U.S. that's valid for five years. He thinks he probably won't be able to use it. Think about this. He's been through the process, he's been cleared and checked out by our government, but now may not be able to use it. If this happened to me I'd really be outraged. Yet doesn't Egypt have the same right to protect itself as we do?

Egypt monitors my whereabouts. Before 9/11, did anyone know where a visitor to the U.S. went after they left the airport? Would Mo have as easily obtained a one-year resident visa to the U.S. as I did here? I doubt it.

Although I know my attitude isn't half as bad as many of the expats I've met who think Egypt should create a microcosm of their homeland to make their lives easier, I now see that I too fall into the "But I'm an American used to 'freedom' so welcome me to your country, protect me, but don't ask me any questions I think can be categorized as intrusive." Damn mirror! It's time to get out the Windex.

I've read two books you might find as enlightening as I did, *Gideon's Spies: The Secret History of the Mossad*, by Gordon Thomas. Although it deals with the Mossad in-depth, it also talks a lot about intelligence networks around the world and the dirty little games they play. Scary stuff, but reality often is. The other, *The Gold of Exodus*, by Howard Blum, tells the story of what may be the real location of Mount Sinai and what two treasure hunters went through with the Saudi government and the Mossad to prove it.

Mo took me to another orphanage. It's very dear to him. Until it can be repaired, major structural damage that threatens to collapse its largest building has forced the founder/director to farm the children out to homes in the village. Mo didn't have the opportunity to show me the building that also houses a clinic, classrooms, and a computer learning center. From what he's told me, the staff is doing an amazing job training the children for a career.

On the way home we stopped to buy kitty litter. Since it's imported, the cost is astronomical. This afternoon, as I was preparing a batch of homemade cat food, I realized that my cats are fed better than a lot of the children in the world. I spend more on litter in one week than some families do on food!

I believe the cats have been brought to me for a reason: to love, to nurture, and to care for. I truly believe God loves all living things, no matter how many legs they have. Yet a part of me feels really terrible I'm not feeding a family, too. I wonder what would happen if every pet owner came to the same conclusion and did something about it: fed, housed and loved an abandoned, homeless, hungry human being.

The founder of the orphanage is only one man, yet each day he makes life richer and happier for a group of homeless kids and the people who live in the village that surrounds his institution. This is something to ponder as the New Year begins and the old one becomes a memory. May every New Year bring to each of you joy, peace, love, a zillion daily acts of kindness, and reasons to laugh from your heart until your stomach hurts.

Mine began with a lovely party hosted by friends of Tim

and Molly. Tim and Molly gave me a gorgeous lavender shell and matching beaded top for Christmas so I got gussied up. I ended up talking to two oil guys. We had a great conversation about Egypt, her future and past. I stayed until midnight, but was home and asleep before one.

If everything that happens to us is a "choice," I must have been having some masochistic moments. There is no other possible explanation for Om, Chakra, and her babies coming into my life!

I feel like the cleaning lady hired by my crew of cats to take care of them. Many times each day I scoop out the litter box. With the kittens now using it, it's an active place. Tonight, to take a break from writing, I decided to change the litter. As soon as I put the box back on the floor, they literally lined up to use it! I was not pleased. "For heaven's sake couldn't you let it stay clean until I leave the room?" I hissed! At least they appear not to have the need to go through the human stool-smearing stage. Actually, I realize I should be grateful. It's a lot easier to clean and empty one box rather than the whole apartment, but if Chakra had her way, she'd ask for separate accommodations. Maybe that's what all her talk is about. Thankfully, she and the rest of the herd understand the spray bottle. I'm using it to deter their undesirable behavior. Thus far I've only succeeded in making the kittens afraid of me. Om and Chakra already know I'm harmless. Since they've discovered that there's a world beyond the bathroom, I use the spray bottle to get the kittens to stop scratching the furniture, to leave me alone when it's time for me to eat, and to keep Om from walking across the keyboard of my computer. She's able to do things with a single leap that I didn't think possible!

Last week I spent most of one day and part of another with my landlady Salwa and her twelve-year-old daughter, Ranya. She's a great kid. Her English is so good you'd think she was American. She even says, "Oh my God!" in that teenage, Valley girl way.

On my second visit with them I went to their apartment for lunch where I met her brother, sister, and brother-in-law. Her sister, Fifi, is a marvelous cook. She prepared roasted chicken, potatoes, pasta fried with yellow raisins and *molukhaya* (an Egyptian green that's similar to kale). It's chopped fine, laced with garlic and served as soup. Molly thinks it's nasty. Even with Fifi's skill as a cook, I thought it was a little too bland.

Salwa has been showering me with presents. I'm a bit embarrassed. She keeps telling me "how happy I am with you." Things didn't start off very well. I'll have to write about it in the next chapter. She's really trying to make amends and is a sweet, kind person.

On our first outing we went we went to the fancy country club in Zamalek she belongs to, had lunch, walked around, and met a fascinating elderly Egyptian gentleman who is an encyclopedia of Egyptian history and a former Petroleum Minister of Egypt. We're invited to his home for "lunch" tomorrow.

He agrees with me, Egypt is ready to explode. Every week the dollar exchange rate rises, the pound becomes weaker. In March it was worth 3.65 to the U.S. dollars. Today it's almost 5 to 1! Yes, it's great for me, but certainly not for Egyptians who find that they have even less buying power on declining income. The former minister believes that a revolution is in the offing. As traumatic as it will be to the people of Egypt, perhaps this is the only way for the pendulum to swing more to center before those, who would like Egypt to become like the rest of the Middle East, have the opportunity to take control. My only fear is that history will repeat itself and they'll end up with an even stricter fundamentalist government.

My other Egyptian friends believe there will be no revolution, that the strength of the Egyptian people will enable them to weather the storm. I think they're being optimistic.

I'm just coming out from under some sort of flu/cold thing. I haven't slept this much in a year. Thankfully, my friend and physician, Marie, sent me off with heavy-duty antibiotics that I broke down and took.

After being gone for over two months, darling Camilla and Yosef have arrived back in Cairo! Molly is the ringmaster of her own circus now that her mother-in-law, Mary and youngest daughter Jan have arrived for a visit.

Daughter Liz leaves next week, Jan in a few days. Mary will be here until March.

I spent a good part of the day directing my own four-ring circus. Four workmen showed up to finish the stuff that's needed to be fixed: the toilet seat that plays musical chairs and pinches when you sit on it, the toilet that runs, the bathroom sinks whose stoppers don't open, the phone jacks that don't work, the lights that are burned out and too high to reach, and the doors that lock themselves. They even cleaned the filters on my heater/air conditioners. They got everything done except the phone jacks. They have to come back Wednesday morning to finish the job. It turns out that the outlets in both bedrooms were never wired.

The cats were in an uproar over the commotion. I finally rounded them all up and put them in the bathroom that's fixed, but only after smacking my bad knee on the floor while trying to retrieve a kitten from under the refrigerator. In any case, the workmen, recommended by Molly, were great. They actually cleaned up after themselves! Amazing!

Make the bread maker do his job even if he eats half the bread.

~ Egyptian Proverb

265

There is no sweet time
without going through hell.

~ Egyptian Proverb

Chapter 35

January 2002

Belly dancing is awesome! I wiggled, thrust, bumped, slid, shook, and soared. The next morning I was unable to walk upright! Where did the provocative woman in the imaginary veil go? I want her back!

Over the years, I've discovered that nothing I've learned is useless; somehow, someday it will come in handy, or serve as a foundation to be built upon. This is true of belly dancing. The steps are a lot like jazz or tap, but you do them barefooted. Instead of keeping your hips silent and generating happy feet, you keep your feet quiet and let your hips and pelvis rip! The reason you wear so few clothes is a simple one. It's the only way to prevent heat stroke from the exertion! For the first time, I'm actually grateful for the torture I experienced when practicing dance routines for a community theater production. I've been vindicated! I made a terrible "dancing skeleton." However, as a result of what I learned in each humiliating performance, there really is hope that my body can actually move in harmony with itself. I think my knee brace could be used as a marketing tool: "Come see the world's oldest belly dancer with a decorated knee!" I wonder if I could have a cover made for the brace. It would be decorated with beads. Could I get them to go in the opposite direction from my hips? Hum!

I promised to tell you about the initial problem my landlady Salwa and I had after I signed the lease. When I visited El Maadi in early December to look for a flat, I had the opportunity to see some places I wouldn't want anyone but the owner to live in.

The night I arrived, my produce guy took me to see his friend, a Realtor (of sorts). He showed me one place. It's the one I ended up renting, but before I would do so, I wanted to look at a few more that Mo and other friends had arranged for me to see.

I didn't like the "agent." While we were in Salwa's apartment, he called a man he said was the owner. He wasn't. He told him I was going to take the apartment when in fact I'd said no such thing. Turns out he also lied about what the rent "had" been.

I looked all day Friday with another Realtor, a "friend" of my friend Ali. The last place he showed me was Salwa's apartment, which I had seen with the first agent. I tried to explain to him that I'd already seen it with another agent and liked it. He doesn't speak any English, so he had his "boss" come along. "No problem!" I've learned that when an Egyptian says this it's like a curse! Once uttered, only compound problems will follow!

On Saturday, after dragging Mo around for six hours, we called the Friday night agent and asked him to show us the apartment again. Mo agreed that it was a great, secure apartment at an incredible rent, and best of all close to Camilla and Molly.

The owner was not available to meet us, but her friend, the former Egyptian ambassador, agreed to meet us at his store after iftar to sign a lease.

When we sat down over tea for the negotiation "ceremony," I told Maher that I had seen the apartment with two agents and wanted to make sure I was not being unethical by renting it through the second agent. "What is the custom here?" I asked. He called Salwa, who agreed that the agent who wrote the lease was the one who deserved the commission. I still didn't feel comfortable and decided that when I moved back to El Maadi I would stop by the Thursday night real estate agent's office and give him some money. Subsequent events changed my mind. He can eat dirt!

We wrote the lease. I left Sunday afternoon to return to Alex, happy, but exhausted. While in El Maadi I picked up some more USAID writing assignments. I was going to have a very busy two weeks before moving back to Cairo.

Sunday evening, my new landlord Salwa called me in Alex. She was frantic. She told me that she couldn't rent the apartment to me because she had just learned that the building had structural damage. I thought this odd. She offered to refund my money and apologized profusely. Something didn't feel right. I told her I'd get back to her.

I called Mo. "She's lying," he said. "She probably found someone who's willing to pay more. Let me call the ambassador." A few moments later, my mobile rang.

"The ambassador says it's 'bullshit.' He says you should threaten her, tell her if she doesn't rent you the apartment you will go to the police, then sue her and threaten to involve him! If she won't rent you the apartment it will cost her 10,000 LE!" These are *big* threats. Egyptians are afraid of the police, the courts, and of dragging someone who's important into the fray. Ten thousand LE is also a lot of money.

Mo then called Salwa and told her how "important" I am; basically that I would have her blackballed by the American Embassy, then sue her. "I was a little bit hard with her," he told me in his understated gentle way. I knew that he'd torn her up one side and down the other. She now knew that I was not without protection.

My mobile rang again. This time it was Salwa's "cousin." Things smelled so bad I'd begun to look for a gas mask to protect me. "We are so sorry," he gushed. "Please, you have to help us."

"Why?" I asked incredulously.

"We are in big trouble," he replied.

I lost it in my head, but kept my voice even but as cold as a bare bottom sitting on a snowdrift in Siberia. "Look. I think you and your cousin are not telling me the truth. Perhaps if we go back to the beginning and you tell me what's really going on we can work things out. I am kind, but I am also smart. Don't mess with me!"

"Okay," he said. "My cousin signed another lease Thursday night. You signed a lease Saturday night. She didn't understand what she was doing. She has to cancel your lease or she will be in terrible trouble. Please help us!"

Thoughts of the Thursday night real estate agent flashed through my head. I sensed his greedy hand and suspected that Salwa thought she had signed two leases, both with me (the ambassador signed my lease on her behalf and she "thought" the other real estate agent had signed another in her name). In the U.S. this wouldn't have held water. It's different here.

The cousin didn't know who the "first" lessee was. He offered to find me another place. He even promised to come to Maamora to bring me to El Maadi to look for a flat. He was begging! I was tired and distrustful. I didn't have time to deal with finding another place, but I also didn't want to live where I wasn't welcome. What the cousin didn't tell me, as I later learned, is that he wasn't a cousin but another person who wanted the flat!

In exasperation I said, "I'm going to bed. I have no desire to help your cousin. She has caused a big problem for me. I do not have time to look for another flat. I have a valid lease and expect her to honor it. If she doesn't, there are two other options: She can pay me 10,000 LE for my trouble (about $2,000.00 U.S.), or she can go to court with me to solve the problem. I will report this to the police and the American Embassy. Let me know tomorrow what her choice is. Do not call me again tonight."

I was really upset, but put it aside. "Okay God. Please handle this. It's out of my hands," I said and actually went to sleep and slept soundly.

The next morning Salwa called. I almost hung up on her, but I'm glad I didn't because the "whole" truth came out and I would have lost a wonderful friend.

It turns out that the Thursday night agent, having discovered that she had rented the flat, told Salwa that he'd signed a lease with me on Thursday night. When he learned that it was rented on Saturday night, he concocted the story about the building being in terrible condition. Because she believed him, this sent Salwa into a tailspin. Drama takes on new meaning! She spoke with government engineers who told her the real estate agent was crazy. "It's a new building!" they exclaimed. Salwa and her "cousin" went to the Thursday night agent's office to "see" the lease he said he had. Of course there wasn't one. Salwa was calling to apologize. "The flat is yours. Please, put what happened behind you."

"I'm happy to do that," I agreed sincerely. "But in the future, you'll find that if you tell me the truth upfront I'll be easy to work with. A problem can't be solved when both sides don't know the truth."

So, since I moved in, Salwa has gone out of her way to welcome me and to make my life easier. She has taken me to her club, introduced me to some fascinating people, had me to dinner at her home, and took me out to lunch today. She's showered me with gifts and incredible kindness. I feel a little bit uncomfortable with all the attention and generosity. Her kindness is more than enough.

Once again, I need to take things at "face value" and to become more open to receiving, not just giving. I read somewhere that those who only like to give do so because they're in control. Yep. Sounds like my bell's ringing the truth! Her daughter Ranya told me that her mom said I "add color to their lives." I think this is a compliment.

Ranya loves anything American and asks many questions about the meaning of different words. One day she took me aside to ask a question. She was squirming in her seat. I thought she was going to ask about sex; she did but not in the context I thought she would. She wanted to know what "hard-core" means. She sees the word a lot on the Internet! How does anyone handle letting his or her child use the Internet these days? Even with parental controls in place, friends tell me that clever pornographers can get around them.

It constantly amazes me that even though we approach things differently, our experiences and attitudes aren't really all that dissimilar, like our opinion of other drivers when weather conditions are difficult. In the U.S. everyone laments that no one else knows how to drive in the snow. Here, they say the same thing about driving in the rain! The ambassador is supposed to buy me a desk, but he won't go anywhere by car in the rain. The traffic is terrible (okay, worse than the normal terrible). It rained yesterday and today, mostly at night, so I haven't seen my desk yet!

I've set up a temporary office. Instead of a desk, I'm using the small plastic café table Salwa bought for my balcony. I hope that doing this will manifest a desk more quickly. The problem is, not only is the table unstable and half the size I requested, the height is wrong. It's so low that after a few hours working at my computer, my back hurts. Combined with my bout with the flu, I've fallen behind on everything.

I finished another E-magazine article for the USAID group. Thankfully, my editor has been happy with the pieces I've written for her. She's a no-nonsense kind of chick so I'm doubly pleased. This week I'm going to finish a project for Rick's group, then go back to editing one of my manuscripts.

I taught Ranya how to make pancakes. Because they're so American, she's thrilled! I was surprised to discover that her mom's kitchen lacks what I would consider basic equipment: measuring cups and spoons and a bowl to mix the batter in. From what I've seen, large baking pans and Dutch ovens in a few sizes are considered basic equipment. None of my flats have come equipped with any baking pans. The few I do have are ones I've purchased. It's a good excuse not to bake, though sometimes I fear I'll lose the knack for making bread, cookies, pies, and cakes. Since the ovens here are "sort of" calibrated on centigrade, without a Western oven thermometer, it makes baking even more of a challenge. My stepmom sent me back with one and it's been a real blessing! Ranya and I were going to make brownies from a mix her mom bought, but we could not do it at her house without the measuring cups, a baking pan, and oven thermometer so I took the mix home and made them here. Based upon my new oven thermometer, I think, in this oven, 350°F is about 240°C.

I've found a great Egyptian dentist. He's going to do some major reconstruction at a price that's better than the U.S., but not as low as I would have hoped. No need for knicker twisting; he practices Western hygienic standards.

Dr. R. is probably in his late thirties. He works from a wheelchair. I haven't asked him, but was told by an acquaintance that he became paralyzed in an accident. He's quite a dynamo. His sunlit smile and matter-of-fact acceptance of his disability puts one immediately at ease. Actually, it's nice to recline in his exam chair and communicate with him at eye level. His wheelchair isn't motorized and he doesn't have an overly developed upper body, yet he moves like greased lightening.

One of the most disconcerting practices of some devout Muslims is the refusal to shake hands. I was reminded of this when I heard construction commotion outside my door. Curiosity got the best of me so I went to see what was going on.

My neighbors, whom I'd never met (there are only two apartments on each floor), were installing a light over their door. This is good. Hallway lights in apartment buildings are on short timers—fifteen to thirty seconds. This saves electricity, but it's a real pain in the behind when your arms are full and you're trying to put your key in the door when it goes out. I could leave my light on all the time, but I'm too cheap. I've been looking for a motion detector. That could solve the dilemma, at least for me. Anyway, he introduced himself and his wife (she didn't bother to turn around until he gently, but forcibly, turned her). I extended my right hand to him. He grasped my arm just above my wrist. I felt my hackles going into gear, and then swallowed hard. I believe the practice stems from not wanting to have physical contact with a woman other than his wife, but also touching someone ungodly and unclean could "soil" him before praying! Ha. He thinks my hand is dirty! He has no idea where my forearm has been!

One of the products I miss most is ammonia. In the U.S., I bought it by the gallon. Mixed with vinegar and a little soap it makes a really good cleaner. You can't find it in the supermarket, but they sell a concentrate in, of all places, the pharmacy. It comes in a glass jar the size of an individual serving of juice. I don't know what medicinal use it has other than to revive someone who's fainted. Until recently, you couldn't buy baking soda in the grocery store either! You bought a little paper bag of bicarbonate of soda at the pharmacy. It's expensive.

I've finished cleaning about 85 percent of the ceramic floors in my living area. The areas I've finished look great! I really don't mind cleaning. To me it's one of the few things I can do that provides instant gratification.

When I was working full-time in D.C., I had a housekeeper who came once a week. Years later I was distressed to discover that when she cleaned for a mutual friend, she made a point of telling her how often my husband and I had, ah, "mingled" the previous week. Apparently she could read sheets like some people read tea leaves! This has only reinforced my desire to not have a housekeeper here.

My bawaabs know who comes to see me; taxi drivers know where my friends live; the delivery boy knows how many cats I have and what I eat and drink; the government knows how much cash I need each month and who I talk to on the phone. Enough is enough! When I stopped to say hello to my first bawaab, Mohamed, he already knew where I lived and about the cats. By the way, unfortunately, he never received the letter I mailed him from the U.S.

My landlady picked me up to go buy a desk. The ambassador is sick, so she was kind enough to push the process along. It's really an oblong folding table, but it's stable and the correct height when matched with a dining room chair. She also bought me a huge handmade basket to hide my files in. Not fancy, but it does the trick. She was thrilled that the table cost only 56 LE. When I move, she'll be able to use it in her home when she needs an extra table.

Wash your face to feel better;
clean your house to free your mind.

~ Egyptian Proverb

Chapter 36

February 2002

I've come to believe that each of us comes into the world accompanied by our own symbolic litter box. As we grow, it does too. How much waste it contains at any given time is entirely up to us.

Our box is filled with good as well as nasty stuff. It just depends upon how we choose to view it. For example, each time we overcome a life lesson, the petals of pain, anguish and history associated with the lesson are deposited in our box. Although they are lighter and no longer reek, they still take up space and need to be removed. And, when we hold onto our anger, keep repeating the same mistakes or allow others to dump their stuff into our box it causes it to overflow with their weight and terrible odor.

Our litter box is comparable to the Hermetic principle of polarity contained in *The Kybalion: Hermetic Philosophy*, by Three Intiates, where there is light there is darkness; where there is darkness there is light; where there is pain there is joy; where there is a lesson learned there is a lesson unlearned. The poop of our lives may not look or smell the same, but eventually it all needs to be disposed of.

Until the moment of our soul's final release, the same box stays with us. Over our lifetime it needs to be emptied, cleaned and then refilled many, many times.

It's easy, actually a joy, to clean our litter box when it contains the debris from lessons learned. But when it's filled with our unwillingness to question why we're continuously surrounded by waste and allow everyone around us to fill our box, it becomes too heavy to lift, to empty and to clean. It holds us by the ankles. It makes it impossible for us to move forward.

However, when we finally surrender and release ourselves from the layers of manure that hold us back from being the best we can be, our overflowing box becomes as weightless as a strand of hair. I think this is the "removing the clothespin from our nose" stage of life.

The bad news is, the more we face things, the quicker our box refills; the good news is, each lesson learned instantly delivers a fresh bag of litter and the tools we need to deal with the next round of waste.

One of the lessons I've been dissecting in my life is the issue of staying balanced no matter what others try to dump in my litter box. The cats have been helping me to see how easily I still fall into the trap of allowing the negative behavior of another to distract and unhinge me.

Lately, dung seems to drop from the trees I walk beneath; even the sky is suffering from the trots. But no one forced me to allow it to come home with me and land in my box; I chose to let it enter my sacred space of self-love and peace.

This insight has felt both overwhelming and sweetly liberating. While I can't control what someone wants to drop in my box, I can refuse to let anyone else use it. I can put a lid on it.

There's a group of women here who are like kittens being directed by a "mother" who has teeth as deadly as a serpent's fangs. Their behavior is similar to that of a high school clique, cubed.

Because her kittens are more vulnerable than she is, the mother uses them to eliminate anyone who refuses to join her litter. To protect themselves from becoming one of her victims, as soon as they see their mother's claws and fangs begin to extend, to protect themselves from being attacked, they do the dirty work for her.

What her kittens don't see is that their mother feels just as insecure as they do. She puts out her claws to keep the world from finding out that she's afraid of not being liked and appreciated. If she can get them to scratch someone who makes her feel inadequate, she can blame them if things get out of hand and she won't have to face her own fears. It makes her feel more powerful, but the opposite is true. In hurting another, she only brings, like a boomerang, more pain, more fear back to herself.

In the past, I've chosen to circumvent the negative behavior of this particular litter. I've done it by avoiding them. But if I (and every other human being) is here to show love, to teach love, to be loved, avoiding the claws won't change anything.

I found another scratching post for my cats. They're finally using it. Through positive reinforcement I've been teaching them that they can scratch all they want, but they have to do it in a way that isn't destructive.

What if I did the same thing with the human litter by allowing them to watch me use my post? Each time they try to extend their claws towards me or someone else, I can smile and show them how beautiful my post is. With love and a firm example, maybe they'll go out and buy their own! These women aren't bad. They just don't see that the only way to bring love and acceptance into their lives is to love and accept themselves. It all begins with their choosing to empty their own litter box. If those around them respond to their negative behavior by gently picking them up and putting them in front of their scratching posts, maybe they'll get it. My cats have. They can too.

$$\triangle \, \triangle \, \triangle$$

Speaking of litter, it's really great having someone available to carry my groceries. When my boys were still at home, I tried to time my arrival with our groceries when they were available to carry them. I don't know if they ever figured this out. Here, I either have them put into a cab and my bawaab brings them upstairs, or a guy on a bicycle delivers them right to my door and into my kitchen.

Today, since I was short on time and kitty litter, rather than going to Road 9, I walked down the street to the local Western-style market. Litter is heavy so I opted to have everything delivered. To my surprise, as I was walking home, voices called to me. I turned around and discovered two guys running toward me. One was carrying a large container of bleach and the huge bag of litter, the other the smaller bag of litter and an undersized metal basket filled with my other groceries.

We walked to my apartment. I led. They trailed single file behind me. Their bicycles are broken, or they don't have any. It was good they came with me because my building isn't numbered. This makes it difficult to tell people how to find me. Salwa said she'd talk to the management company about this. Apparently there was a number, but it blew off or someone took it, or there never was one and to save face the bawaab said there had been one. You never know what the real truth is, not that it really matters. I don't know what my flat number is either. No one seems to be able to tell me, but since I'm the only single Western woman in the building, the bawaabs know where I live.

My friend Karen from Alex is in town for job interviews. She doesn't plan to move here but hopes she can work for the Alex branch of one of the organizations. She had an appointment with UNICEF. She arrived on time and discovered that "It is impossible for you to be interviewed today." The woman she was supposed to meet with wasn't there. Apparently she had an emergency, but if Karen comes back this afternoon someone may see her. I hope she calls first. The person she spoke with may have been doing the polite Egyptian thing to save face and not admit that she messed up. Anyway, because of this problem we may not get together after all. She said that our friend Carla had a fabulous party at her new flat complete with a disco and belly dancer! It lasted until 3:00 a.m. Knowing what a wonderful hostess Carla is, I'm sure it was lovely! How come all the fun stuff happens after I leave town?

A reader asked how I deal with the issue of confidentiality when sharing stories with you. Great question!

This is an ethical battle I imagine every writer has to face. Like an artist, a writer draws upon his or her life experiences to create word pictures. How can a fiction writer construct believable characters and plots without using bits and pieces of the people and experiences of his or her own life? I don't think it's possible.

When writing nonfiction, maintaining a high level of confidentiality is even more difficult. Yes, you can change names and locations to protect those who have given the incredible gift of opening their lives up to the whole world, but the actual events usually cannot be changed without losing the heartbeat of the story.

I Am Happier to Know You is about real people and situations specific to the culture of Egypt. What you read has been filtered through a fine sieve. If I didn't carefully pick and choose who and what I write about, I wouldn't have any friends here or there! I haven't always been as wise, but as I've grown and worked on loving myself, I've become more acutely aware of the depth of meaning behind the phrase, "The pen is mightier than the sword." Words, both written and spoken can be used to express love, to teach, and to heal. They can also be used to destroy or wound another so deeply they may never heal.

As I've grown, so has my code of personal and professional conduct. If someone asks me not to repeat something (personally or professionally), I don't. More often than not, the subject never comes up. If a close friend or family member is having a problem, they have a right to assume they won't read about it in my next chapter.

I've also come to believe that what is said in love and trust between family and friends shouldn't be repeated, even if the relationship ends. I expect the same in return. When someone is honoring me by sharing an intimate detail of their life, as soon as the conversation ends, I literally try and forget it. In this way, I can't accidentally divulge a confidence. Sometimes I screw up. But in general, I've forgotten far more than I've retained!

That said, like a psychologist, I've also trained myself to retain the insights gained from watching my own behavior and that of others. This isn't done as a judgment, but as a way of observing and understanding the ways in which we cope with the debris of life.

The personal heart-wrenching stories I've told have been with the consent of the persons who shared them with me. Other real stories have been written in a way that won't divulge the source, or I've combined information I've gathered from many sources to use as background. In other cases, if someone's behavior is typical of the culture, if a conversation occurs in a situation where the person is speaking publicly, or if the circumstances could easily become part of the public record, I tell it just as it happened in what I hope is the fairest, most balanced way possible.

I'm not what I call a "slice and dice" journalist who looks for opportunities to hurt someone else. My goal is to teach and to heal, not to maim; yet I'll probably hurt someone. I'm human with the average judgment lapses and periods when I feel like the contents of a litter box. When I'm feeling terrible about myself, my judgment goes out the window. This is when I have to use an even finer sieve. It takes practice, perseverance and sometimes crazy glue to keep my fingers off the keyboard and my mouth shut!

Cultural differences and misperceptions cause major and minor annoyances, sometimes laughter. Sometimes they damage relationships between expats and Egyptians.

When an Egyptian dials the wrong telephone number, they refuse to believe it. A conversation with the misdialed party can go on for some time and be repeated so many times, you end up leaving your phone off the hook.

In most cases, if you buy something, you can't return it without a major battle. Sometimes you win. Other times you don't! If the merchant does take back your purchase because the product is defective, more than likely he'll put it right back on the shelf! I find this extremely annoying.

If the product isn't damaged and you've changed your mind about purchasing it, good luck! When I come across this practice in the U.S. (when they'll only give you a store credit), I don't shop in that establishment again.

Recently I had to return a flat scratching tray. The cats would not go near it. Fortunately, I saved the original bag. You definitely can't return anything without the original carton or bag. The lady at the pet store said she could not give me back my money without the consent of the shop owner. Unfortunately, she had no idea when he would be in. Of course, she could take my money if I bought something else! I didn't appreciate this logic.

I asked my grocery delivery guy to handle the return for me. His shop is right nearby. Even though he's young, being male, I knew he'd have a better chance at success than I would. He did, but only after a major argument with the owner who tried to say the tray was "dirty," etc. I gave him 25 percent of the refund. We were both happy!

One expat decided to order pizza for dinner. She called the local Pizza Hut and asked for home delivery. When she requested a large ham pizza, the voice on the other end replied coolly "Madame. We do not sell ham! It is against Islam." Whoops!

When an Egyptian baby is born, friends and relatives will stand over the child and coo in loving voices. If you don't understand Arabic and the culture, as you eavesdrop, you'd think, by the sweet tone of their voices that they're telling the baby how, "beautiful, healthy, and brilliant" it is. Not!

What they're cooing is that it's "ugly, stupid, and sickly." This is done to keep the "evil eye" away from the child! The belief is that if you say aloud how special the child is, it will attract jealousy and a curse from a childless woman or one whose child has problems. In fact, shortly after birth, to protect the child, the women of the family perform a whole evil eye ceremony. The evil eye superstition is not limited to any segment of Egyptian society. It's believed by most everyone, no matter how well educated and sophisticated.

It's kind of an extension of our "knock on wood." One day when I was visiting with an expat and the wife of a high-ranking diplomat, we were talking about which emergency we would go home for. I said something along the lines of: "If something happened to one of my children . . ." They visibly shuddered and looked at each other. In horror they frantically searched until they found wood to knock upon!

Misconceptions flow both ways. While an Egyptian female periodontal professional was cleaning my teeth, between disparaging comments about the number of meals she was excavating from beneath my gums, she shared details of her frustrating day.

Just before coming to work, she and her husband met with a Korean couple that wanted to lease the flat they had purchased as an investment. After protracted negotiations, during which the Asians asked for and received many concessions, they all sat down at the dining room table in the flat to write a lease. Just as it was about to be signed, prayer call sounded from the neighborhood mosque. The couple looked at each other, stood up, and said they'd changed their minds! The Egyptian couple was horrified and angry. In addition to feeling that they'd wasted their time, they assumed the couple hates Islam.

I tried to explain to her that noise from mosques is a big issue for expats who aren't accustomed to a loudspeaker blowing them out of bed before dawn. Since mosques have loudspeakers mounted on top, if you're close to one where they all work, the noise is appalling.

I heard one story about a friend from the U.S. visiting an expat. When she was awakened by the pre-dawn prayer call, she jumped out of bed, put on her robe, and fled outside. She thought the prayer call was a warning of a fire or other disaster!

As the tooth cleaner continued to torture me, she said that since the flat she's trying to lease is in New El Maadi where many middle-class Egyptians own property rather than Digla/El Maadi where more foreigners live, they couldn't find an American family to rent it. "I think all Americans live in Digla or El Maadi because their government tells them to. They also like to be together . . . but Koreans like New El Maadi. . . ."

Yes, some expats want to live only with other expats, but those with school-aged children want to live close by the American school in Digla and where its convenient to find taxis and walk to neighborhood shops. New Maadi is in the middle of nowhere. Location, location, location!

She's also asking $1,100 U.S. Granted, I got a great deal. But, I'm paying about four times less than what she's asking and the location of my flat is excellent. Perception is often not reality.

It seems to me that one of the few legal ways for an Egyptian to make a good living is as a landlord to a foreigner. Of course, with the world as unstable as it is, if there's an evacuation, the gravy train is going to dry up. Because things are unstable, I added a "diplomatic/out of my control" clause to my lease. Otherwise, if I have to leave, I will still owe rent.

In addition to not dressing respectfully, expats can be thoughtless in other ways about showing consideration for the culture. I was surprised by how many Western women in my belly dancing class don't shave their legs or under their arms. This must be shocking and insulting to the Egyptian women in the class who remove all their body hair.

Speaking of belly dancing, I think I have to retire. Even though I wear a knee brace, the exercise is causing a lot of pain and weakness to my injured knee. I'm not willing to risk another injury . . . sigh! I guess I need to start doing the physical therapy exercises again.

I've been a bit of a khroof about tipping. Karen explained to me that one is supposed to tip a small amount whenever someone provides a service you requested, and sometimes, even when you didn't. This includes the guy who wraps the flowers you've purchased or the man in the grocery store who packages your meat or slices your cheese. I used to worry about being taken advantage of, now I just give a little bit more. In this way I never have to worry about being unfair or cheap.

The exchange rate has gone up again. Several Egyptians told me they believe it won't stop before it hits eight to the dollar. Every extra pound I give can make the difference between a family having bread on the table or nothing. I used to pay the taxi driver the going rate, now I add to it. It's my way of trying to help, small as it may be.

I had lunch in Zamalek with Salwa and Ranya. She's having major car trouble. I encouraged her to stop at the gas station. They said they could fix it in fifteen minutes, but Egyptian minutes are longer than the ones I'm used to, and the mechanics here are not like those who serviced my car at my friend Gina's station on Capitol Hill, so I took a taxi home. El Maadi is a long way from Salwa's apartment in Dokki. I worried that her mechanic wouldn't do a good job, and feared we'd all end up on the side of the road.

Traffic wasn't too bad. The driver wasn't weaving in and out of traffic the way most usually do so my knuckles weren't white and my stomach was calm. Many empty wagons drawn by donkeys were heading home after a day at the market. The sun was beginning to set on the Nile. The air was mild. I didn't shiver once. I felt a breath of peacefulness enshroud me.

It's difficult to share the depth of my feelings for Egypt

and her people. It's kind of like trying to explain why you're in love with someone when your friends can only see that his pants are too short and his barber appears to have learned his trade on the Internet.

Coming here has been one of the greatest gifts of my life. Sometimes I think it will be impossible for me to leave; yet I know that no matter where I am, I will carry Egypt within my heart and soul. God, in his time, will lead me. This I know without a doubt. I hope your journey is as beautiful and rich as mine.

*A good Muslim will
leave what is not his.*

~ Prophet Mohammed

Chapter 37

February 2002

The average Egyptian is gentle and kind. Many are also exceptional B.S. artists who use flattery to manipulate— usually so they can make some extra money. In this economy, it's become even more prevalent. Whatever works will put food on the table and change in the pocket.

The problem is, when we first arrive, we expats like being fawned over. It feels really good to think that people like you for you! There's no hidden "power" or "how can they help my career" agenda, only a financial or sexual one.

I think it's part of the adjustment process. When you first arrive you don't have a sieve, but before long, one's delivered to your door. Out of necessity, it's a huge one. At first you overuse it, then you begin to shake it more selectively until you develop a balance.

My brother John, who has lived overseas, warned me about this. He told me that at first I'd love everything about Egypt, and then I'd begin to see things realistically and go to the other extreme. He cautioned me to wait it out; eventually I'd reach a balance. It was wonderful advice from a guy who is my baby brother, one of my best friends, and a consistently loving supporter.

By Western standards, Egyptians are also extremely expressive and emotional. When they're really upset, they'll scream, keen, argue, and cry until their emotional systems have been purged. Men feel no shame in allowing tears of rage or total joy to slide down their cheeks. The people have a delectably subtle sense of humor. Their language shows a mastery of both under and overstatement.

Sometimes they think it best to soften how they feel. The euphemisms they use reflect this. When someone is too embarrassed to ask for something, such as money that is owed to them, they'll say, "I was a little bit shy." If they find themselves in a difficult situation they may explain, "I was a little bit afraid." When they're angry with a friend or acquaintance, they may later say, "I was a little bit angry." When something terrible happens, such as the World Trade Center and Pentagon attacks, they refer to the incident as an *accident*. I've had several go-rounds with Egyptian friends about the use of this word to describe the events of 9/11. For just as George W. Bush climbed up to his neck in manure when he used the word *crusade* that brought up a lot of cultural and religious fears in this part of the world, Egyptians don't understand the rage the use of the word *accident* can cause in the West. I've also heard 9/11 described as a war. This, I suppose, is closer to the truth.

The Arabic language is difficult to translate, for a single word or phrase can have numerous, flowery, subtle meanings. For example, *roh Masri* means "Spirit of Egypt." But the translation doesn't end there. It also describes the love, purity, compassion, sweetness, kindness, and angelic quality of her people.

Egyptians like to say that in one or two words they can speak paragraphs. This isn't always true. In Arabic, "please" is "*Min fadlak*" (or *Min fadlik* depending upon gender).

Speaking of gender, everything, even inanimate objects, has a gender. This makes learning the language even more difficult. There seem to be few logical rules; it's kind of hit or miss. You have a 50 chance of being right.

Although inquisitive to the point of being nosy or rude by Western standards, Egyptians are also extremely polite and effusive. A warm response to *Sabah el-kheir* (good morning) is *Sabah el-ful* (greetings of the morning filled with flowers) or *Sabah el-noor* (greetings of the light). If something terrible has happened to someone, it is not appropriate to just say, "*Asfa*," (I'm sorry). There's a whole expression that goes on and on about how upset you are for their pain.

A stranger is *raebe*, but *raebe* is also used to ask, "What happened?" or to describe a strange situation and as a sign of astonishment. A person who's strange is *raeba*. In English, when an Egyptian is describing a situation that seems odd, they'll say, "This is very strange."

If an Egyptian tells you, "You're very dear to me," they're paying you the highest compliment. Someone who is very *dear* is like family, the ultimate connection. And of course there are dozens of expressions for wishing another God's blessings.

I had an Egyptian morning. My mouse was worn out so I decided to show my face at Radio Shack. As you may recall, since I've returned several purchases there, I'm no longer really welcome. We're beyond the fawning stage.

Using pidgin Arabic, I got there just fine. The trick to use is to give the taxi driver a landmark. Most won't know Radio Shack, but they will know Mo'men, a wonderful Egyptian sandwich shop. Radio Shack is in the same block.

Anyway, they weren't open and wouldn't be for another hour. I hailed another taxi and went to Road 9. The guys at the stationery store had a mouse with the right connector. Great! By the way, it was only 15 LE (a little over $3.00 U.S.). I ran a few more errands and went home to try it out. It was broken. I got back in another taxi and returned it. Since I deal with these guys all the time, returning it was not a problem. They didn't have any more so I went across the street to see my friends at Amin's market. I had not realized, until I stopped for groceries on my first trip this morning, he now sells lots of computer stuff, too. I brought my computer with me and placed it on top of the ice cream freezer. Everyone crowded around to see if it worked. Ah ha! Success!

The taxi driver who brought me home earned a rather large tip. This is because he took it upon himself to teach me more Arabic. Hassin, a fatherly man who drives the newest taxi I've ever seen here, beamed each time I answered a question correctly. "*Kwayyis!*" (Good) or "*Kwayyis awi*" (Very good)! he exclaimed. Thus far my favorite Arabic words are *awi* and *ayiza* (want).

I've come to realize that in many ways my classes at Alexandria University did me more harm than good. Our professors were so intent upon us memorizing and teaching us sentence structure, they didn't spend enough time on pronunciation. So, when I tried to use a new word and the person I was speaking to couldn't understand me, I became even more frustrated and lost my confidence. Eventually, unless I was desperate, I stopped trying. Since most shop owners speak at least a little English, with some ingenuity I can get by in El Maadi. I couldn't in Maamora. Hardly anyone spoke English there.

The good news is, because I now have a basic understanding of Arabic sentence structure, it's helping me in a project I'm doing for Rick.

I'm editing a manual that was translated from Arabic into English. Most of the sentences are backwards and utilize words in the wrong context. Since the document will probably be translated back into Arabic, I need to keep some of the flowery stuff in, but make it clearer and far less redundant. It's really hard work. I've finished two-thirds of the first edit, but have a crazy week ahead of me so I'll have to put off the last section until next week.

I had a ladies' luncheon. In addition to not having copies of most of the recipes I wanted to use, I was thwarted by mishap after mishap. The filling for the strawberry pie fell out of the refrigerator and spilled all over the floor. I had to make another batch. The first piecrust came out of the oven like concrete. I threw it out and made a tart crust. It wasn't much better. Although it's supposed to be an American brand, there's something about the flour here. It's heavier and denser. Molly told me she always sifts it first. I'll try that next time.

My five "helpers" were constantly underfoot. I almost lost a finger in the food processor. Even worse, I barely avoided contaminating the yeast dough with blood that spurted everywhere. Despite it all, the luncheon went off beautifully, but next time I'll make Egyptian kusheri or a stew. Enough is enough!

It's a real challenge to cook a nice meal. There's the tiny refrigerator thing, the ingredients thing (what's available is hit and miss so you have to be really creative and very flexible) and the lack of basic equipment like pots, pans, and utensils. I have one mixing bowl. I used it to make each dish! It's never been cleaner.

Since everyone is in the same boat, guests help. I needed five-spice powder for the chicken salad. Joan had some. I couldn't find sesame oil. Fiona brought hers, but it was rancid so we tossed it. I didn't have enough dessert plates, forks, serving dishes, or a tablecloth. Molly brought them. I didn't have any wine; three bottles appeared! Most of us don't have matching anything. No one cares. Can you imagine the comments if you set your table with mismatched, chipped china in the U.S.?

Since I'm on a roll, tomorrow I'm having my landlady, her daughter, brother, and an Egyptian-American friend of theirs who's visiting from New York over for lunch. Salwa asked me to cook an American meal. I'm making meatloaf, mashed potatoes, fresh creamed spinach, homemade yeast rolls, and another attempt at a fresh strawberry pie. After preparing the first luncheon, this one will be a snap.

One of many reasons I adore Mo is because he's so wise. His analogies are marvelous. He can say in a few words what I fail to communicate in a full page.

Between parties, he came by to visit and we talked about Bin Laden. "The relationship between Bin Laden and the U.S. government is similar to that of two bank robbers. After robbing a bank and splitting the spoils, they turn against each other," he reflected.

Then we talked about religion. I have felt that Muslims are suffering from a little bit of paranoia, Mo replied thoughtfully, "Jeanne, not everyone believes as you do that everyone has the right to worship as they please. There are many who believe that only their religion is the right one. They don't like other religions and want to eliminate them." Of course, he's right. The ramifications are being played out around the world. When I said that I believe most religions have lost God's basic message, his desire for us to show our love for him by loving each other, he replied, "Religions didn't lose the message; people did."

I met a charming older Egyptian woman. She was wary of me. I quickly saw through her warrior woman costume. Although Salwa had vouched for me, she was defensive. I think she feared that I, like so many Westerners, spend my time bashing Egypt and Egyptians.

She graduated from a Seven Sisters' school with a degree in social work. Rather than remaining in the U.S., she chose to return to Egypt to help her people. She told me that her grandmother was a feminist who helped the women of Egypt attain the right to vote. She doesn't believe that Egyptian women are all that far behind the women of the U.S. "After all," she said, "We have equal pay for equal work. You don't!" She added, "We may be behind technologically, but maybe it's not so bad. Perhaps we won't make the same mistakes that have been created by the West in its progress." Wow! She has a point! Some Egyptians, while admiring the freedom guaranteed by our Constitution, also believe it allows too many excesses, in particular when it comes to creating sexually explicit, "in-your-face" materials.

I attended a meeting of the El Maadi Women's Guild. The guest speaker, Medhat Zakhary, is the head of the Prevention and Social Departments for the Assiut Burn Center in Upper Egypt. Double wow!

His program is located in a rural area where people live in one-room houses with no running water or electricity. To cook, they use small stoves fueled by kerosene. The stoves look like a cross between a poorly made camping range and a Bunsen burner. The burn center's mission is to rehabilitate burn victims socially, physically, and spiritually. Another component of their program is burn prevention by conducting four educational home visits.

More than 50 percent of their clients burned themselves when they tried to commit suicide; some were victims of domestic violence that turned into attempted murder. The stoves were used as weapons. The rest were injured when they tried to add kerosene while the stove was lit, used it for more than the recommended one-hour limit or, since it's usually placed on the floor in the middle of the room, they knocked it over by accident.

His program is a remarkable one. Some of the women make beaded jewelry to sell. This provides them with a little income, but handiwork also helps them to learn how to reuse their injured fingers. However, by and far, the most difficult task his program faces is to help the victims heal their spirit.

Parts of Lower Egypt are similar to poverty belts in the U.S. where education, decent housing, medical care, and other services, aren't available. Women who have been badly scarred are often shunned by their families, divorced by their husbands, and abandoned by their friends. For those who used kerosene to try and end their lives, the issues are even more complex.

These women work hard; still they have nothing. They take care of their children, their husbands, work in the fields, clean their homes, grow their own food, and since they have no money, they make whatever they can or do without what they cannot afford to buy. They're exhausted. They're without hope. Each day is like the last, a struggle to survive.

The burn staff mentors and works with the women to develop their self-esteem. They use many unorthodox methods social workers in the U.S. are unable to avail themselves of. For example, a teenage girl, when she could no longer take her father and stepmother's physical and emotional abuse, decided to take her own life. She was badly burned. Her father said it would be better if she had died. He no longer wanted anything to do with her. He refused to support her.

Medhat went to visit the father's employer. After hearing the whole story, the employer agreed to give half of the man's salary directly to his daughter! But the girl has other problems. Due to the rejection of her family, she retaliated and became promiscuous. In a society that values a woman's virtue above all else, her life continues to spiral downward.

I also attended a lecture about a program founded by a local journalist to provide food and clothing for the babies of women in prison. Under Egyptian law, until the child turns two, a woman who is incarcerated is allowed to keep her baby with her. This is because Islam encourages women to nurse. Nursing ends at two. After that, the baby is taken from the mother and placed with family, or if the family can't or won't take it, it's placed in an orphanage. Thereafter, once each month, the child is brought to visit its mother.

The program was created when the journalist, Noelle,

was doing research to write a story about women in prison. When she learned that the government pays to feed and house the mother, but not her child, she decided to do something about it. Children had no clothing or food beyond their mothers' milk. Thus far, she's raised millions of pounds for her foundation.

Salwa brought her Egyptian-American friend for lunch. We had a grand time! George, a tall thin man in his mid-fifties, works for U.S. Treasury in N.Y.C. It was a golden opportunity to share cultural shock experiences. A naturalized American, George has lived in the U.S. for twenty-five years. I sensed that he feels the same cultural pulls I do, only they're reversed. Not surprisingly, he told me that his Egyptian-American community was as devastated by what happened on 9/11 as every other American. His office is so close to the World Trade Center that a friend and coworker was killed when flying debris hit him in the back.

We talked about the need to educate each culture about the other. He agreed that it is the best way to begin to create a level of compassion and understanding that will lead to peace. I hope to see him again and to have many more conversations. In particular, I want to understand the parts of our culture that he has found most difficult to adjust to. He did say that "Yes, the U.S. is an economically materialistic society, but the American people have a wonderful spirit and big hearts that pulled them together during the crisis."

I'm becoming quite fond of my dentist. Yesterday he told me about the accident that placed him in a wheelchair sixteen years ago.

He was riding a motorcycle in the desert. He wasn't going very fast when he found himself propelled through the air like a paper airplane. He said that his body bounced over rocks until he landed on one with such force that it broke his back leaving him paralyzed from the waist down.

After treatment and rehab here in Egypt, his family took him to Switzerland for advanced physical therapy. In addition to the horror of suddenly being paralyzed from the waist down, he said recurrent dreams that he could walk again were devastating. Actually, it wasn't the dreams that were disturbing; they were wonderful. What was horrific was waking up each morning to reality. He said the average person who is paralyzed in an accident needs about five years to adjust and accept the fact that they'll never walk again. It took him half that amount of time, but the dreams continued.

It's been about two years since the dreams stopped. His attitude, his energy, his gentleness in the face of his disability is a wonderful inspiration. I'm so blessed to have met him.

As with many of the people I meet, my dentist's experience is a reflection of my life. In this case, I realized that like him, I often don't want to face reality. Some of my dreams are just dreams; they feel so good that I refuse to open my eyes and to see that what I want isn't necessarily reality or for my highest good.

△ △ △

When I opened my junk mail box this morning, I was shocked to see a message from someone with my exact e-mail name, but a different service. Thankfully, they were advertising debt consolidation, not porn! If those who use their creativity in this way, channeled it into something useful, so many miracles could be created.

My propane tank, which I use for cooking, was getting low. I asked Ramadan, my daytime bawaab, to get me a full one. As the propane truck came by, Ramadan stopped it and escorted the propane guy up to my flat. To my surprise, the man didn't have the right tools and had to go downstairs to get them! He expected me to have a wrench. This is not unusual. Every expat should arrive with a complete toolbox.

Anyway, I left the kitchen when they tested it. Instead of putting soap around the coupler that would bubble if the tank wasn't tightly connected, they used a match! I think the tank guys need a burn center prevention class, too!

This morning when I used the stovetop I noticed that when I turned off the gas at the tank, the burner on the stovetop remained on! I turned it off and opened all the windows. I'm waiting for the guys who did other repairs in my unit to come and check for a leak. I decided to pass on having my bawaab or a tank guy come and fix it. There are some things I won't compromise on having fixed properly. This is one of them. I hope your day, as well as mine, is non-explosive!

*If you do not take
the whole peach, you'll
end up with only its juice.*

~ Egyptian Proverb

Chapter 38

February 2002

I haven't been able to forget what my dentist told me about finally letting go of the recurrent dream that he could walk. Yesterday, as I was removing another layer of crud from the ceramic floor in my hallway, I understood why his words turned like a merry-go-round in my head. He could not let go of what he wanted reality to be until he saw that it was holding him back from appreciating what he still had, what life even now has to offer. Those who are never ready to let go never adjust and never again live life to the fullest. Their spirits become as crippled as their bodies.

In looking back over my life, I see that I too have held onto dreams that flew in the face of reality. I was so focused upon forcing what I wanted that I let numerous opportunities pass me by. I didn't end up in a wheelchair, but more than once my spirit was paralyzed. Sometimes it took a horrific dose of truth to get me to let go and to appreciate what I did have.

I am beginning to see that when I want something but find every road blocked, it's an indication that I'm supposed to stop and look at my goal. Maybe the goal is attainable, but the way I'm approaching it isn't the right way; or maybe the dream is one I need to let go of. Maybe I've had so many challenges because I was too busy to learn from the little lessons placed in my path. The only way God could get me to "get it" was to hit me over the head with a mega example of the lesson I chose to repeatedly ignore!

I think it's kind of like consistently driving the wrong

way on a one-way street. Eventually, reality in the form of a ticket or a head-on collision makes us sit up and take notice.

This all comes back to living in the moment. When we live in the moment rather than in the past or future, we're given all the information we need to solve any problem in our lives. We are only required to listen. If we don't, we won't hear the answer. The quandary is that Western society has taught us to always think in the future as well as behind us so we can beat ourselves up for our mistakes.

Somehow we've missed out on cherishing the moment. The present is a gift. "That's why," as one of the remarkable hospice patients I had the privilege of working with said, "It is called the *present*." Egypt has taught me to slow down, to witness each moment with wonder, to clearly see that all the wisdom I need is available if I just take the time to close my mouth, open my mind and listen.

I've begun to see life as a huge puzzle. Each day, pieces of the puzzle are placed in my hand for me to examine. However, if I just toss them in my puzzle box, I miss the opportunity to experience the wonder of seeing how everything fits together perfectly. Everything is for a reason. There are no coincidences, only opportunities to grow by learning or teaching.

The cats are helping me. I've seen firsthand that when I'm calm and serene, they are too. They don't stick a paw in an electrical outlet more than once. They learn much more quickly than I. They're often smarter, more compassionate and saner than humans.

Yesterday I trimmed each cat's front claws. No one was happy about this, including me. Each time I took on the claws of one cat, the others surrounded it to offer comfort. They talked to it, kissed it, and stood watch as if to say, "We know this is scary, but you'll be okay."

Have you ever noticed how groups of animals protect each other? One bird in a flock will serve as a lookout to alert the others of danger. It's the same with the fish I saw when snorkeling. Yes, they'll fight over food, but when the whole group is in danger, they don't close the windows, turn on the television and pretend they're separate from their school.

Cats can't clean the top of their backs, behind their head, or their noses so they do it for each other. When it's cold, they snuggle together to stay warm. No one gets upset because someone is sitting on his or her head. When Chakra is nursing her kittens, she lets Om sit on top of her and nip at her ears. As if to make Om feel welcome, she cleans her while she's nursing the kittens. They never try to really physically hurt each other or me. If they're annoyed, they show it and get over it. They're never in a bad mood. They never say anything unkind. If they don't want to be bothered with me, they hide. If they want to be held, they jump into my lap. They ask for what they want. They have no hidden agendas.

Sure, they get a lot from me: a clean litter box, good food to fill their bellies and a safe place to sleep. But they give me even more. They show me the effortless joy of turning a piece of cellophane into a fantastic new toy. They teach me patience and allow me to see the wisdom of the simple, but significant ways they express kindness, love and trust.

Maybe God created animals for reasons other than to provide food, clothing, and companionship. Maybe he wanted them around us so we'd remember all that our complicated civilization has caused us to forget. I read somewhere that if an animal threatens you, rather than running or responding with aggression, if you stand still, close your eyes and consciously send it love, it will simply walk away. Merely by being in touch with the energy being directed towards them, they know whether or not they are in any real danger.

What I've learned from the cats has been worth all the money I've spent on convoys of trucks filled with litter. They've given me many small moments of laughter and a lifetime of learning by example. I just had to stop long enough to watch and listen to all they have to teach me as I do when dealing with human teachers.

△ △ △

I received an offer to make some extra cash. I declined. An American woman whom I've met only once e-mailed to ask if I would help her to identify Egyptian doctors and professionals who are experts in cosmetic/plastic surgery and permanent physical enhancements. In exchange for my research, I would receive half of the kickbacks she would charge the physician for each client/patient successfully referred.

My first reaction to her proposal was one of horror, but probably not for the reasons you might imagine. Her scheme was a marketing add-on to the spiritual tours of Egypt she leads. Since such treatments are cheaper here than in the West, and she'd like to undergo a few herself, she saw this as an opportunity to fill her tour and to, as they say in parts of the U.S., "get beautified "

When I responded to her query by saying that I believe the focus of spirituality is inner work, she wrote back, and in a thinly veiled manipulative way, accused me of wanting to put a guilt trip on people who want to feel better about themselves. She hit an all-time low when she added that I'm obviously not as spiritually advanced as she. I bit my tongue.

My response was short and sweet. I acknowledged that everyone has free will and the opportunity to choose their own path and how they use their energy. I ended by saying that my energy "is focused elsewhere" and wished her luck.

Of course, her letter was a wonderful opportunity to look at my beliefs as they were beamed, via reflection, back to me.

First, I saw that she was right. I was being judgmental. Rather than sharing my philosophical outrage, it would have been better if I'd just politely declined. Her choices, how she chooses to "walk the talk," are entirely up to her. I let my ego get in the way. I neither needed to explain nor defend myself and I certainly don't have to agree with her, but if I wish my views to be respected, don't I owe her the same courtesy?

Second, because she is a facilitator for an international program whose work I admire, I had placed her on a pedestal. Because of her "advanced" spiritual work, I saw her as "better" than me. I expected more from her. I forgot that she's human, too. Her arrogance reflected back to me my belief that because someone has studied longer than I have, they're better or more advanced. She showed me that people walk the path that's right for them. What's right for her doesn't have to be right for me; what's right for me isn't necessarily right for her.

Third, she forced me to revisit my feelings about aging. This is the part I really didn't want to look at. Because I continue to be blessed with a high energy level, a fast metabolism, and skin I was lucky to inherit, I often forget that I'm fifty-five, not thirty-five—until some "thoughtless" kid, or a mirror strategically placed in harsh sunlight, catches me off-guard, and reminds me.

Plastic surgery and hair dye are sometimes appealing, but most of the time I work really hard to take the road best for me and to say to myself, "Get over it!" You can have everything lifted and tucked, but you'll still be your age and the same woman inside. Conversely, if you continue to work on loving yourself and all others, the glow that comes from inside will never go away." Unfortunately, Western society doesn't really reinforce this belief; older men are sexy, older women are just old, so sometimes I feel as if I'm kidding myself.

Upon departing from our marriage, my ex said something along the lines of (I've added the humor) "The only men who will want you are those who can't walk unassisted and can't leave the house without a diaper. Men want a younger woman." Thankfully, this has not been my experience, but I know the time is coming when it may be true and I'll need to settle for a knight in shining armor who hires a "second" to whisk me off my feet.

Several years ago a single woman I knew who was about to turn sixty confided that she had begun to wonder if aging meant that she would no longer have the opportunity to be desired, to express her sexuality.

Another friend recently recalled the shock she felt when for the first time she realized that the men she found attractive were suddenly looking past her at the woman coming along behind her. Once she adjusted to the reality of aging, she discovered that it felt really liberating to no longer have to play the male-female game.

In the book, *Tuesdays with Morrie*, by Mitch Albom, Morrie is quoted as saying that he sees himself as every age. I understand. Each age has its benefits and I too can be any age no matter what society says.

I can still feel like a little kid and squeal in delight when I'm in the local market and find a product I haven't seen since I came here. I can still feel the joy of learning something new. I can kick a soccer ball back to the kids in the street when it goes out of bounds. I can still laugh really hard without having to run to the bathroom. I can put on black pantyhose, a pretty dress, and "hooker pumps" and feel beautiful even if the moonlight picks up my natural gray highlights rather than the colors of the night. I can still wear pretty underwear just for me, even a thong (though it takes me five minutes to figure out how to put it on).

Andy Rooney recently did a piece about why he loves older women. It was beautiful, but coming from a guy who's almost older than God, it wasn't all that reassuring and he defined older as fifty plus!

I can embrace the fifty-five-year-old who is wiser, kinder, more gentle and loving; but it still twists my knickers when I realize that I didn't appreciate "it" and took "it" for granted while I had "it." Sometime I feel a little sad that I'll never again have the opportunity to do a better job raising my children, to be a better friend to those who have sailed on without me, to be a more compassionate daughter, to undo many of the choices I've made, to have lived a life where I learned at an early age to love and accept myself and everyone I have ever met.

That's living in the past. I can't turn back the clock. Where I was at the time was where I was supposed to be and every experience I've ever had has brought me closer to the woman I want to be.

I can dye my hair, I can work out ten times a week so that from the tip of my toes to the top of my head everything heads north instead of south, or I can pay a surgeon to do it for me. But a bigger part of me believes that aging is natural, it's not always kind, but it's a stage of life we are fortunate to reach. It's all in how we look at it: a gift or a theft.

My path is not what many would choose. It's up to each of us to decide. I want to embrace all of who I am. I want to use the wisdom I've gained to get beyond the surface, to always remember that it's what's inside me and everyone else I meet that's important. I'm working on incorporating this belief system and for the most part, I feel more beautiful than I ever have.

When I responded to "the proposal," I did so from my heart and from my belief system, but also I now see from a place of judgment based upon a speck of fear of loss.

By the way, if you're inclined to go out and buy a thong for yourself or someone else, it's much easier to figure out how to put it on if there's a tag still in it. There should also be a warning label that says: "The discomfort associated with wearing this garment can lead to one's questioning the sanity of putting it on in the first place."

I wasn't surprised to receive a flotilla of e-mails about aging and cosmetic intervention. It reminded me that when I react strongly to something, it's usually because I'm ready to look at the fear I associate with it. Since the majority of you who receive these e-mails are part of the boomer generation, I wonder if the redefinition of aging isn't another issue we can take on as a group. We've certainly done this with menopause and erectile dysfunction, aspects of aging that no other generation has been willing to discuss openly.

△△△

"Nip and tuck" pretty well describes the challenges I'm facing right now with my Internet connection. It took six attempts after being kicked off-line before I succeeded in sending it. The provider I paid for is now offering the same service for "free." Ever since the switchover, I've had major problems. I can no longer access Hotmail through Netscape, and Internet Explorer needs Preparation H.

A friend of mine has been involved in a family drama that shows no signs of abating. This person's father-in-law (a widower in his mid-seventies) decided to remarry. He's been telling his daughters for some time that he wanted to remarry. I can't remember exactly how many daughters he has, but several are married and two, in their early twenties, live at home with him. Apparently he wants a younger wife because she'd still be interested in sex. I've been told that many women beyond childbearing age would rather put their sexuality along with their fertility behind them. His daughters think he shouldn't be interested in sex. According to them, "He's too old."

The girls told him they would help him find a wife. They never got around to it so he came home one day and announced that he had not only found a woman, he married her! The result of this revelation has been mass hysteria.

The younger ones have consistently said that if he remarries they'll leave home or commit suicide. After his announcement, one moved in with an aunt. As far as I know, the other has not taken her life. Why are they so upset? The youngest daughters can't go off and live on their own and they don't want to live under the same roof with a "wicked" stepmother. In this culture, until they marry, young women are expected to remain with their father or another relative to protect their virtue.

Baba (Dad) stormed out of the house, returned, left, returned, left. The husbands of the married sisters are trying their best to stay neutral as their wives cry and carry on. As things escalate, they're attempting to keep their children far away from the situation. Things are often discussed openly in front of children. In this case, the grandchildren are already hysterical about what grandpa has done.

As they join together to try and pressure Baba into seeing the error of his ways (they want him to divorce his new wife), normal life has been suspended. Baba is apoplectic. He can't bring his wife home because his children will eat her for lunch.

There have been a billion family war councils. They consider the new wife to be a "little bit dirty" (because she's twice divorced and has children younger than they). They also believe she's only after his money.

They may be right about her wanting money, or perhaps she's just smart. Apparently, she knew what she was getting into. She negotiated a marriage contract (everyone has marriage contracts) that required the payment of some money up-front. The agreement states that if they divorce, she will receive an additional lump sum. She also got him to agree to be "a little bit patient" about consummating the marriage.

Thus far, no one has asked him if he loves this woman, nor do they care if she makes him happy. This situation reminds me that children of every age often forget that their parent is a person first with needs and dreams separate and apart from theirs.

The other side of the family is dealing with a similar situation, but with a twist. The grandfather needed a live-in housekeeper. He's in his eighties. Since he's frail, the family decided it would be a good idea to have someone live in to care for him. They can't hire a woman to do this. Even with his advanced age, there would be "talk." The solution was to *buy* him a wife.

They searched for a new wife in Upper Egypt where poor women, for a price, will marry a man older than their grandfather. They found a sweet, young girl from a poor family. They paid her about 10,000 LE up-front (a little more than $2,000 U.S.). Very quickly, things turned bad. No one knows if the marriage was consummated, but grandpa quickly became tired of his new wife. He refuses to give her money to buy food. He uses his cane to beat her. Family meetings have taken place with little success in protecting her.

△△△

In the hope of finding good homes for them, I took a picture of the cats to the local animal rescue league. My landlady was supposed to take all or some of them but keeps putting it off so I think she's "a little bit shy" about saying she thinks I'm out of my bloody mind for even suggesting she do so. I have to agree. I think I was a little bit obnoxious in hoping she'd take them all. They aren't her responsibility; they're mine.

My friends in Alex (Karen and Berhan) who were going to adopt Om and Chakra just moved into a new flat. The landlord doesn't allow pets. I'd rather place them with Egyptian families or people who will stay here even if other expats are evacuated. Please pray that I find good homes for them. I'm beginning to feel like an eccentric midlife cat woman. At a minimum, I need to place the kittens.

There's another problem. Two of the kittens have suddenly developed extra body parts! I think I have one girl and two boys! Does anyone know how old boy cats are when they are able to become impregnators?

△ △ △

I had a great Valentine's Day. I bought a hot evening dress and joined Molly, Tim, Camilla, and Yosef at a formal dinner dance. We had a blast. Karen and Berhan came from Alex and stayed overnight so they could go to a salsa party in Cairo. It was great having my first houseguests!

Yesterday, we went on a Hash House Harrier walk. Apparently, there are Hash groups around the world. Members meet weekly to walk or run a course in the country, and then celebrate by getting tanked. It's an opportunity to get drunk in the afternoon using the pretext of exercise.

The group is rather bawdy, mostly expats from the UK. I think they'll teach me to loosen up a bit. Molly, Tim, Tim's mom Mary, and I went to the site about forty-five minutes outside Cairo. The course ended at what was billed as the oldest dam ever built. I was told that it lasted for 1,300 years before it collapsed. It was a beautiful day. Some of the terrain was harsh, but we made it through like champions. It was a real treat to see the desert begin to bloom.

There's a holiday next weekend, *Eid al-Adha* (Feast of the Sacrifice) where most families slaughter a goat to share with their family and the poor. I was supposed to travel to the White Desert with a group from the local Community Center. Unfortunately, there weren't enough people signed up so it was cancelled. Pooh! We're all scrambling to come up with some day trips that don't include running into bloody goat stuff on every street corner.

△ △ △

Last week a bunch of conservative Muslims got ticked off when Christians in their town rang their church bells.

There was some violence, but I don't know the details. Why this upset the local Muslims I have no idea. One would think that Egyptian Christians have the right to ring the bells in their church as the Muslims do to blast prayer call over loudspeakers. I also see this incident as positive. Many Muslims think that the rights of the Christian minority are respected. This episode offers an opportunity for those who are more balanced to see through the illusion perpetuated throughout Egypt. Other than this, things are normal and quiet here. I have never felt uncomfortable or unsafe even on a train, but that's because I have the luxury of going first class. Many Egyptians aren't as lucky.

By now, most of you have read about the burning train traveling from Cairo to Upper Egypt that carried Egyptians going home to share the Feast of the Sacrifice with their families.

It was a third-class local train, the only kind the average Egyptian can afford to travel on. I've taken a train numerous times to Alexandria, but I'm fortunate. I take the first-class express train. It costs me about $12.00 round-trip. Only those who have seats on those trains are allowed on. Each car has three rows of seats, two together and a row of singles across the aisle. There are bathrooms at the ends of each car and a rack if you want to store your luggage.

A man comes through with a cart filled with sandwiches and drinks. Except for the incessant singing of mobile phones, it's a quiet, peaceful trip. One can sleep, read, visit with their traveling companion, daydream, or watch passing farmland and areas of appalling poverty that skirt the train tracks as they do everywhere in the world.

I've seen many trains like the one that burned. The possibility that someone started the fire while cooking on a kerosene stove is a real one.

Any train would be difficult to evacuate in an emergency, but these trains carry so many people there would have had to be a stampede of terror. Regular trains look old and dilapidated. There's a bar across each open window, probably to keep people from falling out as they seek space and air. I've seen men and children riding on top of the train or hanging on to handles on the outside as it flies by.

There are no assigned seats. Those on first get the few

available seats. The rest are packed in like cattle on the way to market, yet surprisingly people are good humored and happy because they're going home to visit their families.

Imagine for a minute a subway car at the pinnacle of rush hour. Now imagine that in addition to too many adult passengers, a zillion small children try to cradle in their mothers' arms, or climb and squirm over strangers. Crates of food, perhaps a few chickens, maybe even some goats and baskets of gifts and clothing fill every inch of space. Imagine what it's like to be on this train for upwards of twenty or more hours, standing or crushed on the floor by your fellow citizens. There is no air-conditioning. All the windows are completely open. Thankfully the weather is cool, but with so many people surrounding you, it's stifling. The train stops at most towns between Cairo and Aswan. I've taken this trip by express sleeper. It took twelve hours!

When the fire broke out, with superhuman strength, men were able to pull some of the bars off some of the windows. They jumped, fell, or threw people out of the moving train. Many died from the fall. Those who remained were burned beyond recognition; the feet of those trying to escape undoubtedly crushed others. Because there is no communication between the conductor and individual cars on these trains, it kept going for several miles before the conductor saw that several cars were on fire. The open windows and doorways turned it into an inferno.

Each person who died or escaped but is now suffering from terrible burns is part of a larger extended family. Nearly four hundred died, but thousands are in mourning. There aren't enough burn units to treat everyone properly. I can only imagine with a shudder the terrible pain those still alive are experiencing. A friend of mine was burned on his hands, face, and arms. He told me that the pain was so terrible he had to choose whether to live or die. Your prayers are really needed for their healing or quick death.

△ △ △

Then there were two. Last Wednesday, Bashful, the female kitten, was adopted. A young man from Animal

Friends, a rescue organization, brought an Egyptian man to my flat to look at the kittens. He chose Bashful. I named her Bashful for a reason. She is not friendly. She only comes to you when she wants to. I had trouble catching her and when I did, she went nuts. She scratched and bit me. Blood was flying everywhere . . . mine. The animal rescue kid was horrified and asked if she would attack the children of the man who wanted to adopt her. Thankfully the Egyptian said, "She's a cat, not a lion. She's just afraid." I think it was more traumatic for me to let her go than for her mother or siblings. I expected major retaliation from Chakra, but she seems relieved. This afternoon I took the two male kittens to the shelter. Another Egyptian family adopted them. I'm down to Chakra and Om.

I've made friends with a woman from my Arabic class. Anita is from New Jersey. She's been in Egypt for a short time. Her husband, an Egyptian, works for an American company that has a marketing contract here. Anita has a cat, Dusty. He's identical to Om. They even have the same nose. We've already switched off baby-sitting! Things are looking up.

I went to another Hash event. I had a blast! I met many new people from around the world and didn't get home until late last night because some of us went out for dinner after the race then to of all places, a Korean pool parlor/bar.

Molly, Tim, Tim's mom, and I went to Camilla and Yosef's for dinner. Their daughter and future son-in-law were in town. It was fun to meet them.

Last Monday I went on a Nile cruise to celebrate Molly's birthday. It was a nice evening complete with a belly dancer. I have to admit I was itching to get up and join her. I'm sure Molly's guests are delighted that I didn't.

I attended a lecture at the American University with a new friend from the Hash, Fatma. The subject was a Ph.D. dissertation of an Arab-American anthropologist who studied the cultural challenges of Arab-Americans living in the United States. What struck me strongly is that Arabs living in the U.S. have transported the same cultural conflicts from here to there that I've been writing to you about.

Friday, I joined a group from the Maadi Community

Center for an overnight trip to Fayoum. It's fairly close to Cairo. The main attractions are water wheels that are used to pump water into the fields, a sweet water lake, and a saltwater lake adjacent to the desert. The scenery was lovely. I bought too many baskets, ate too much good food, and made several new friends who shared with me some interesting insights about the legal ramifications of a Western woman marrying an Egyptian. It blew my socks off!

The first wife is better even if she's a piece of mud.

~ Egyptian Proverb

Chapter 39

March 2002

While on the trip to Fayoum, I had the opportunity to speak with four Western women who are, or have been married to Egyptians.

While it's not required of a Western woman (as it is of a Western man because Islam passes from father to child) to convert to Islam when she marries a Muslim, many Western women do, at least on "paper." To convert they only need to say that they believe in only one God and that Mohamed is his messenger.

Some women convert to make their husbands and his family happy while continuing to eat pork and to drink alcohol. Many women have told me that converting wasn't "a big deal." They did it to keep peace, but still do their own thing. Others take their conversion seriously and embrace Islam into ever fiber of their lives. It's judging on my part when I feel a cold shiver each time I see a Western woman wearing a *hijab* (a head covering). I fear that which we betray in the name of love ends up betraying who we are. Our past will eventually arise, like a substantial shadow in a cemetery that turns fear into terror.

Two of the women are widows. When their Egyptian husbands died, although they each had good relationships with his family, before his body was shrouded in a white cloth, the family began to clean out their homes and investment properties. One woman, seven years later, is still fighting with his family over his estate.

My understanding of Egyptian law is that if a woman does not convert to Islam she is entitled to nothing. If she does, she is entitled to only one-eighth of his estate, even if she contributed to most of it. If there are children from a prior marriage or the current marriage, things become even more complicated.

One woman, probably in her late sixties, was shocked to come home one day shortly after her husband died to discover that only a bed and desk remained in their home. His family had taken everything. They told her that they were going to move into the other rooms. This confused her. They already had homes of their own.

Her husband owned several apartment buildings, but only his name or the name of the original developer was on the titles. This is because Egyptians go to extremes to avoid paying taxes. Rather than having the property put in their names at settlement, they keep it in the name of the developer so they won't have to pay transfer taxes. It's also my understanding that another issue involves not being able to put a property in your name unless it is paid for in cash and/or all the other units have sold. To later change the names on the deed is expensive and apparently takes years to accomplish. I guess there's no title insurance or a way to establish a clear chain of title either. Given its ancient history, trying to set up a chain of ownership would be an amazing challenge for title abstractors!

In this particular case, without her knowledge or consent, the family had a power of attorney drawn up, giving them the "right" to represent her so they could steal all the property. When she discovered the existence of the POA, she began to fight back. They retaliated by putting poisonous snakes in her lone bed. She decided that her life was more important than the property and gave up. Greed knows no nationality.

The second widow, a slender, bitter woman who's probably in her fifties, has been through several hundred lawyers. This is no exaggeration! Apparently, many Egyptian lawyers play both sides against the middle. They sell confidential documents to the other party! In an effort to regain what is rightfully hers, this year, she's already been through at least thirty-five lawyers.

When a woman marries an Egyptian and has children with him, the children legally belong to him. This is true for Egyptian wives as well. She cannot take the children out of the country without his permission, and since Islam passes from the father to the child, the child can only be Muslim. If the woman is a non-Muslim she has no say in raising her children in her faith.

If any woman asks for a divorce and her husband agrees, she leaves the marriage with *nothing* unless a marriage contract says otherwise. He doesn't have to pay a dowry to a Western wife, but he does have to pay one to an Egyptian wife before they marry. If she divorces him, she doesn't get to keep this either unless they stipulate it in the marriage contract. This is probably why many Egyptian women who work keep everything they make rather than contributing to the financial support of the family. It's allowed. This is their only protection and why so many women own property in their names only. Unless she has become a citizen, once she divorces, a Western woman can be forced to leave the country and her children!

The third woman is German, happily married to an Egyptian, but she feels great sadness, a sense of loss, that her children are not equally German.The fourth woman is Filipino. After they had been married a while, her husband took a second wife. He wanted children. I don't know if she didn't want more (she has at least one from a previous marriage) or if she couldn't have more. He told her that they would all stay together for just a few months. A child was born to the second wife who, four years later, is still in the house.

To his shock, one day the husband came home and found his first wife gone. She felt that he didn't appreciate her. She reached her limit. She leased her own flat. She is an Egyptian citizen so she isn't worried about being deported, but she's stayed married for the financial convenience. They have a "date" once a week. She's really quite happy having things on her terms for a change.

One of the hardest adjustments a Western woman is faced with when she marries an Egyptian man is his tie to his family. Even if he isn't the only son, if he makes more money than his brother(s), he is expected to contribute to the support of his mother and married or unmarried sisters. If there is a family "problem," he's expected to drop everything and rush to their aid, no matter how petty. His wife suffers.

What's interesting is that men who have lived in the West for years will often fall back into the cultural norm upon returning to Egypt. Many have no plans to return to Egypt from the West but do so when a family member becomes ill. The Western wife, used to Western values, is then faced with a husband who may revert back to his cultural background. In some cases, when their Western children reach a certain age, some Egyptian men begin to fear that the morals of the West will harm their children and decide to return to Egypt before it's "too late."

Egyptian men are raised to see themselves as the head of the family, the protectors. A huge responsibility is placed upon their shoulders. From childhood, they're taught to honor their responsibilities. This is one of the reasons that a male child is so valued. It's his responsibility to take care of everyone else. In exchange, from the moment he's born, he's treated like a little king. His mother does everything for him. Few know how to cook or clean. There's no need. A woman will always be available to do it for him.

I've seen young boys hit their sisters while their mother stands silently by. In certain segments of this society, they're allowed to beat their adult sisters when they do something they don't approve of. Put succinctly, they're the boss with the responsibility of protecting and punishing. Even a brother-in-law is allowed to discipline his wife's sisters.

Morality extends to the wife's friends. My friend from Alex has an American friend who recently married an Egyptian. She is allowed to visit her, but if her live-in boyfriend comes along, they're not allowed in the house.

The male members of her family protect an Egyptian woman. If she has a problem with her husband, they will intercede on her behalf. Since her family is usually not in Egypt, a Western woman does not have the same help available to her. Therefore, she is at the mercy of his famiy when conflicts need to be resolved. It is rare that she will find a voice to stand beside hers. Although everyone writes and agrees to a marriage contract, even if she dots all the i's and crosses all the t's, to the bride, apparently, it isn't always worth the paper it's written on. I've seen very few happy mixed marriages. This isn't because the men here are bad. Egyptian men are loving and kind. It's more about the cultural differences being so vast that a Western woman is often required to lose herself to fit into his family and society. Part of the loss can be to give up the "rights" she is used to.

All of this reminds me for relationships to work, individuals need to make compromises that don't require them to lose themselves. This happens in the West as often as it does here. Perhaps we don't see it that way because it's much more subtle in the West. In any case, it really comes down to valuing oneself and giving what we can without losing who we are.

$$\triangle \triangle \triangle$$

More frequently I'm thankful for every experience I have, no matter how painful or bittersweet. Once I get to the other side, it now seems easier to look back objectively and to ask, "What was I to learn from this?" I usually request an answer before falling off to sleep. As I awaken the next morning, it's there for me to embrace.

After encountering a major life hurdle, have you ever looked back and thanked God for the experience?

I don't know if it's Egypt or just the place I've grown into, but I've come to see that everything is a gift. The trouble is that the initial package is usually wrapped in a used grocery bag secured by twisted, icky duct tape. Madison Avenue has done its job well.

All around me, here and there, friends are uncovering the same kinds of presents. Several are watching helplessly those closest to them bleed from the wounds of their life lessons. Some are offering gentle sight and a heart beating with compassion. Some are trying to *fix* the problem. I understand. I always tried to fix things, too. But along the road I began to ask, "What if, in fixing the problem, I remove the opportunity for the person I love to grow into a happier, healthy human being? What if their experience is necessary for their ultimate good? What if, by coping with a challenge, new opportunities and options will become available to them? What if, in trying to control and *fix* others, I'm only hurting them? What if a part of me is using the crisis to avoid looking at my own ugly boxes that are stacked up outside my door?"

Now, instead of trying to fix, I pray. I never ask that the problem or obstacle be removed, only that I, or the person involved, be given the wisdom and strength to get through it.

I have a theory. I believe we are born with our own personal pan pizza. It's been created just for us. No two are alike. God keeps our pizza hot for us, but he only gives it to us a tiny sliver at a time. He's the only one who's able to see the whole pie, the complete picture. Each sliver has its own unique topping. There's stuff on it we could never begin to imagine. It's perfect!

Sometimes a sliver is delivered in a box retrieved from a dumpster. Other times it arrives wrapped in gold encased in jewels. It's funny how we usually remember the dumpster presentation rather than the gold box. We waste so much energy trying to throw the ugly box away rather than embracing it and asking for the strength and wisdom to successfully digest its contents. Maybe this is because the dumpster version is the hardest to swallow and chew. Because the beautiful one is easier to digest, we take it for granted and expend all our energy complaining about the cold, greasy pieces. Yet, each piece is from the exact same pie. The wrapping is different, but each one is a gift filled with the jewels of love and wisdom.

△ △ △

I had a rather mild week. The approaching one promises to be less bland with school, lunches, dinners, excursions, and an early St. Patrick's Day party.

The weather is glorious! It's been warmer than normal. I went on another Hash yesterday. We did a five-mile hike through incredible wadis. A *wadi* is a dry riverbed. The ones I've seen on Hash walks are nestled beneath incredibly massive rock formations, more like mountains than hills. The sand is firm but spongy, which makes it easy to walk on and to grip with your feet.

I've been doing a bit of shopping, too much really. I've been to the tentmakers twice. Tentmakers create beautiful canvas umbrellas and tote bags; they also make magnificent quilt-type handmade appliqué wall hangings, bedspreads, and throw pillows.

There are souks where you can also buy fabric. For about $40.00 I purchased fifteen yards each of upholstery and dress fabric. I also bought two smallish handmade wool rugs and a cotton throw runner, all for less than $30.00. I haven't done much shopping up till now, but as I become more attuned to the best Egyptian products, I'm beginning to indulge. Camilla had an excellent point. She reminded me that many expats buy so much stuff that when they try to incorporate it into their Western homes; they lose the flavor of the West. Since the things I'm buying are more universal in nature, I'm not too concerned, but her point is one to keep in mind.

This reminds me that many stores advertise *oriental* (Eastern) products. I'm also amazed at the cost of prescription drugs. They can be purchased over the counter without a prescription. Premarin costs approximately $2.20 for thirty pills! Apparently, the Egyptian government subsidizes medicines.

I've found another pork store. It's only a block or so away from my flat. This week they had fresh American bacon and pork scaloppini. Molly showed me where the closest government-subsidized bread store is. For 1 LE you can buy a bag of sandwich rolls hot out of the oven. They don't have quite as rich a flavor as Western bread, but they're good.

Salwa, and Ranya, are coming for lunch this afternoon. They want to try different American foods. They made a special request for macaroni and cheese and creamed spinach, which I've made for them before. I'm also serving American barbecue chicken (Egyptian barbecue chicken has no sauce on it. It's coated with spices and salt and cooked on a grill or spit), garlic bread, avocado-tomato salad, and homemade brownies with vanilla ice cream. It should be fun.

Trying to cook "American" food is a challenge. More and more I realize what a melting pot our culture is. I thought the food here would be totally foreign to me, but most of it isn't. In one day we Americans eat foods whose source ranges from China to Mexico. Egyptian food is a mixture of Middle Eastern foods such as shish kabob, tahini, eggplant dip, stuffed grape leaves, stuffed cabbage, spaghetti with meat sauce, and so on. The spices used are a bit different (they use a lot of cinnamon and mint as well as cumin), but the product is pretty much the same.

Even if the speaker is crazy, the listener should be wise.

~ Egyptian Proverb

Chapter 40

March 2002

March 11 marked the first anniversary of my arrival in Egypt and six months since 9/11. I've spent some quiet time thinking and reflecting back upon the past year because I've wanted to share with you my perspective of how Egypt has changed my life without sounding like an expert on Egypt, her culture and people, or an escapee from a self-imposed life lesson workshop.

Over the past year, I've written from my heart. I guess it's not time to start approaching things differently. Some of what I'm going to say is harsh. I believe it's also the truth.

I've changed in many major as well as minor ways. I have come to the realization that I no longer see myself as only an "American." I've become *Ana Amrikaniyya wi Masriyya bell elb* (I am an American and an Egyptian in my heart). In my soul, I've also become a citizen of the world.

Egypt and her magnificent people have taught me so much. By staying open to understanding this culture, I saw how much misunderstanding. has been created by the differences in our cultural norms, our religious beliefs, our governments, and the media. We're all sitting in the same box of assumptions and judgments that are based upon half-truths.

I have learned by putting aside what I thought I knew, by looking at Egyptians with newborn eyes and hearing them with virgin ears, my prejudices, assumptions, and misconceptions fell away. Only then did my journey toward love truly begin; only then did I see with clarity the one truth that can heal the world and those who inhabit it; we are all the same. We are all one. I have come to believe that if one person is hungry, if one person is homeless, if one person is starving for love, their need reflects back upon me and, in turn, the rest of the world.

If one person is hated because of their culture, their faith, their beliefs, or their skin color, then we are all at risk of being hated, hungry, or homeless.

Like love, intolerance, judgment, violence, and hate can begin or end with one person. Everything we think, express or feel is spread like a ripple on a pond that feeds into the nearest stream, then to a lake. It flows onward until it eventually reaches the water that sustains *all* life. If the water is filled with love, it nourishes. If it is polluted, it suffocates and kills not only the body but also the spirit. Egypt and the expats I've met from around the world have taught me that our fears and needs are basically the same. It's only a matter of degree and how our cultures teach us to express them.

Our physical needs are simple. To stay physically healthy we all need clean water and air. We all need rich soil to grow our food. We need sunshine and rain, shelter and clothing to protect us. We also need arms to encircle us and the wisdom and strength to embrace and climb over the obstacle courses of our lives. Hate, misunderstanding, intolerance, and unkindness of any kind pollute our spirit and deplete the love we were born to give and receive.

If I could choose to have one wish fulfilled, it would be that only words of love that come from the heart would be carried upon the lips of every man, woman, and child on earth. If we spoke only love to each other, we would have no need for laws; we would have no need for war or the rage that creates terrorism. No one would want to be more powerful than another. No one would ever be hungry, homeless, sad, angry, or afraid. When we come from love, we become more loving in our thoughts and actions, and our fears evaporate.

There is no black, no white, and no absolutes. Balance is created from the ability to stay centered, to rock gently with the imbalances rather than to fight them head-on.

When I left the U.S. I believed that I needed to protect myself from the feelings of loss I experienced. I accomplished this by putting everyone I love in a box. When I visited the U.S. last fall, the box happily exploded. I discovered that distance and separation are an illusion Whomever you love is always with you. All you need to do is think of them and they are there. I know it's been hard for my family and close friends to have me so far away, yet they've given me the gift of freedom to do what is right for me, without a guilt trip.

I have faced my own prejudices, fears, and feelings of inadequacy, negativity, and hopelessness as well as those of people from around the world.

I have also seen my strength and capacity to love. I've learned to ask for help, to swallow my fear of rejection, and to overcome my shyness when meeting new people. I've done a lot of listening and a lot less judging.

I finished cleaning the ceramic floor in my apartment, but I left one square as it was. I did this to remind myself that no matter how hard I work, no matter how much I learn there will always be more to see, discover and understand. As my wise friend, Anita, said recently about her own journey, "I'm not trying to be perfect, just better."

Egypt has taught me to slow down, to experience life more fully in the moment, not in the future or in the past.

Most of all I've learned to stand on my own two feet and to know that if I greet life with an open heart and a smile, others will usually respond in the same way. If they don't, that's their decision.

I've learned to choose friends more wisely, to see that I'm better off alone than with people who aren't really my friends; it's the quality that counts. My friendships in Cairo have been consistent blessings, as have the love and support of those in Alexandria and my friends around the world.

I arrived with only four suitcases. I now know that the only things I can't survive without are human contact, laughter, and love.

I've learned to honor my instincts and myself. I've learned that if I want to be myself I must allow others to be themselves, to help when I can and to keep silent when someone isn't ready to receive what I have to offer. I cannot fix. I can only share if someone is open to hearing what I have learned.

I've used this opportunity to cherish each new day as an adventure waiting to happen. I constantly remember that laughter is indeed the best medicine for whatever ails me. I've learned that every challenge is a chance to grow just waiting to be unveiled.

I came here believing that how I act is a reflection of not only me, but also every other American. It has not been easy. I really believed that citizens from around the world saw the kindness and generosity of the American people and appreciated it. Once I stopped being defensive and opened my ears and eyes, I lost my patriotic virginity. Our formal government is a democracy, but the stuff going on within our government that we do not know about, that we never have the opportunity to vote on, isn't. I've seen first-hand how hated our government is, not just by Egyptians, but also by just about every culture in the world. This broke my heart for I love my country and I am responsible for what my government does.

I've learned that if I see or hear something that makes me question its accuracy, I need to climb out of my box and look and listen more carefully. Every belief contains a grain of truth; every belief contains a grain of mistruth. Where there is darkness, there is light; where there is light there is darkness.

I Am Happier to Know You has been my gift to you. I didn't set out to write it. It created itself. I've been told that it has entertained you and given you the opportunity to see, understand, and appreciate another culture. It has made you laugh aloud, cry in sorrow, scream in outrage, put you to sleep, given you hives, twisted your shorts, and made you think... sometimes far more than you wanted to. As I've said in an earlier chapter, gifts often come in dirty pizza boxes as well as solid gold ones!

I'm still not entirely sure if I know all the reasons for my coming here, or if this part of my journey is to continue or to fade like the sun behind the Pyramids. I do know that I can trust God to tell me when, and if, it is time to move on. From my heart, I wish each of you love and blessings on the journey that is yours alone to live and experience.

Jeanne

I Am Happier to Know You

GLOSSARY OF ARABIC WORDS/SAYINGS
AND THEIR ENGLISH TRANSLATION

Abbaya: A full-length black robe worn by women over their clothing
Al Ahram: The Pyramids
Al Hamdulilah: Praise God
Ala tuul: Straight ahead/right away
Alam: A pen or a pain in the body
Alf shoke: A thousand thanks
Allah: The first of ninety-nine names of God
Ana: I
Ana Amrikaniyaa wi Masriyya bell elb: I am an American and an Egyptian in my heart (f)
Ana Asaad: I am happier to know you
Ana Asfa: I'm sorry
Ana min hena: I am from here
Ana Mus Ray-a: I am Egyptian (f)
Awi: Very
Aywa: Yes
Ayiza: Want (f)
Baba: Dad
Baksheesh: A tip/bribe
Baladi: Native/local
Bara: Outside/outdoors/outside the country
Bawaab: Building guard/virtue protector
Bent: Girl
Bikam: How much
Bod Bokra: After tomorrow
Corsi: Chair
Coptic: Egyptian Christian
Eid: Feast around a religious holiday
El Maadi: The area of Cairo where I live—the word means riverboat crossing
Enti: You (f)

322

Enti kwayyisa: You good (to a female)
Enta: You (m)
Felucca: A native sailboat
Faloose: Money
Galabaya: A full-length native robe worn by both men
and women
Gamb: Beside/next to
Gamoosa: Water buffalo
Gazma: Shoe
Gharam: Love you're willing to pay the price for
Ghee: Clarified butter-shortening used to fry and bake
native dishes
Habibi: My sweetheart (m)
Haram: Forbidden under Islam
Harami: A thief
Hawa: Shares love with air and falling
Hayman: Love that wanders the earth
Hena: Here
Hena kwayyis: Here is good
Hijab: Any scarf a woman wears to cover her hair
Iftar: The sundown fast breaking meal during Ramadan
Imshii! Imshii!: Go away
Inshallah: God willing
Ishq: Love that entwines two people together
Kefya: Enough
Kelb: Dog
Khamasiin: Strong spring winds that cause dust storms
Khroof: Sheep/lamb
Kilo: 2.2 pounds
Kusheri: A delicious native dish made from rice,
macaroni and lentils topped with fried onions
and tomato sauce.
Kwayyisa: Good/okay (f)
La-a: No
Mafish: There are not/there are no/there is no
Mashkilla: Problem
Massa el kheir: Good evening
Men: From
Min fadlak/fadlak: Please

Mish: Used before a word, it negates the meaning
Mish kiteer: Not a lot
Molukhaya: An Egyptian vegetable similar to kale that is finely chopped, cooked with garlic, then served as soup, oftentimes with rice
Mus: Egypt: (*roh Musri*...the spirit of Egypt)
Muslim: A member of Islam (pronounced mus-lamb)
Om: Mother
Pasha: Honorary title to show a man's importance
Piastres: Small change
Raebe: A stranger, or also used as What happened
Raeba: Someone who is strange
Sabbah el kheir: Good morning.
Sababah: Love exudes from your pores
Salaam: Hello
Shaghaf: Love that nests in the heart
Shara: Road/street
Sharmoota: The original definition is a dirty rag, but it is frequently used to describe a loose woman
Shartra: Clever/smart
Shay: Tea
Sheikh: Muslim religious authority
Sheisha: A native water pipe used to smoke tobacco
Shimel: Left
Shokran: Thank you
Souk: Street market
Sufi: The mystical arm of Islam
Tamaya: Bean cake
Tech: Losing yourself in love
Tessa: Nine
Wadi: Dry riverbed
Walah: Love with sorrow
Waldeen: Boys
Walad! Imshi! Imshi!: Boy go away
Ya Kelb!: You dog
Yemeen: Right
Zakat: Giving a portion of your income to the poor is one of the Five Pillars of Islam

Reading I Am Happier to Know You
Book Group Questions for Discussion

I Am Happier to Know You is the inspiring story of Jeanne M. Eck's courageous journey to Egypt; in the process of learning about another culture and faith, she discovered that our true home is built upon our relationship with ourselves.

Throughout I Am Happier to Know You, Ms. Eck shares the challenges and joys of her journey while weaving a mantle of hope that with faith, personal power, grace, and love, peace achieved through mutual respect and understanding can envelop the world.

1. Discuss the cultural differences between the East and the West that you found most difficult to respect and why.

2. What differences do you think Middle Easterners find most difficult to understand about your culture?

3. Compare the similarities between the people of Egypt and the Middle East and your culture.

4. After arriving in Egypt, the author came face-to-face with her personal prejudices and assumptions. Discuss what they were, how she overcame them and what she learned from them.

5. Share how I Am Happier to Know You has changed the ways in which you look at the people and challenges in your life.

6. Discuss which stories touched you the most and what you learned from them.

7. Discuss how I Am Happier to Know You has expanded your definition of love, faith, and peace and what you can do as an individual to bring us all closer together.

8. Share how fear has touched and touches your life.

The Five Pillars of Islam

A Muslim must:

-Publicly declare that: "There is no God other than Allah, and Mohammed is his messenger."

-Pray 5 times each day

-Fast from sunrise to sunset during the month of Ramadan

-Pay 2.5% of their income as a tithe for the poor.

-At least once in their lifetime (if money and health permit) go on a pilgrimage to Mecca at a specific time of the year.

For information about the author, photos, copies of the Book Group Questions and Glossary of Arabic words, please visit Jeanne's website at: www.jeanneeck.com

The author welcomes your emails and comments at Iamhappiertoknowyou@hotmail.com